The
Wreck
of the
Penn Central

The Wreck of the Penn Central

Joseph R. Daughen and Peter Binzen

BeardBooks

Washington, DC

Library of Congress Cataloging-in-Publication Data

Daughen, Joseph R.
   The wreck of the Penn Central / Joseph R. Daughen and Peter Binzen.
      p.   cm.
   Originally published: Boston : Little, Brown, 1971.
   Includes index.
   1. Pennsylvania Central Transportation Company.   I. Binzen, Peter.
II. Title.
HE2791.P2755.D37   1999
385'.06'574—dc21   99-12646
                                                        CIP

Copyright ©1999 Beard Books, Washington, D.C.

ISBN 1-893122-08-5

All rights reserved. No part of this publication may be reproduced,
stored in a retrieval system, or transmitted in any form, by any means,
without the prior written consent of the publisher.

Printed in the United States of America

For Virginia, Lucy, Jenny,
Jonny, Kate and Harriet

For Joan and Joan Patrice

Saunders said, "As soon as the merger takes place, I'll be the boss." But he never exercised authority. He seemed to be afraid of Perlman.

—David C. Bevan

To me it was not a merger; it was a takeover, frankly.

—Alfred E. Perlman

Personally, I like Perlman. I really do. And he's got a lovely wife. She's a nice woman. A real lady. And he's got nice children. I like Perlman. I really do.

—Stuart T. Saunders

Acknowledgments

We are indebted to a number of individuals for the assistance and encouragement they offered us during the writing of *The Wreck of the Penn Central.*

Among them are the Penn Central insiders and others close to the railroad and its board of directors, as well as government officials, who were willing to discuss what happened to the railroad. Some of them necessarily spoke on a not-for-attribution basis.

We are grateful for the help we received from our colleagues at the Philadelphia *Bulletin.* A. Joseph Newman, Jr., the financial editor, helped fill in gaps in our knowledge and steered us to needed documents and key figures in the story. William B. Dickinson, George R. Packard and Samuel J. Boyle, the *Bulletin*'s executive editor, managing editor and assistant managing editor, respectively, gave us the time, and the tolerance, we needed to complete the book. B. A. Bergman, the book editor, gave us encouragement at the outset.

Harry Sions, our editor at Little, Brown, played an important role at every stage. Without his careful editing, advice and continued interest, our job would have been much more difficult.

Finally, we must thank our wives, Virginia Binzen and Joan Daughen, who helped in so many ways — with the typing, with the chapter layouts, and by ungrudgingly giving us the time to work on the railroad.

Contents

List of Illustrations

The Wreck
of the
Penn Central

1

A Head of Steam: February 1, 1968

The underground concourse running west from beneath Philadelphia's City Hall was nearly deserted.

The shops and restaurants that lined the walls of the subterranean passage were closed. A policeman, his hand imprisoned on the halter of a deceptively passive-looking German shepherd, plodded through his rounds. Occasionally, the *thock-thock-thock* of heels could be heard echoing along the concourse as someone made his way to the stairs leading to the commuter platforms, one level below, of the Pennsylvania Railroad's Penn Center Station.

It was almost midnight, January 31, 1968. On that day, the Pennsylvania Railroad had carried about thirty thousand passengers into Penn Center Station. It was now preparing to transport the last of them back home again.

But before these late travelers reached their destinations the Pennsylvania Railroad would cease to exist.

Down on the platform beside Track One, nine persons stood waiting, collars turned up against the chilly, thirty-three-degree air that swept along the rails. Directly in front of them was a luxurious private railroad car, its windows shielded by tightly drawn shades, opaque eyes set in steel. Most of those in the group were railroad officials, but some newsmen were also present.

On the side of the car, the word CENTRAL was painted in huge white letters. To the left of this was a large, rough patch of black masking tape.

Some commuters, bound for the 11:59 Paoli Local, the last

train the Pennsylvania would ever run, noticed the activity at Track One. A curious few approached the group waiting outside the private car and asked what was going on.

A historic event is about to occur, the commuters were told. At 12:01 A.M., just a few minutes away, the merger of the Pennsylvania and New York Central railroads, the largest merger in the nation's history, would become effective.

The commuters were not impressed. A few feet from the gleaming private car stood the equipment that made up the 11:59 Paoli Local. Two weatherbeaten coaches, each more than fifty years old, vulnerable to ice and rain, or a penny on the tracks.

Arnold Day, lately of Great Britain, was one of the sixty passengers to ride the last Pennsylvania train. Before he climbed aboard for the trip to his residence at the Merion Cricket Club in Haverford, Day told a reporter what he thought of the railroad: "The trains are absolutely disgusting. They're filthy. They're invariably too warm and too late. The timekeeping is shocking. I spent twenty-six years commuting in London and I can count on one hand the times the trains were late. My normal greeting to the trainman here is, 'Hello, you're late again.' "

And Miss Louise Mogab, an employee of the N. W. Ayer advertising firm, who lived in Wynnewood: "You never know when you're going to get to work on that train. I'm late on the average about three times a week. It's always breaking down. I certainly hope things improve with the merger. Things can't get any worse. Some of the cars they use are so old that I'm always afraid that they're going to fall apart before I get off."

Alfred E. Perlman did not hear the complaints. He was locked, safely and snugly, inside the private car. It was his private car, a $175,000 haven, where the heat was carefully regulated, the floor was clean, and the plumbing worked.

Perlman was president of the New York Central and, at one minute after midnight, he would become president of the merged Penn Central. He had been a reluctant partner in the marriage of the two giants. His mistrust of his colleagues on the Pennsylvania was no secret. He was comfortable in the New York Central's board room on the thirty-second floor of 230 Park Avenue in Manhattan. The new Penn Central board room on the eighteenth floor of Six Penn Center in Philadelphia, the old Pennsylvania board room, was in the wrong city and belonged to the wrong railroad. The railroad he was supposed to run would be headquartered in Philadelphia, but Perlman had long since decided that he would continue to live in Larchmont, New York, and would work out of Park Avenue.

And on this cold winter night, when the brief ceremony symbolizing the union of the two railroads was to take place, Perlman refused to leave the warmth of his private car. A porter told the group that Perlman was asleep. He had left word that he was not to be disturbed. The ceremony would be conducted outside. The president would remain inside.

John J. McMurrough, a foreman in the Pennsylvania's coach yard, walked up to the private car. He grasped a corner of the patch of black masking tape, peeled the tape away, and the letters P E N N popped into view, like rubber fingers suddenly straightening up. PENN CENTRAL. In big white letters. The railroad officials grinned and exchanged handshakes. No one mentioned the fact that McMurrough had performed the ceremony at 12:04 A.M., three minutes late.

Thursday, February 1, 1968, dawned bleak and chilly. By the time Perlman left his sanctuary on wheels the rain had started. It would continue throughout the day. As he walked into the board room, lushly paneled and plushly carpeted, dominated by a vast, polished table, there was nothing in Perlman's demeanor to suggest anything but enthusiasm for the merger. This was, after all, a day of triumph, the first meeting of the Penn Central board of directors, ten years aborning. But the executive waiting to greet him was a man whom he believed to be a politician rather than a railroad man, a man to whom he would have to play second fiddle.

Stuart T. Saunders, the new chairman of the board and chief executive officer of the Penn Central, who ran the Pennsylvania and who now was Perlman's boss, bustled toward Perlman, a broad smile on his face and his hand outstretched. Perlman smiled back and extended his own hand. If any man was responsible for bringing off the merger that Perlman didn't want, it was Saunders.

Newspaper photographers and television cameramen crowded into the room. For their benefit, Saunders and Perlman beamed benignly at each other and posed together, like warm friends, in front of an engine bell, beside a Penn Central pennant, behind a model train, before a large photograph of a train, anywhere the cameramen suggested. But most of the men in the room may have suspected that if Saunders and Perlman were playing penny ante poker to pass the time, not a hand would be dealt unless the cards were cut.

The first board meeting passed without incident. The general atmosphere was jovial, although there were tensions and undercurrents that did not go unnoticed. Everything had been prearranged. There were twenty-five directors, fourteen from the Pennsylvania, eleven from the Central. The battle to have fifteen Pennsylvania directors, against ten from the Central, had been fought and lost long before.

The new Penn Central stock certificates had finally been released from the vault of the Security-Columbian Banknote Company, in West Philadelphia, where they had rested since their engraving in July 1966. The new certificates showed clearly the direction in which the nation's largest railroad company intended to go. The face of each certificate was adorned with drawings of a locomotive, an airplane, a ship, a pipeline, a truck, and clusters of houses and office buildings. It would not take a particularly alert shareholder to sense, upon receiving one of these certificates, that the Penn Central was thinking conglomerate.

The old Central certificates, which were to be traded in for the new ones, bore the likeness of Commodore Cornelius Vanderbilt, the company's founder. Pennsylvania shareholders did not have to trade in their old certificates, decorated with a picture of the storied Horseshoe Curve, near Altoona. The new certificates cost $10,000 for each batch of 116,000. Penn Central had 23,016,274 shares outstanding on February 1, 1968. Pennsylvania shareholders owned almost 61 percent of them.

Quickly, the board zipped through its agenda, ratifying decisions already made by Saunders and Perlman and the board's committee on officers' salaries. Saunders would be paid $225,000 annually, plus $15,600 in additional funds which would go into a deferred compensation plan for tax purposes. Saunders, in the past few months, had taken advantage of a stock option benefit and pur-

Stuart T. Saunders (left), chairman, and Alfred E. Perlman, president, oblige photographers by posing with a model of a Penn Central freight car on Merger Day, February 1, 1968. (Philadelphia *Bulletin* photo)

The chairman of the board of the Penn Central, Stuart Saunders
(left), and the president, Alfred Perlman, shake hands on Merger Day.
They came out fighting later. (Philadelphia *Bulletin* photo)

chased 40,500 shares at an average price of $23.17 per share, a total cost of $938,385. He had borrowed heavily to make the purchase. Pennsylvania stock had been selling at $56.75 at the time, and Saunders thought it a propitious time to add to the 5,176 shares he already owned. The merger, he believed, would make him a truly wealthy man.

Perlman, as the number-two executive, would receive $170,000 plus $9,450 in deferred compensation.

The number-three man was David C. Bevan, a fact that made both Perlman and Saunders uneasy. Bevan, like Saunders and Perlman, was proud and arrogant. He was not asked to pose for photographs on February 1, 1968. Bevan had been a member of the Pennsylvania board of directors before the merger. After the merger, he would no longer be a director. Saunders had seen to it that Bevan would not be offered a seat on the new board. It was a rebuke that Bevan would never forget.

As Penn Central's finance chairman, Bevan's salary was to be $116,306 plus $22,730 in deferred compensation.

The Penn Central's board gave its approval to the salaries, as it was to give its approval to everything suggested by the management over the next two years — blindly and unquestioningly. The board stamped its imprimatur on the proposed table of organization, a matter far more serious than the salaries and fringe benefits of officers, a matter so serious that it became a vital factor in the subsequent events that were to overtake the company.

The first meeting of the board ended. It was expected to take five to eight years to physically integrate the two railroads, but as they left the board room, the directors were satisfied that the merger had indeed taken place.

Saunders went to his office quite pleased with the way things had gone. He had an operating man — Perlman — to run the railroad. He had a financial expert — Bevan — to take care of raising the money and dealing with the banks. Relieved of those two major responsibilities, Saunders would be free to do what he did best — negotiate with the leaders in government and politics who could help, or hurt, the Penn Central.

Bevan was not even mildly pleased. February 1, 1968, had been a day of agony for him. He was angry and humiliated, but he was

David C. Bevan addresses a stockholders' meeting less than a month before he was fired from his job as chief finance officer for the Penn Central. Seated at his right is grim-faced Stuart Saunders. (Philadelphia *Bulletin* photo)

Mr. Saunders

determined to do something to better his position vis-à-vis Saunders and Perlman. He was depending on his friend, billionaire Richard King Mellon, the senior member of the Penn Central board by virtue of his thirty-five years as a Pennsylvania Railroad director, to help him.

Perlman went back to Track One, boarded his private car, and returned to Manhattan.

The Penn Central had survived its first day.

For 871 days more the Penn Central held together. But tensions flared up that were barely perceptible on February 1, 1968. Problems that nobody foresaw or bothered about on opening day, swelled to unmanageable proportions. On June 21, 1970, with a sickening crash that frightened Wall Street, jarred both the United States economy and its government, and scared off foreign investors, the nation's largest railroad went broke.

The history of American railroading is marked by wildly cyclical ups and downs, but never before had there been a cataclysm as stunning as this. The wreck of the Penn Central reached far beyond railroads, challenging deep-rooted and basic assumptions of American corporate life.

This single bankruptcy caused the nation and its business and political leaders to take a fresh look, not only at railroads, but at mergers in general and, more importantly, at the future of the country's transportation industry. The collapse of the Penn Central raised questions about conglomerates and diversification programs; about the role of boards of directors and how they function, or fail to function; about the inherent conflicts of interest that arise as a result of incestuous, interlocking directorates between financiers who supply money, managers who borrow the money, and brokers who traffic with both; about the relationship between big government and big business. And about the condition of American capitalism.

The dimensions of the disaster that befell the Penn Central Transportation Company, its 100,000 creditors, its 118,000 stockholders, and the hundreds of lesser companies tied economically to the railroad will provide food for thought for students of business history for years to come.

Because of the collapse, the railroad was placed under the protection of the courts. Judge John P. Fullam, of the U.S. District Court for Eastern Pennsylvania, on July 22, 1970, appointed four trustees to oversee the reorganization of the Penn Central. To them fell the staggering task of recruiting new management to operate the massive $4.5 billion complex — 20,570 miles of track winding through sixteen states, two Canadian provinces and Washington, D.C.,[1] rolling stock that would form a 1,780-mile-long train, stretching from Grand Central Terminal in Manhattan to Denver and beyond, 94,453 employees, an annual payroll exceeding one billion dollars, more than the gross national product of Bolivia or Panama or a dozen other countries.

The judgment behind Penn Central's accumulation of vast non-railroad holdings was also brought under suspicion as a result of the collapse. Was it wise for a railroad whose very life depended on a fast flow of cash to own five New York hotels, huge chunks of real estate in California and Florida, pipeline and trucking companies, amusement parks, and interests in Madison Square Garden, the New York Knickerbockers basketball team and the New York Rangers ice hockey team?

Nobody — not even David Bevan, the erstwhile financial wizard who was toppled from his exalted position amid whispers of misconduct — could name the 186 different companies that were brought under the Penn Central's umbrella on February 1, 1968. Nor could anyone identify, without the aid of complex corporate charts, Penn Central's stake in these companies, or state with assurance the debts on each.

The Penn Central was like a gigantic octopus, its tentacles

---

[1] Miles of track owned and/or operated by Penn Central:

Connecticut	627.48	New Jersey	364.24
Delaware	232.07	New York	2,862.09
District of Columbia	13.03	Ohio	3,731.15
Illinois	1,347.97	Pennsylvania	4,282.25
Indiana	2,968.86	Rhode Island	136.95
Kentucky	4.97	Virginia	81.21
Maryland	455.73	West Virginia	373.32
Massachusetts	817.74	Ontario	284.24
Michigan	1,898.20	Quebec	70.74
Missouri	18.05	TOTAL	20,570.29

reaching into hundreds of board rooms, affecting universities, touching virtually every major bank in the nation, influencing government. When the Department of Transportation attempted to retain attorneys and accountants to untangle the corporate spaghetti, it was forced to search for days before it could locate firms that did not, in one way or another, have some relationship with the railroad or its subsidiaries.

During the course of the research for this account, several persons involved with the Penn Central said the story of the collapse could not be told because of the immensity of the subject, or because it was premature. Some refused to cooperate.

Carroll R. Wetzel handled legal matters for the railroad during the tense, final days before the petition for reorganization under Section 77 of the Bankruptcy Act was filed. Wetzel drafted the petition and arranged to have it presented to a judge at the judge's home on a late Sunday afternoon. Later, Wetzel complained that press reports about these events were filled with "distortions" and "gross inaccuracies." But he refused to help set the record straight. Wetzel was a partner in Dechert Price & Rhoads, one of the largest and most prestigious law firms in Philadelphia. Interestingly enough, another member of the firm was Stuart T. Saunders, Jr., son of the head of the Penn Central.

"I could write a book about the Penn Central," Wetzel told us. "But I'd have to wait twenty-five years or until a hundred persons were dead."

In twenty-five years, perhaps some things might become clearer. But memories become fuzzy, principal figures die, records disappear, lawyers impose their version of truth upon events, and the lesson to be learned today is conceded to history. There are also certain advantages in getting onto the track of a big story while the scent — and this one had quite a scent — is still warm.

The Penn Central story is one that reflects credit on nobody. The railroad's three top officers scarcely spoke to one another. They could not, or would not, work together. After the railroad failed, each sought to place blame on the other two. The railroad, the victim, paid these three men salaries which totaled almost $600,000 annually and provided them with stock options which, under different circumstances, could have made them millionaires.

The New York Rangers in action, against the Philadelphia Flyers. The Penn Central empire included ownership of 25 percent of the Rangers. (Philadelphia *Bulletin* photo)

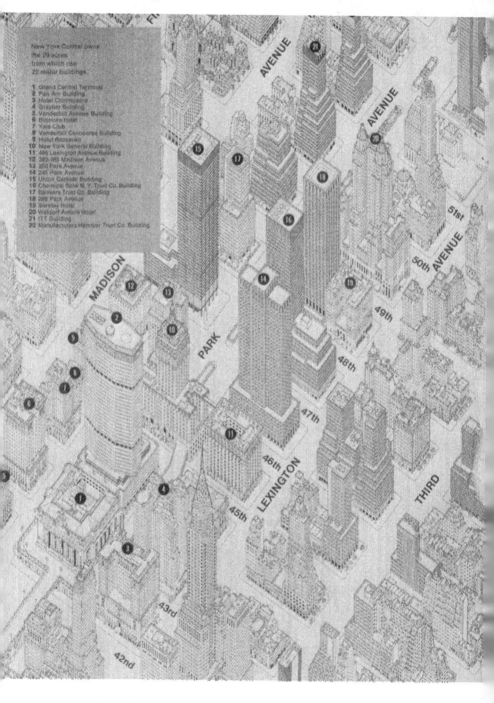

New York Central owns
the 29 acres
from which rise
22 major buildings

1 Grand Central Terminal
2 Pan Am Building
3 Hotel Commodore
4 Graybar Building
5 Vanderbilt Avenue Building
6 Biltmore Hotel
7 Yale Club
8 Vanderbilt Concourse Building
9 Hotel Roosevelt
10 New York General Building
11 466 Lexington Avenue Building
12 383-385 Madison Avenue
13 250 Park Avenue
14 245 Park Avenue
15 Union Carbide Building
16 Chemical Bank N. Y. Trust Co. Building
17 Bankers Trust Co. Building
18 299 Park Avenue
19 Shelley Hotel
20 Waldorf-Astoria Hotel
21 ITT Building
22 Manufacturers Hanover Trust Co. Building

An indication of how the Penn Central came to be the nation's largest real estate company is this map of twenty-nine skyscraper-filled acres in mid-Manhattan owned by the railroad. The value of this property in 1970 was more than $400 million. The railroad placed all of these properties, except for Grand Central Terminal, up for sale in June 1971. (© Anderson Isometric Maps)

The backbiting that characterized the three top men was reflected downward throughout the corporate structure. Morale was nonexistent.

Penn Central's directors seem to have done very little to earn the $200 each received every time he attended a board meeting. They sat around the big polished table as representatives of the railroad's stockholders, whose interests they were supposed to protect. But in most cases all they did was sit. With few exceptions, they appeared to be blind to the onrushing events that sent the Penn Central hurtling off the tracks.

The Interstate Commerce Commission, through its endless hearings and months-long delays in granting needed freight rate increases, and its insistence that the railroad continue to operate little-used and unprofitable passenger trains, made life difficult for the Penn Central, as it has for all railroads. By the time the Penn Central went under, there was a growing feeling in Washington that the ICC had outlived its usefulness.

The Nixon Administration, by reneging on its agreement to provide loan guarantees to the Penn Central at a crucial time, precipitated the move into bankruptcy court. Whether its refusal to provide the guarantees at that point was a sound decision — and a good many railroad men as well as most of the Congress came to believe that it was — the indecisiveness with which it approached the problem, and the apprehension it felt over the political implications of its act, indicated that the Nixon Administration simply had no real policy toward railroads in trouble.

The White House position was complicated by the fact that cabinet officers, an ambassador and a former associate of President Nixon's were all involved with the Penn Central.

Committees of Congress showed great zeal in exposing wrongdoing on the Penn Central. They even managed to get some sex into their reports — always a surefire method of gaining space on the front pages rather than the business pages of the newspapers. But Congress itself did little to help the railroad before it collapsed, even though its growing financial dilemma had been well known, and well publicized, for at least a decade.

The wreck of the Penn Central is a story of tragic dimensions. To a certain extent, events were beyond the control of the principal characters. But these same characters, whether through bad judgment, personal vanity or for baser reasons, contributed significantly to their own, and the railroad's, downfall.

It is a story that doesn't really begin on February 1, 1968, or on November 1, 1957, when the Pennsylvania and the New York Central first announced they were studying the possibility of merger. It begins back in railroading's distant past, when robber barons threw tracks across plains and mountains, and started fouling the environment with the smoke from their engines.

2

Ties to the Past

Putting the Penn Central together took more than ten years. It took 128 Interstate Commerce Commission hearings involving 276 interested parties in eighteen cities. It took seemingly endless court litigation and millions of dollars in legal fees paid to more than five hundred attorneys. It took careful bargaining with unions and skillful negotiations with politicians at all levels of government, including the, White House. Despite all these efforts it was touch and go until almost the last minute whether the merger would ever be approved.

When the final obstacle was overcome and twenty-five newly named Penn Central directors met in Philadelphia on February 1, 1968, to launch the largest corporate merger in American history, observers might well have pondered what a couple of nineteenth-century railroad executives named George B. Roberts and Chauncey Depew and a financier named J. P. Morgan would have thought of the agonizingly extended dickering.

In 1885 Roberts headed the PRR and Depew the Central.[1] On a single July day that year they reached an agreement that must have seemed almost as momentous to them as the 1968 merger did to Penn Central's board. Roberts and Depew didn't agree to merge their railroads, then the two mightiest in the United States. That would have been out of the question. But they did agree to quit the cutthroat competition that threatened the survival of both. They

---

[1] Depew was sitting in for the ailing William H. Vanderbilt, who died in December 1885.

George B. Roberts, PRR president in 1885, reached an historic accord with Chauncey Depew of the Central aboard J. P. Morgan's yacht, *Corsair*. (Penn Central portrait, from the *Centennial History of the Pennsylvania Railroad*)

When asked about the upkeep of his sleek black seagoing yacht, *Corsair*, J. P. Morgan, Sr., is supposed to have replied: "Nobody who has to ask what a yacht costs has any business owning one." (Lucius Beebe, *The Big Spenders*)

Chauncey Depew, lawyer and advisor to William H. Vanderbilt, later became president of the Central. (*Dictionary of American Portraits*)

J. P. Morgan, Sr., the financier with close ties to both the Central and PRR, came to control more railroads than either of them. (Courtesy of the Library of Congress. Portrait from the *Dictionary of American Portraits*)

reached this historic accord without help or hindrance from the ICC (it didn't exist) or the courts (they never got involved in such matters then) or even lawyers or politicians.

They managed it in the space of a few hours aboard John Pierpont Morgan's yacht, *Corsair,* cruising in outer New York harbor and up the Hudson as far as West Point. Morgan was there, too. In fact, he more or less forced the agreement, one of many he was to hammer out in his role as unofficial U.S. railroad czar. In his time Morgan proved far more formidable as an arbiter of railroad disputes than today's ICC examiners or judges or high-priced legal talent. But corporate life was simpler in 1885. Simpler and much more savage. There was no federal regulation of freight or passenger rates and there were few controls over stock issues. The railroad industry, like much of American business, was a jungle whose rulers, to quote Stewart H. Holbrook, "fought their way encased in rhinoceros hides and filled the air with their mad bellowings and cries of the wounded."

In the summer of '85 the PRR, then the nation's largest railroad, and the Central, which was number two, were deliberately plotting to wreck one another. The Pennsylvania held a monopoly over the traffic, the industry and even the lawmaking in its state. But now the Central was challenging this monopoly. Central construction crews were leveling mountains, building bridges, and laying track for a competing railroad which was to run, roughly, from Reading to Pittsburgh. The Central had floated $40 million in bonds to finance this venture across the Alleghenies. In the meantime, PRR interests were buying up depreciated bonds of a bankrupt railroad, the West Shore Railroad, that ran along the west shore of the Hudson to Albany, in direct competition with Central lines across the river. Despite its financial problems, the West Shore Railroad could hurt the Central and help the PRR extend its sway into New York.

From his banking house in Manhattan, J. P. Morgan, then a forty-eight-year-old, two-hundred pounder with a fondness for big black cigars, saw what was happening and didn't like it. For the previous three summers, blastings of construction gangs working on the West Shore line had disturbed Morgan's vacations at his nearby country seat. More important, he was a director of the

Central, and he and his associates were beginning to loan vast sums to railroad builders. They could see nothing but trouble resulting from such rivalries as the PRR and Central were locked in. He wanted hostilities stopped. And on his terms. Morgan decided what had to be done and then invited the railroad magnates aboard the *Corsair* to ratify the agreement. The PRR was to drop all interest in the West Shore line, letting the Central buy it out of bankruptcy. In return, the PRR was to purchase the Central's South Pennsylvania line for the estimated $3 million that had already been spent on construction. Both sides would be gaining essentially worthless properties that duplicated existing railroads, but Morgan could see no other way out of the impasse.

In addition to George Roberts, the PRR was represented aboard Morgan's sleek, black, 175-foot oceangoing steam yacht by Frank Thomson, vice president and the nephew of the great J. Edgar Thomson, who had converted the Pennsylvania from a local carrier into the nation's mightiest railroad. Chauncey Depew, a New York lawyer who, after heading the Central was to serve as a U.S. senator, was his railroad's lone representative.

As the *Corsair* steamed down the Hudson and into New York harbor as far as Sandy Hook, the rail titans talked. Roberts was wary. He was trained as an engineer and he didn't trust New York money men. He viewed the Central's South Pennsylvania enterprise as a "hole in the ground." He suspected his rival would get the better of the bargain. Morgan promised that the Central wouldn't "get out whole." Gradually, Roberts came around. In early evening he and Depew disembarked with handshakes at the dock at Jersey City. Roberts told Morgan: "I will agree to your plan and do my part."

Having achieved in a few hours on the water what might take years before today's courts and regulatory agencies, Morgan promptly set about reorganizing the two pirate properties. The West Shore line was bid in by Morgan and Depew at foreclosure sale for $22 million and leased to the Central for 999 years. When Morgan sought to arrange the Pennsy's purchase of the Central-owned South Pennsylvania property, a hitch developed. Pennsylvania's constitution forbade railroads from buying competing lines within the state. To get around this law, Morgan allowed his name to be used as purchaser and signed the necessary papers as straw party for the PRR. By September of 1885 all construction had stopped. The South Pennsylvania's embankments and tunnels remained unused for fifty years until the Pennsylvania Turnpike Commission bought some of them for its first toll road. The PRR then got back about $1 million from the purchase Roberts had reluctantly agreed to.

The *Corsair Compact,* as it came to be known, provided a measure of order and stability to an industry that badly needed both. The *Commercial and Financial Chronicle* hailed the agreement for removing "the chief source of discord to the whole railroad system of the country."

From the days of their founding to their shipboard peace treaty and on up to their climactic merger of 1968, the Pennsylvania Railroad and the New York Central reflected basic differences in corporate personalities, in styles and operating methods. The Central bore the stamp of one man, the remarkable if not always admirable Commodore Cornelius Vanderbilt. In an era of rascality and rugged individualism, the old commodore had few peers. Manipulating stocks and bonds in ways that would bring long prison terms by today's more stringent rules of business activity, he built the biggest fortune in the New World — close to $100 million — and then his son, William H., doubled it. The Vanderbilts were feared and hated, but their competitors underrated them at their own peril. The Central was the Vanderbilts' railroad and their name became synonymous with it.

The Pennsylvania, by contrast, was always, in sociologist E. Digby Baltzell's view, "a very Proper Philadelphia business enterprise." There was never much flash or flair to the PRR, and its managers were a colorless lot. But it always paid a dividend, and small children in the City of Brotherly Love were brought up to pray for the railroad along with the Girard Bank and the Republican Party. It was an upper-class institution and it generally behaved like one.[2]

---

[2] Of the PRR, Louis M. Hacker has written: "The fraud which made the history of many of the rails a byword in American economic life was unknown to its annals; the stock manipulations of the Vanderbilts never had their parallel in its steady growth."

The Pennsylvania engaged, of course, in the same ruthless rate wars and underhanded "rebates" to favored shippers as its competitors. But at its founding, at least, it appears to have had broader civic objectives than most of the others. It was started, in fact, to save Philadelphia. The Quaker city on the Delaware, once America's largest metropolis and most prosperous port, began to lose ground when the nation expanded westward. Trade was largely by water rather than overland. With the opening of the Erie Canal in 1825, the riches of the West moved down that waterway to New York, bypassing Pennsylvania. Barges also plied the Mississippi to New Orleans, and mule skinners drove wagon trains over the "National Road" to Baltimore. Philadelphia, lacking a good connection across the mountains, was effectively shut out.

Railroading was then in its infancy. The first U.S. railway opened in 1826 in Quincy, Massachusetts. Its horse-drawn cars carried granite four miles from quarries to docks for shipment to Boston for construction of Charlestown's Bunker Hill Monument. The following year a nine-mile coal-carrying railroad began running in Carbon County, Pennsylvania. In 1829, the first English locomotive was imported. And in the following fifteen years numerous small railroads began operating in New York and New England. In 1842, a distinguished foreign visitor rode the rails from Boston to Lowell, Massachusetts, and was duly impressed. He was Charles Dickens. In his *American Notes* he graphically described his ride:

> There is a great deal of jolting, a great deal of noise, a great deal of wall, not much window, a locomotive engine, a shriek and a bell. The cars are like shabby omnibuses, but larger: holding 30, 40, 50 people . . . In the centre of the carriage there is usually a stove, fed with charcoal or anthracite coal; which is for the most part red-hot. It is insufferably close . . . In the ladies' car there are a great many gentlemen who have ladies with them. There are also a great many ladies who have nobody with them: for any lady may travel alone, from one end of the United States to the other, and be certain of the most courteous and considerate treatment everywhere. The conductor, or checktaker, or guard, or whatever he may be, wears no uniform. He walks up and down the car, and in and out of it, as his fancy dictates; leans against the door with his hands in his pockets and

stares at you, if you chance to be a stranger; or enters into conversation with the passengers about him. A great many newspapers are pulled out, and a few of them are read. Everybody talks to you, or to anybody else who hits his fancy.

Back in Pennsylvania, Quaker traders were struggling to keep pace with New York and Baltimore. After the Revolution New York had quickly outgrown Philadelphia. The 1820 census counted 152,000 New Yorkers while Philadelphia, with 63,800 people, led Baltimore by a scant thousand. Up to then the three cities had not been competitive; the trade of each was limited to its hinterland. But as the country grew the competition became heated. Philadelphians were alarmed not only by the increasing Erie Canal traffic but also by the progress of the New York & Erie Railroad and by Baltimore's plans to replace its National Pike with a steam railroad to the West.

At that time, travel between Philadelphia and Pittsburgh was by horse and wagon only. A hard-surface toll road ran from Philadelphia to Lancaster but the country beyond Lancaster was largely wilderness. A team of horses needed eighteen to thirty-five days to reach Pittsburgh. In 1824 the Pennsylvania legislature appointed a commission to develop plans for a network of canals across the Alleghenies. This led to the so-called "Main Line of Public Works" with its publicly financed canals and "inclined-plane" railroads. The inclined-plane railroad was a means of getting horse-drawn trains over mountains. The principle was similar to that of the rope tow on the ski slope. Cars were attached to a rope by clamps and moved along as a stationary engine pulled the rope over a drum. The plane was usually no more than half a mile long at a grade of seven to ten feet per hundred.

Using inclined planes and canals, Pennsylvania opened in the spring of 1834 a through route between Philadelphia and Pittsburgh. The hardy traveler boarded a railroad car at Broad and Vine streets, Philadelphia, at 8 A.M. and was delivered in Pittsburgh — more dead than alive, one suspects — on the afternoon of the fourth day. He rode the train eighty-two miles to Columbia, near Lancaster, then took a canalboat 172 miles to Hollidaysburg. There he transferred to a "Portage Railroad" train for a thirty-six-mile ride over the mountains to Johnstown, where he caught a second canalboat down the Conemaugh and Allegheny rivers, 104 miles to Pittsburgh. On the Portage Railroad there were ten planes, five on each side of the summit, and eleven "levels." Delays resulting from the transfer of freight from cars to canalboats and back again made the trip even longer. Soon, however, the operators of the Main Line of Public Works developed an ingenious piggyback system. Canalboats were made in detachable sections which could be loaded on trains. Cargo thus could make it to Pittsburgh without being unloaded.

Nevertheless, the Main Line failed to attract the desired trade and travel of the West. Its natural difficulties were compounded by inefficient management and a reluctance on the state legislature's part to provide adequate funds for repairs and improvements. Gradually, Pennsylvania concluded that it needed a genuine east-west railroad. Several years of legislative debate led to the development of two principal plans. One called for the Baltimore & Ohio Railroad, which dated from 1827, to extend its line from Cumberland, Maryland, to Pittsburgh. The other called for the founding of an entirely new railroad company to link eastern and western Pennsylvania. In March 1846, after fierce debate and lobbying by rival proponents, the legislature adopted the second plan by chartering the Pennsylvania Railroad. It warned the new railroad's backers, however, that if they didn't raise $3 million in twelve months the B&O's lapsed privileges to build in Pennsylvania would be revived and it would be free to construct its Cumberland-Pittsburgh line.

Two weeks after Governor Francis R. Shunk signed the PRR's charter on April 13, 1846, a group of leading Philadelphians met in the city's Chinese Museum to plan the raising of funds. Samuel Vaughan Merrick, a businessman who became the railroad's first president, urged citizens to subscribe to its stock "not so much," as he explained later, "with the hope of direct profit as with a patriotic intent to save the trade of the great West to Pennsylvania . . . for the sake of public improvement, and the advance of general prosperity."

Thousands of citizens did subscribe and the state's condition was met. The city of Philadelphia put up more than $5 million of the first $12 million raised — and was given three seats on the PRR's board, which it held until the railroad bought back the stock in 1879. Allegheny County, in western Pennsylvania, subscribed to $1 million and got two seats. The Pennsylvania Railroad opened for business in 1849 with sixty-one miles of track from Harrisburg northwest to Lewistown, two locomotives, two passenger cars and one baggage car. In less than thirty years it was to become what the London *Economist* called the world's largest corporation, twice over.

Governor Milton J. Shapp of Pennsylvania, chief individual critic of the 1968 merger, has termed the PRR's founding "an outstanding example of Government and private citizens joining forces in response to an economic challenge." Perhaps even more important, the merchants who originally backed the railroad were either lucky or wise in their choice of a man to run it. He was John Edgar Thomson, the PRR's first chief engineer and its third president. Thomson proved to be, in Stewart Holbrook's estimation, "one of the greatest all-around railroad men America has known." He had technical skill, vision, determination and great qualities of leadership. Beyond that, he was first, last and always a railroader who willed the income from his estate for the education of daughters of railroaders killed in accidents.

What Baltzell terms "Proper Philadelphia's proudest accomplishment — opening trade to the West with the 'Pennsy' " — took shape during Thomson's long term, from 1852–1874, as president. The Pennsylvania first purchased the state-owned Philadelphia and Columbia Railroad, then extended its rails to Harrisburg and on to Pittsburgh. Thomson selected the route over the mountains, including the famed Horseshoe Curve, with such virtuosity that it has never had to be resurveyed. On July 18, 1858, a PRR passenger train inaugurated travel over the Philadelphia-Pittsburgh right-of-way.

Thomson pushed lines to Chicago, St. Louis and Cincinnati, bought other railroads, and purchased terminals on the Hudson River in New Jersey which set the stage for the PRR's turn-of-the-century thrust into New York City itself. He and his associates also organized, in 1870, what may have been the nation's first holding company, one that was to become a storm center of controversy a century later. This was the Pennsylvania Company, formed to control all PRR properties west of Pittsburgh. These included a direct line to St. Louis, second lines to Chicago and Cincinnati and much new territory.

In this way, the Railroad, as Philadelphians called it, catapulted into the front rank of American industry. Under Thomson it was transformed from a local Philadelphia-Pittsburgh carrier into a sprawling 6,000-mile system with a virtual monopoly on traffic in grain, oil, coal, iron and machinery. It was the first railroad to use steel rails and probably the first to use air brakes and a block-signal system. For its passengers, then a major source of revenue, it provided the first smoking cars in America. Its conductors in cutaway coats of blue broadcloth, with shiny brass buttons, buff vests and black trousers, were acclaimed for their courtesy. For its stockholders it provided dividends — 6 percent at the outset — and never missed a payment. The PRR was well established before the Civil War and profited greatly from the war. Its trains carried Union troops, armaments and supplies to the fighting zone. Its revenues rose from $5.9 million in 1860 to $19.5 million in 1865. After that, there was no stopping the Pennsylvania Railroad.

The New York Central's beginnings were less respectable but a lot more colorful. It was the creation not of civic-minded merchants but of corporation lawyers and speculators. It started not as one railroad but as ten small ones; the sixteen-mile Mohawk & Hudson Railroad, for example, the first section of what was to become the Central, was built in 1831 to connect the Erie Canal with the Hudson River. Its success led to the construction by nine other companies of nine more railroads. Running end to end they linked Albany and Buffalo. But timetables were not synchronized and travelers never knew when they could catch connecting trains. In 1853, Erastus Corning, an Albany nail maker and politician, headed a syndicate which consolidated the ten railroads into one, the New York Central, with 542 miles of track and capitalization of $23 million. Service subsequently improved, traffic increased, and profits soared. What was needed, though, was a line down the Hudson to New York City. The man who made this possible was Cornelius Vanderbilt. He came late to railroading but proved astonishingly adept at it.

Vanderbilt, a native of Staten Island, had made his name and early fortune as an operator of ferryboats, sailing schooners and steamers. His methods, though often ruthless, were usually effective. When gold was discovered in California he entered into private negotiations with the dictator of Nicaragua. The deal the two worked out permitted gold prospectors from the East Coast to sail on Vanderbilt's ships to Central America and then travel across Nicaragua to the Pacific. Because of a change of government in Nicaragua the deal fell through. Vanderbilt, undaunted, got four neighboring republics to organize a "defensive alliance" against the new rulers of Nicaragua. Next he persuaded Washington to send in the Marines to protect "American [i.e., Vanderbilt's] interests." Prospectors continued to travel West according to Vanderbilt's original plan. He made a lot of money.

As the Union's shipping agent in New York during the Civil War, Commodore Vanderbilt saw his fortune mount. But he saw something else: Railways were replacing waterways as a major means both of transport and moneymaking. The old man — he was sixty-eight in 1864 — first bought two small railroads running between New York City, Poughkeepsie and Albany. Then he set about acquiring the Central at the lowest possible price. He devised a simple plan to drive the Central's stock down. His trains coming up the Hudson's east bank from Manhattan were supposed to connect with Central trains on the west bank in Albany for transfer of passengers. On a bitter day in winter when the Hudson was frozen and the commodore was playing whist at home, his trains abruptly stopped on the East Albany side of the river. This premature halt — ordered by Vanderbilt for all of his trains thereafter — forced Central riders bound for New York to slough two miles through snow across a railroad bridge to reach Vanderbilt's trains. In the ensuing brouhaha in the New York state legislature, Vanderbilt, with feigned regrets, pointed out that a long-forgotten state law prohibited his trains from crossing the river. And the law, he noted, was enacted at the Central's behest to avoid crippling competition.

As the Central's passengers kept walking, the Central's stock kept falling. When it had dropped to what Vanderbilt considered a fair price he bought $18 million worth and took over the railroad.

After becoming president of the Central in 1867, he extended its rails from Buffalo to Chicago, thus establishing the basic outline of the road that was later to merge with the Pennsylvania.

Commodore Vanderbilt, who acquired the Central through stock manipulation, soon discovered that others could play the same game. A favorite ploy of moguls and would-be moguls in those days was to start a nuisance railroad and then unload it on a bigger railroad at a good price. Edward H. Harriman got his start this way: He sold the small Ogdensburg & Lake Champlain Railroad in New York to the Pennsylvania, which bought it only to keep the road out of the hands of Vanderbilt. In the case of the New York & Erie Railroad, Vanderbilt himself faced three master plunderers in corporate finance — Jay Gould, Jim Fisk and Daniel Drew.

Gould, Fisk and Drew controlled the Erie, which ran from New York City to Dunkirk, in the western part of the state. When Vanderbilt tried to move in they proved more than a match for him. Gould's presses changed $10 million worth of Erie bonds into 100,000 shares of common stock, thus making it that much more difficult and costly for the commodore to acquire controlling interest. Finally, Vanderbilt got a judge to order the arrest of the three crooked capitalists. At Erie's head office in New York, Gould, Fisk and Drew stuffed $6 million in greenbacks — from the sale of printing-press stock — into bundles and drove furiously by hack to the Jersey ferry slip. They managed to board a boat just ahead of lawmen whom Vanderbilt had sent after them.

In Jersey City they installed themselves in a hotel, mounted three small cannon on the waterfront nearby, and commandeered four lifeboats with forty-eight armed men as their "shore patrol." Fisk placed his mistress, Josie Mansfield, in a lavish suite — at the Erie stockholders' expense — and held court for reporters with cigars, champagne and lively quips about the latest fusillade in the "Erie War." After some weeks, Gould filled a suitcase with $500,000 in greenbacks and went to Albany, where he bribed legislators to legalize his conversion of Erie bonds to stock. The lawmakers did what Gould paid them to do. With the threat of unlimited stock issues confronting him, Commodore Vanderbilt

J. Edgar Thomson, president of the Pennsylvania Railroad from 1852–1874, converted the local carrier into a national institution. (*Dictionary of American Portraits*)

Commodore Cornelius Vanderbilt built the Central into a great competitor of the Pennsylvania. (Engraving by Alexander H. Ritchie. From the *Dictionary of American Portraits*)

Jay Gould, the speculator, is supposed to have kept a cow in a baggage car while traveling in his private railroad car to make sure he had milk for his ulcers. (*Dictionary of American Portraits*)

Jim Fisk died as he lived — spectacularly. He was shot dead by the man who succeeded him in the affections of Josie Mansfield. (*Dictionary of American Portraits*)

Daniel Drew had few peers in the nineteenth-century game of railroad stock manipulation. (After a photograph by Matthew Brady. From the *Dictionary of American Portraits*)

William H. Vanderbilt denied having uttered them but rail ritics recall the words attributed him: "The public be damned!" (Engraving by Alexander H. Ritchie. From the *Dictionary of American Portraits)*

gave up. He sold back his Erie stock to the trio at a loss of $1 million.[3]

On his death in 1877, Cornelius Vanderbilt was said to be the richest man in America. He willed most of his fortune, including 87 percent of the New York Central's outstanding stock, to his eldest son, William Henry. William Henry Vanderbilt, though a milder man than the commodore and a more public-spirited one, nevertheless is remembered principally for four words that he uttered on October 8, 1882. Answering a reporter's needling question whether railroad trains weren't supposed to be run for the public's benefit, the Central's president replied that he was working for his stockholders and he added: "The public be damned!" When criticized for his candor, Vanderbilt later denied having used profanity, but the damage was done. Since that episode, railroads that raise rates or reduce passenger service — and that includes about all of them — are accused of perpetuating William Henry Vanderbilt's "public-be-damned" attitude.

William Henry Vanderbilt is also remembered for his racehorse, Maud S., which he kept fenced in a private pasture in the city block where the Penn Central–owned Biltmore Hotel now stands. From his office in Grand Central Terminal, built by his father in 1870–1871, Vanderbilt kept his eye on Maud S. For travel, he used his $50,000 private rail car, painted circus-wagon yellow with red trim and decorated with garish renderings of Niagara Falls and other sights along the Central's route.

In the matter of private railroad cars, William Henry Vanderbilt had plenty of competition. Mrs. E. T. Stotesbury ordered gold-plated plumbing fixtures for her car, according to Lucius Beebe, and Lily Langtry's *Lalee* contained a food locker capable of holding an entire stag. Chilled beer was piped under pressure into every apartment in Adolphus Busch's *Adolphus*. And to soothe Jay Gould's ulcers his cow, with a ready supply of butterfat, was said to ride in a baggage car up ahead of the speculator's private car.

The rich indulged themselves and paid no taxes. J. P. Morgan,

[3] Fisk was subsequently shot to death by Josie Mansfield's later paramour, Edward S. Stokes. The Erie's funded debt rose by $64 million, and the railroad was so depleted by Gould, Fisk and Drew that it didn't pay a common-stock dividend for sixty-nine years.

when asked about the upkeep of his yacht, *Corsair,* is supposed to have responded grumpily: "Nobody who has to ask what a yacht costs has any business owning one." Railroads reigned supreme in the American transportation industry, and railroad magnates enjoyed enormous power. "These railroad kings," observed James Bryce in his classic study, *The American Commonwealth,* "are among the greatest men, perhaps I may say, *the* greatest men in America." Richard T. Ely agreed. "You cannot turn in any direction in American politics," he wrote in 1890, "without discovering the railway power. It is the power behind the throne."

Sometimes the railway power wasn't so very far behind the throne. "Before the doors of the Pennsylvania's office," Matthew Josephson wrote of the PRR, "politicians scraped their feet respectfully. At the bidding of the railroad, the Pennsylvania legislature passed necessary measures with noticeable speed. When Mr. [Thomas A.] Scott [PRR president from 1874–1880], according to legend, had 'no further business' for the legislature, it would promptly adjourn." Even the Pennsy's Centennial History, commissioned by the railroad, termed Scott the "most skillful politician" among PRR presidents, and told of the state senator who, after two bills of great benefit to the railroad had been enacted, rose to ask: "Mr. Speaker, may we now go Scott free?"

With such political backing plus an ideal location in the heart of the nation's most rapidly industrializing zone, between New York and Chicago, the PRR could hardly have missed. And it didn't. In only six of the sixty years from 1860–1920 did it pay cash dividends of less than 5 percent per annum. In seven years it was 10 percent. Through the decades the price of its securities remained remarkably steady. From 1880 to 1919 PRR common stock never fell below 40 or rose above 85. In twenty-two of those years it varied less than ten points between January 1 and December 31. In some years there was hardly any movement at all. For example, in 1892 the high was 57⅜ and the low was 53.

The Central's record was more volatile and its management, in the view of some observers, more predatory. Of Commodore Vanderbilt, Gustavus Myers, a contemporary of Lincoln Steffens, Ida Tarbell and other muckrakers, wrote: "Each new million that he seized was an additional resource by which he could bribe and manipulate; progressively his power advanced; and it became ridiculously easier to get possession of more and more property. His very name became a terror to those of lesser capital, and the mere threat of pitting his enormous wealth against competitors whom he sought to destroy was generally a sufficient warrant for their surrender."

William Henry Vanderbilt inherited his father's Midas touch. In the eight years following the elder Vanderbilt's death in 1877 to the son's demise "after board hours" on December 8, 1885, the family fortune grew from $100 million to roughly $200 million, diversified in hundreds of enterprises. In those years the Central earned from 16 to 20 percent on its real capital.

Yet while the bellwether Central and PRR were prospering, the unregulated industry as a whole underwent cataclysmic ups and downs. Speculators in railroad stocks and bonds took such a drubbing that much of the time it's hard to understand why they kept coming back for more. In 1876, 40 percent of all U.S. railroad bonds were said to be in default, and between 1873–1879 European investors lost an estimated $600 million through this country's railroad bankruptcies and frauds. In 1879 alone sixty-five railroads were foreclosed. "By the 1880's," wrote John Moody, "about twice as many railroad lines had been built as the country could profitably employ." In 1884, Poor's Manual reported that the entire capital stock of U.S. railroads, then about $4 billion, represented water. In 1895, a total of 169 railroads with 37,855 miles of track — more than one-fifth the national trackage — were being operated by receivers. Among the bankrupt roads then were the B&O, Erie, Northern Pacific, Union Pacific, Santa Fe, Reading and Norfolk & Western.

The PRR and Central may have survived because of their size and their ability to work closely with John D. Rockefeller, Andrew Carnegie and other industrialists. To keep the business of favored shippers, the railroads offered secret rate reductions, called rebates. Rebates were not against the law because there were no laws. Rockefeller himself once explained how the system worked:

A public rate was made and collected by the railroad companies, but so far as my knowledge extends, was seldom retained in full; a portion of it was repaid to the shipper as a rebate. By this method the real rate of freight which any shipper paid was not known by the competitors, nor by other railroads, the amount being a matter of bargain with the carrying companies.

Rebates saved millions for shippers and also appeared to have worked wonders for certain railroads like the Central and Pennsy. In those days there was money to be made as well, of course, in passenger traffic. The railroads competed furiously for long-haul riders. By 1884, says Josephson, five trunk lines ran between New York and Chicago and two more were under construction, "though three would have been ample, and most of these roads were on the verge of bankruptcy." To the delight of riders, the competition drove down rates. At one time, the Central charged only $7 for the New York–Chicago run, and the "immigrant" rate fell to $1.

In this period, too, the railroads began to develop their suburban service. Whole suburbs were created as a direct result of railroad action. An example is Philadelphia's lush, monied western suburbs known as the Main Line — for the late Main Line of Public Works. In the 1860's the PRR ran double tracks twenty-five miles out to Paoli and began operating six daily trains lighted with oil lamps and heated with hot coals. It bought up land near the present Bryn Mawr station, marked off streets, planted trees, set zoning regulations, and built middle-income houses. It also erected and operated a hotel in Bryn Mawr which is now used by a girls' private school. With only one or two exceptions, its presidents up to and including Stuart T. Saunders lived on the Main Line. And some, but not all, rode the Paoli Local to work. In 1884, the PRR built its commuter line to Chestnut Hill, a bluestocking residential district inside the city. It was probably no accident that a PRR director, Henry H. Houston, then owned much of the land in Chestnut Hill and stood to gain enormously from a rail tie to center city.[4]

Largely unsung in this railroad-building era were the actual rail-

---

[4] The Houston Estate still owns hundreds of houses in Chestnut Hill which it rents. Many of its tenants ride Penn Central commuter trains to town every day.

road builders. Many of the common laborers who drove the spikes, laid the rails, dug the tunnels, and flattened the mountains were immigrants, detested by "native Americans" and savagely discriminated against. They were paid very little for their backbreaking labors. And when Jim Fisk, in combating a strike of Erie brakemen dispatched a gang of toughs with orders to shoot resisters, his act drew praise and his courage was hailed. But the brutal disparity between enormous railroad profits and starvation railroad wages made trouble inevitable. It came in the summer of 1877, four months after Commodore Vanderbilt's death. Claiming a financial pinch, the railroads cut wages. In addition, the Pennsylvania and B&O doubled the length of freight trains to be operated by train crews whose pay had just been reduced. Thousands of their workers struck first. The stoppage spread quickly to the Central, Lake Shore and other railroads. Soon railroad workers were rioting in cities all over the country. In Pittsburgh, federal troops were summoned to deal with 15,000 rampaging PRR workers and their allies, many of them armed. The angry mob killed some of the soldiers, burned rail yards, and destroyed 104 locomotives and 500 boxcars and passenger coaches. Flames engulfed Pittsburgh's Union Hotel and depot and downtown office buildings. Windblown embers fell on long stretches of the Monongahela.

In Reading, 3,000 regulars under General Winfield Scott Hancock shot and killed at least ten civilians. Disorders flared in Altoona, Easton, Bethlehem and Buffalo. In Chicago, crowds stormed rail terminals and forced a halt to all rail traffic. To get the trains running again, General Phil Sheridan dispatched a full regiment of soldiers. In Omaha, locomotives and rail cars were wrecked. Blood was shed in St. Louis and St. Paul. The rioting appeared contagious, yet communications were primitive. Newspapers alone carried accounts of the violence. Vast numbers of workers were either illiterate or, being newly arrived immigrants, couldn't read English. One wonders what effect full-scale national television, in color, might have had on events. Seeing their brothers shot in Reading, would the Chicago rioters have reacted even more violently? Or viewing troops slain in Pittsburgh would middle-America nativists have demanded more repressive retaliatory measures? Judging from recent experience, one might surmise that comprehensive TV coverage then might have served only to increase the polarization — a term not used in those days — between workers and rulers, railroad bosses and yardhands.

In any event, although the strikers didn't win their demands they gained something that in the long run was far more important: unionization. The railroad brotherhoods dated from this period. Over the succeeding decades, they grew and prospered — prospered to the extent that they were later to be blamed for overloading the Penn Central merger of 1968 with padded payrolls that doomed it to disaster.

From the outset, critics assailed the brotherhoods. "Laborers' unions," cried Henry Ward Beecher, that "eminent preacher," in 1877, "are the worst form of despotism and tyranny in the history of Christendom." But the savage outbursts in '77 subjected the rail magnates themselves to close scrutiny for the first time. Many observers were appalled at what they saw. After the destruction in his own city, a Chicago editor charged that the railroads had been run "wholly outside the United States Constitution." Another complained that the railroad operators, "having found nothing more to get out of stockholders and bondholders . . . have commenced raiding not only the general public but their own employees."

So great was the public reaction that the entire railroad industry was quietly transformed. An era was ended. "From then onward," Stewart Holbrook has written of the post–1877 period, "capitalists and industrialists of all degree had to use more ingenuity than before. They had to fight harder. They were watched more closely. They were harassed infinitely more." But Holbrook also notes that the most successful of them "quickly developed new abilities of survival amidst the new complexities." Certainly this was true of the Pennsylvania and the Central. Despite tough times for other railroads, they continued to make money. The PRR's stock dividends fell from 8 percent in 1876 to 3.5 percent in 1877 and 2 percent in '78 — a low that was not to be repeated until the depression-ridden 1930's. By 1881, however, the rate was back to 8 percent. In the following dozen years, the railroad six times added stock and scrip dividends to its regular cash dividends. It's a fact, though, that after 1877 PRR profits never returned to previous levels when, in seven years in the 1864–1874 decade, it paid 10 percent dividends on common stock.

William H. Vanderbilt, at the Central, became wiser in the ways of public relations. He responded to the public outcry over the 1877 rioting by dividing $100,000 in cash "among the loyal men of the New York Central & Hudson Railroad" — the Central's full name at that time. Two years later, in 1879, Vanderbilt sold 250,000 of his 400,000 Central shares in a record-setting divestiture. J. P. Morgan headed the syndicate that secretly disposed of the huge block of stock with such skill that the market was unaffected. Vanderbilt got $30 million for the stock and Morgan's group was said to have been paid $3 million in commissions. As part of the deal, Morgan joined the Central's board of directors, became its fiscal agent, and extracted a pledge that the Central would pay at least $8 a share in dividends for at least five years. Morgan's emergence as a railroad power dated from his role in selling Vanderbilt's stock.

The reason for the huge sale was explained by Chauncey Depew, Vanderbilt's counselor and his successor as president of the Central: "Mr. Vanderbilt, because of assaults made upon him in the Legislature and in the newspapers, came to the conclusion that it was a mistake for one individual to own a controlling interest in a great corporation like the New York Central, and also a mistake to have so many eggs in one basket, and he thought it would be better for himself and for the economy if the ownership were distributed as widely as possible."

By the 1880's, most of the big competing railroads, in the absence of state or federal regulations, had their own pooling arrangements or gentlemen's agreements with one another. Invariably, these understandings were shaky; one mogul never knew when another was going to doublecross him. Collusion and blackmail were common. Into the regulatory vacuum moved Morgan. The Pennsy-Central "peace treaty" aboard his yacht in 1885 marked his first major move as railroad arbitrator. As time passed and his influence grew, Morgan became a kind of one-man government, the government itself being unable or unwilling to act.

Between 1868 and 1886 more than 150 bills and resolutions seeking railroad regulations were introduced in Congress, but the railroads succeeded in blocking all of them. In 1886, the U.S. Supreme Court held that the states had no right to regulate interstate commerce or interfere in any way with traffic crossing their borders. Despite this finding, Congress the following year, in 1887, passed an act establishing certain basic rules for railroads and setting up a regulatory commission, the Interstate Commerce Commission. Among other things, the Interstate Commerce Act forbade railroad rebates and pooling. It said that railroads could not charge higher freight rates for short hauls than for long hauls. (At one time, because of fierce competition for the Chicago freight business, the Pennsy charged twice as much to ship steel from Pittsburgh to the Atlantic Coast than the far greater distance from Chicago to the coast.) The act prohibited discrimination between persons, places or commodities. It required all railroads to submit reports and accounts of their operations to the new commission.

The Interstate Commerce Act outraged the railroads. They complained loudly about government interference in their business and they warned that the legislation threatened the free enterprise system. Initially, their fears proved baseless because the Supreme Court sided with them. In a series of important decisions over twenty years the Court prevented the ICC from fixing rates, limited the commission's powers generally, and defended rights of private property against the rights of citizens.[5] It turned the Interstate Commerce Act into what Charles and Mary Beard called a "scarecrow." As a result, said Josephson, the agrarians and communists had their law and the barons had their railways.

But the barons surely saw that the writing was on the wall. Instead of fighting among themselves they began to seek what Morgan termed a "community of interest." This was a very simple scheme in which big railroads bought out small ones to build combines large enough to combat the inevitable assaults of gov-

---

[5] The Supreme Court decision that had most profound impact upon the nation and its development was undoubtedly Plessy v. Ferguson (1896). In it the court sustained a Louisiana law requiring separate but equal railroad accommodations for Negroes. It held that: "If one race be inferior to the other socially, the Constitution of the United States cannot put them on the same plane . . . ." The "separate but equal" doctrine later was applied to schools as well as railroads. Not until Brown v. Board of Education (1954) was it overthrown.

ernments. In making these purchases, the big railroads often used Morgan money. The result was that the big roads, notably the PRR and Central, grew even larger. By 1893, the Central and lines it controlled comprised at least 12,000 miles of track and earned more than $60 million a year. "All of the best railroad property," wrote John Moody, "outside of New England, Pennsylvania and New Jersey were penetrated by the Vanderbilt lines, and no other railroad system in the country, with the single notable exception of the Pennsylvania Railroad, covered anything like the same amount of rich and settled territory or reached so many towns and cities of importance."

At the turn of the century, American railroading reached its zenith. "It was an institution," Jacques Barzun has written, "an image of man, a tradition, a code of honor, a source of poetry, a nursery of boyhood desires, a sublimest of toys, and the most solemn machine — next to the funeral hearse — that marks the epochs in man's life." It was in this period that the Pennsylvania, under A. J. Cassatt, the European-educated horse breeder and brother of the artist, Mary Cassatt, made some of its most significant investments. In 1900 it purchased controlling interest in the Long Island Rail Road. In that year and the year after it joined with the Central to buy 45 percent of the Chesapeake & Ohio's stock. In the following five years, the PRR bought $17.9 million worth of Norfolk & Western stock, $65 million worth of B&O stock and $21.5 million worth of Reading stock. The purchases came to more than $110 million, and the PRR virtually controlled these competing lines. It was able to do so because the Sherman Anti-Trust Act of 1890 did not at first apply to railroads. In its 1907 report the ICC said that the end result of control by the PRR and Central of the B&O, the N&W and the Reading was to "practically abolish substantial competition between the carriers of coal in the territories under consideration." While working together in these ways, the two mighty railroads continued to compete fiercely for passenger business. On the very day in 1902 that the Central began running its *Twentieth-Century Limited,* New York to Chicago in twenty hours, the Pennsy inaugurated its own new twenty-hour run between the two cities. It was Cassatt who devised the bold plan for the PRR to invade the Central's home base in Manhattan by tunneling under the Hudson and East rivers. Its great Pennsylvania Station opened in 1910.

As the PRR and Central expanded so did the Morgan interests extend their sway over the railroad industry. In the McKinley era, the House of Morgan was said to control or dominate close to half the national railroad mileage. And the biggest independent system, the Pennsylvania, retained Morgan as fiscal agent. Morgan was said to be influential, if not dominant, in councils of the Central, Erie, New Haven, Reading, N&W, the Southern Railway System and the Lehigh Valley; plus, in alliance with James J. Hill, in the Northern Pacific, B&O and Great Northern. An ally dominated the Jersey Central. The PRR, Lackawanna and other smaller roads were in hands friendly to him. Shortly after the turn of the century Morgan partners and allied bankers were said to have held 105 directorships in thirty-two transportation companies. (After the Penn Central's collapse in 1970, Rep. Wright Patman, the Texas populist, attacked Morgan interests and other corporate "interlocks" between bank directors and Penn Central as one of the reasons why the ailing railroad didn't deserve federal assistance.)

Morgan's "community of interest" concept ran into difficulties with President Theodore Roosevelt and eventually with the Supreme Court itself. As a result of these pressures, the PRR and Central yielded their joint control of the C&O. (The Central first sought to buy the Pennsy's interest but they couldn't agree on a price.) Following enactment in 1914 of additional antitrust legislation, the Central sold the Nickel Plate Railroad to two bachelor brothers from Cleveland, Oris Paxton Van Sweringen and Mantis James Van Sweringen. The brothers formed the Alleghany Corp. and built a railroad empire almost as large as the Central's itself, an empire that later came into the hands of Robert R. Young, who parlayed it into control of the Central, after a gigantic struggle.

The expansion of U.S. railroad mileage reached its peak in 1916. Following America's entry into World War I, the U.S. Railroad Administration took over the railroads and ran them for the balance of the conflict. Federal control and operation was no panacea for the industry's mounting miseries. The railroads emerged from the war in worse shape than before, their physical plants deteriorated and balance sheets filled with red ink.

In a surprising turnabout, Washington, recognizing the railroads' plight, concluded that further rail consolidations were desirable and necessary. It breathed new life into J. P. Morgan's discredited "community of interest" principle. The Transportation Act of 1920, besides turning the railroads back to their owners, directed the ICC to plan rail mergers and consolidations needed to develop a workable national transportation network. Railroads complying voluntarily with the consolidation program would be exempt from certain antitrust regulations.

Grandiose in design, the Transportation Act proved unworkable in practice. The ICC couldn't force railroads to consolidate in accordance with a national plan and it couldn't prevent them from ad hoc consolidations through stock purchases, holding companies and other legal means. None of the big roads wanted to take on deficit-ridden smaller ones except in cases where extraordinary tax benefits might result. None of the rail executives wanted to merge themselves out of well-paying positions. Nor would the brotherhoods support mergers if the jobs of union members were threatened.

For these reasons implementation of the transportation act was blocked and the will of Congress was thwarted. All through the 1920's, the ICC delayed developing a consolidation plan. It kept asking Congress to be relieved of responsibility for getting the job done. Meanwhile, the railroads, fearful that the ICC would act at any time, charged ahead with their own combinations. The result was a frantic scramble in which the big eastern roads, as Otto Kahn, of Kuhn, Loeb & Co., later said, "put themselves in a position where possession was nine points of the law."

Accounts of the railroads' scramble for power and position in this period vary. Joseph Borkin's *Robert R. Young, The Populist of Wall Street* says that in the twenties the Central "consistently followed a more conservative policy than the other largest eastern systems during these years." Borkin quotes ICC Commissioner Joseph B. Eastman: "The New York Central has a practically clean record of nonaggression." By contrast, the Pennsy's *Centennial History* by George H. Burgess and Miles C. Kennedy argues that the PRR was "continually on the defensive against a coalition" of the Central, B&O and the Van Sweringens. It's true that the Central bought into the Lackawanna and the Reading in this period, while the Van Sweringens acquired at least eight middle western railroads. But the Pennsy proved that the best defense was a slashing offense. It gained control of the Wabash, the Lehigh Valley, the Pittsburgh & West Virginia and the Detroit, Toledo & Ironton; it tightened its grip on the Norfolk & Western, and bought stock in the New Haven and the Boston & Maine. Most of these purchases were made by a new corporation, Pennroad, formed by PRR stockholders at the railroad's behest in 1929 to buy other rail properties in competition with the Alleghany Corporation and the Central. With sale of $91.1 million worth of stock Pennroad began making purchases at exactly the wrong time — just before many of the railroads it bought felt the effects of the Depression. But the Van Sweringens had their woes, too, and their railroad empire, once worth an estimated $3 billion, was virtually auctioned off at a sheriff's sale in September 1935, shortly before the two brothers died. In April 1937, the former Van Sweringen holdings were sold to a syndicate headed by Robert R. Young. And in 1954, after a titanic proxy fight — the kind that old Commodore Vanderbilt would have reveled in — Young won control of the Central.

By that time, the Central was close to bankruptcy. Indeed, the entire railroad industry was in financial difficulty. The thirties had dealt crushing blows to the railroads. Scores were forced into reorganization and many remained bankrupt for years. Even in 1940, when the worst ravages of the Depression had abated, railroads representing close to one-third the nation's total trackage were being run by trustees or receivers. PRR stock hit a record high of 110 in 1929, then fell to 6½ in 1932. It gradually recovered, but remained in the twenties and thirties until after World War II. Still, the Pennsy managed to pay dividends throughout the 1930's, even though its rate fell to 1 percent in four years.

Ironically, many railroad improvements were made just as the U.S. economy dipped to its lowest ebb. In this period electrification, diesel locomotives, streamlined trains and faster freights were introduced. In 1930 the Pennsy opened two passenger stations in Philadelphia — the classic marble monument at 30th Street and the Broad Street Suburban Station. The following year it began electrifying its New York–Washington run. The project took four years and cost $126 million; 1,405 miles of track were electrified. Through-service with electric passenger trains between the two cities began on February 10, 1935. The trains sped at close to a mile a minute. Runs were reduced from four hours and fifteen minutes to three hours and forty-five minutes. Electrification helped railroads compete more effectively with growing airline travel. But after World War II, the shift from trains to planes and long-distance automobile travel on federally subsidized superhighways became pronounced.

Burgess and Kennedy's *Centennial History* of the PRR, noting mounting problems in 1948, 100 years after the great railroad's founding, warned that trains faced ever stiffer competition from trucks, buses, airplanes and private autos. "Services will have to be made more attractive and costs reduced where possible," they wrote. But they were quietly confident of the future: "The history of the company from its earliest day is notable for the absence of any trace of defeatism. If any prediction may safely be made, it is one soundly based on Pennsylvania tradition, to the effect that its management will face its problems, whatever they are, with unflinching courage and fortitude."

By the decade of the 1950's, however, it became clear to top executives of the PRR, the Central and other railroads that more than courage and fortitude would be needed if their businesses were to survive. What the railroads had to do, it was generally agreed, was consolidate. Consolidations had been necessary in the 1920's, but nothing had been done. Now they were essential. The question was: Who would line up with whom?

3

The Coupling

On October 4, 1957, the Soviet Union fired a twenty-three-inch aluminum ball into earth orbit. As the small satellite sped around the globe, it sent radio signals from a height of 558 miles. *Sputnik I* quickly led to *Lunik II* and *Vostok I* and *Freedom 7* and *Friendship 7*. To compete with the Russians, the United States began pouring billions into this new means of rapid transit. The Space Age had dawned and it was all very exciting.

Meanwhile, back on the ground-hugging railroad tracks, things were going to pot. Train service was a mockery and a joke, a bitter joke for riders and shippers who couldn't understand why the world's richest and most technically proficient nation had to put up with such abominable railroads. The railroads had few friends and they seemed incapable of helping themselves.

Not only were their own policies and public relations inept, but outside factors often conspired against them. In the East, for example, there was a problem beyond the control of the railroads: Much of their former business had simply packed up and moved away. During Alfred E. Perlman's student days at Massachusetts Institute of Technology, Lynn, Massachusetts, was America's shoe-manufacturing center. Worcester was the leather capital. General Electric's heavy machinery was produced in New England. The textile industry was New England–based. Now forty years later, virtually all of this business had left.

Similarly with steel. For years, furnaces in Pittsburgh, Youngstown, Chicago and Buffalo, cities served by the Central and PRR, produced most of the country's steel. This was no longer true. West of the Mississippi there had been just one integrated steel mill; now three lit up the sky. And the agrarian South was making steel, too. Much the same pattern emerged in other industries. Business moved with its markets. And in many cases these relocations cost Eastern railroads dearly needed revenue. Furthermore, the plants in the South and West, being more modern and more highly automated than the older ones in the East, operated at lower unit costs. As a result, recessions generally pinched Eastern industry first. As it happened, there was an economic downturn in 1957, and it drastically reduced PRR and Central freight-car loadings.

Then there were the trucks. There seemed to be more of them every year, seizing a greater share of the intercity freight business. To get from city to city, they traveled over ribbons of concrete built largely with federal funds under President Eisenhower's multibillion-dollar interstate highway program. By making it possible for cars and trucks to get from New York to Chicago and back without encountering a single traffic light, the government virtually guaranteed freight and passenger problems for the PRR and Central. Perlman estimated that within two years of the opening in 1954 of the New York Thruway from Newburgh to Buffalo, the Central's long-haul passenger traffic fell by 51 percent.[1] Another blow came with the opening, in the late fifties, of the St. Lawrence Seaway. While the seaway hasn't succeeded commercially, it "drastically reduced the level of freight rates and sharply cut revenues of competing railroads," Perlman said.

Seeking to win public support in their struggle against the truckers, the Eastern railroads hired a high-pressure public relations firm, Carl Byoir & Associates, of New York. Using railroad money — a reported $425,000 a year in fees and expenses —

---

[1] Perlman was bitter about the New York Thruway for personal family reasons as well. He told the ICC that when he joined the Central in 1954 he and his wife chose Larchmont, New York, for their home partly because it had a "beautiful [railroad] station and lovely flowers around it." The Thruway construction tore out the station, ruined the grounds, and forced his wife to walk through a tunnel under the new superhighway to reach the train platform. Rather than have her do that, said Perlman, he preferred that his wife ride taxis to and from New York City.

Byoir paid professors and other transportation "experts" to produce data attacking the trucking industry and backing the railroads. It secretly organized "civic groups" to peddle the Byoir line.
Its agents worked skillfully in statehouses. Following Byoir's
propagandizing, the governor of Ohio, Frank J. Lausche, based his
1952 reelection campaign, in part, on advocacy of a stiff tax on
truckers. In Pennsylvania, after the legislature passed a Big Trucks
Bill raising from fifty to sixty thousand pounds the maximum gross
weight of truck and load in the state, Governor John S. Fine
vetoed the measure. Fine's veto meant that a reported $5 million
worth of freight would be retained on the PRR, whose executives
had first recommended that the railroads hire Byoir.

When the truckers discovered what was going on they fought
back with a $250 million triple-damage suit, accusing Byoir and
the Eastern Railroads President Conference of vilifying and slan-
dering them. The federal court case was enlivened by the appearance of Miss Sonya Saroyan, an ex-secretary at Byoir. In a letter
to the presiding judge, Thomas J. Clary, Miss Saroyan complained
of her treatment at the hands of the truckers. She said that she had
supplied from Byoir files much of the information on which the
truckers' suit was based but they had reneged on a promise to pay
her $25,000.

Following this startling disclosure, the railroads countered with
their own $140 million suit against the truckers. And so the case
went on for four years in the fifties. For a while, Byoir's ex-secretary was as titillating to newspaper readers as was Miss Golden
Shifter in the Executive Jet scandals of 1970. In the end, though,
the railroads benefited no more from the revelations of Miss
Saroyan than they did from the later ones of Miss Golden Shifter.
On October 11, 1957, one week after the firing of *Sputnik I,* Judge
Clary found for the truckers. He termed the railroads' campaign "a
deliberate attempt to injure a competitor for an illegal purpose by
destroying public confidence in it." He said Byoir "lavishly entertained" public officials at the railroad's expense and used them "as
dupes in the railroads' campaign against the truckers." The Pennsylvania Motor Truck Association was awarded $852,000. Byoir
was ordered to pay 20 percent, and twenty-four Eastern railroads
the other 80 percent. They included the PRR, Central, N&W, C&O

James M. Symes was chairman of the Pennsylvania Railroad before
Stuart Saunders. The Pennsylvania–New York Central merger was
his dream. (Philadelphia *Bulletin* photo)

and B&O. The award was nowhere near what the truckers sought but it was, nevertheless, a moral victory for them and a stinging setback for the railroads. The U.S. Court of Appeals for the Third Circuit sustained this judgment. The U.S. Supreme Court agreed that the railroads' campaign was "vicious" and "reprehensible" but said that it had not violated anti-trust laws. The judgment was reversed, and both sides were back where they started.

For the PRR and Central there were other reverses in 1957. Because of the national economic slump, the Pennsylvania's earnings for the first nine months of the year fell under $20 million — less than two-thirds the total in the same period of 1956. The Central's decline was even more precipitous — from $28 million in earnings through September of 1956 to less than $9 million. And the Central's stock nosedived from 49½ in 1955, the year after Robert R. Young took control and brought in Perlman, to 13½ late in 1957.

It was no wonder, then, considering how badly things were going, that the Eastern railroads began to figure that if they didn't hang together they might hang separately. Merger talk and even merger plans weren't new. Much time and effort had gone into various consolidation schemes since the 1920's. But nothing had ever come of any of them. In the summer of 1957, James Miller Symes, then the PRR's chief executive, mulled over a revolutionary new merger idea. Most of the others had envisioned the Pennsy going in with one group of Eastern roads and the Central with another. In this way, their historic competition would be retained while their chances of survival would be strengthened. Symes' plan was different: He wanted to merge the Central into the PRR as part of a move to establish three competitively balanced rail systems in the East.

As Symes (pronounced Sims) saw it, the two old rivals were really like "two peas in a pod." They served the same general areas; they weren't much different in size; their traffic patterns in freight, passenger, mail and express revenues were similar — and their problems were virtually the same. Symes could think of "no two railroads in the country," he later told the ICC, "in a better position than the Pennsylvania and the Central, by reason of their location, duplicate facilities and services, and similarity of traffic patterns, to consolidate their operations and at the same time substantially increase efficiency and provide an improvement in service at lower cost."

Symes took his idea to the PRR's board of directors and got its okay to open talks with Young. One day late in September 1957, he went to Young's suite in the Waldorf Towers in New York and outlined his grand design. It was the first meeting of the two men. Young, small-town Texas banker's son, scourge of Eastern financial interests, friend of the "little man" and the long-haul railroad passenger, had gained control of the Central after a bitter proxy fight before movie cameras, on TV and radio. "I'm a stock analyst," he once said, "not a railroadman."

Jim Symes was every inch a railroader. He was a Pennsy baggage master's son, the star shortstop on the Sewickley, Pennsylvania, high school baseball team in 1914, and he had risen from a 25-dollar-a-month part-time job in the traffic department to become the boss of the world's largest privately owned railroad (finding his wife, a Pennsy secretary, along the way up). Like Young, Symes made it to the top without benefit of a college degree. The two men got along well; according to Symes, Young "was very enthusiastic right off the bat."

Following the Symes-Young meeting, Perlman was brought into the talks. The three executives spent a long day at White Sulphur Springs, W. Va., analyzing the proposed merger. Then Symes and Young rode north on the train and talked some more. Symes recalls that Young thought savings of as much as $200 million might be possible. On November 1, 1957, Symes and Perlman jointly announced that a merger of their two roads was under study.

Young had been wearied by court suits and proxy fights and depressed by the Central's shrinking revenues and falling stock. He decided to rest during the following January at his Palm Beach mansion. On Thursday, January 23, Symes was at his desk in Philadelphia when Young telephoned, inviting him and his wife down for the weekend. Symes had a cold and didn't feel like a flight to Florida. He declined the invitation. Two days later, on Saturday, January 25, when Robert R. Young might have been entertaining the Symeses, he went alone into his billiards room and killed himself with a shotgun.

With Young's death, his protégé, Perlman, took over at the Central. He too believed in mergers. As an MIT undergraduate, he had been exposed to the views of William Z. Ripley, the renowned transportation expert and early proponent of Eastern railroad consolidations. In the 1930's, Perlman had studied possible rail mergers in the Midwest before going with the Denver & Rio Grande Western, where he made his reputation as a sick-railroad doctor. In one year, he turned the D&RGW around, restoring it not only to solvency but to prosperity after four bankruptcies and seventy-six consecutive years with no common-stock dividends. On joining the Central in 1954, Perlman had been told by Thomas Lamont, of Morgan Guaranty, that it was a "bankrupt railroad." At his first staff meeting in June 1954, the new president was informed of a $9 million deficit for the first five months of the year. His financial advisor warned him that at the year's end the Central would have only $6 million in the bank to meet a $35 million payroll.

Through "cost-saving modernization and mechanization," and by lopping 15,000 men off the payroll in four months, Perlman explained later, he was able to halt the Central's skid.[2] It showed profits of $9 million in 1954 and greater earnings the following year. But Perlman soon became convinced that the magic he had used to rescue the debt-ridden Denver & Rio Grande Western wouldn't work in the East. The changes he instituted at the Central, Perlman said, were merely "postponing the day of reckoning." "The East," he later told the ICC, "can or will no longer support the present and increasing capacity of its railroad system . . . We are rapidly reaching the end of the road."

But while Perlman favored mergers he did not share Symes' enthusiasm for the one Symes had in mind. Perlman wanted the

[2] In telling Congress in 1970 how he had done it, Perlman quoted a letter he had received from Young in October 1954: "Dear Al: The preliminary October 15 man count on the Central is 74,700. This compares with 89,700 June 15 . . . Miracles can still happen with an ownership board and a good all-around organization wrapped up in one man — the president. Sincerely, Bob."

Central to merge with somebody, but with the Pennsylvania? He wasn't so sure. Moreover, he and Symes didn't strike it off as well as Symes and Young had done. Much, much later, after the merger débâcle, Stuart Saunders said: "Symes and Perlman didn't get along at all. Impossible." Saunders thought it was a case of personality conflict. He didn't know whose fault this was but he was convinced of one thing. "There would never have been any merger if Symes and Perlman had stayed there. I'm sure." According to a former Central director, Symes, a Protestant, seemed to consider Perlman, the first Jew to head a major U.S. railroad, his "social inferior."

Despite the coolness between Symes and Perlman, the talks went on. A committee headed by Walter E. Patchell, PRR vice president, reported that a merger, if effected, would produce savings of $80 million. Remember that figure: $80 million. It was first mentioned in 1958. Ten years later, following dramatic changes in wages, rail rates, size of the companies, cost of living hikes and new conditions subsequently added to the merger agreement — following changes which must have thrown the original estimate out of kilter — officers of the newly merged Penn Central were still predicting $80 million in merger savings. Until the bitter end they continued to anticipate such savings. Where the original figure came from was never explained — the ICC wasn't given as much as a scrap of paper. Nor was there ever an explanation of why revisions weren't made as time passed and conditions changed. It was gospel that $80 million would be saved, and the holy writ remained even after the presumed savings vanished.

All through 1958 the PRR and Central continued to talk merger. To the press, they were lovers plighting their troth. The Central was the highly eligible bachelor bidding for the hand of the plump, wealthy and matronly PRR. It turned out, though, that while wooing the Pennsy, the Central was secretly eyeing a couple of Southern belles, the old, impecunious B&O and the upstart, nouveau riche C&O, also known as the Chessie. "Before we marry the girl [the Pennsy]," Perlman was to say later, in explaining why merger talks were halted, "we want to make sure no other heiress will fall into our laps."

What troubled Perlman, to drop the matrimonial metaphor, was

James M. Symes, chairman of the PRR, turns over the railroad key, symbolic of authority, to his successor, Stuart Saunders, on October 1, 1963. (Philadelphia *Bulletin* photo)

the Pennsy's large investment in the coal-rich Norfolk & Western Railway. Both the N&W and the Chessie serve the Pocahontas coal fields of West Virginia and, practically alone among Eastern railroads, they have been consistent money-makers over the years. When the PRR-Central merger talks began in 1957, the Pennsylvania owned more than one-third of the N&W's stock and four of the N&W's twelve directors were PRR connected. (One of the four was Symes.) The N&W board met in Philadelphia. Its executive head, a bright, hard-driving Virginia lawyer named Stuart T. Saunders, also sat on the PRR's board of directors.

Perlman saw all kinds of perils in this setup. If the Penn-Central merger fell through, the PRR could always line up with its country cousin, the N&W. The C&O and B&O could get together; in fact, there already were murmurings that they would. But what about the Central? Who would line up with it? Perlman feared the friendless Central would be left out in the cold. He became even more alarmed when Saunders, at the N&W, moved to take over the Virginian Railroad which, Perlman said later, "had always been one of Central's friendly connections." Now this former "friendly connection" was to become a part of the giant Pennsylvania complex. The N&W-Virginian merger engineered by Saunders was the first of independent railroads of significant size in the twentieth century. And Perlman saw it changing the railroad balance of power. He insisted later that the Central had not talked merger with any other railroads while the PRR talks were progressing because "I felt it would not be fair." PRR officials privately accused him of doing exactly what he said he didn't do. And Perlman accused the N&W of doing it.

At any rate, on January 12, 1959, the Central broke off negotiations with the PRR. Perlman's stated reason was that the huge Pennsy system coupled with the growing N&W network plus the Central would unbalance the Eastern rail network. He conceded that adding the N&W-Virginian combine to the Penn Central "would have made it [the merger] more financially acceptable to us, actually." But he argued against this lineup on grounds that it would have "precluded balanced Eastern systems." If the PRR were to stick with the N&W, he preferred to see the Central join the C&O or the B&O, or both. And in an interview in August

1969, before the Penn Central merger began to fly apart, Perlman said he still would have favored linking the Central to the C&O-B&O, leaving the PRR to join the N&W and its satellites. "I think that would have given us a better balance geographically, physically and trafficwise," he said. "But certain other people didn't feel that way."

With the Central-PRR talks off, Perlman made overtures to the C&O. He viewed a Central-C&O-B&O combination as "an effective counterweight to the Pennsylvania system." But the Chessie wasn't interested. On May 18, 1960, Perlman was "shocked" to learn that a C&O takeover of the B&O had been approved by the boards of both "without notification of the Central."

"The Central thus found itself faced with the possibility of a Pennsylvania system including almost half the Eastern rail mileage on the one hand," Perlman testified later, "and a B&O-C&O combination on the other. If these plans were to be effected, Central would meet destructive competition . . . and would soon lose the ability to continue to provide service on its lines east of Buffalo, New York."

Against this bleak prospect, the Central began buying B&O stock to block the C&O takeover. It got about 20 percent of the voting shares outstanding. But the Chessie acquired, through purchase and under assents to its stock exchange offer, more than half of the B&O's voting stock. About 25 percent of the B&O's shares were held by Swiss investors, who supported the Chessie's takeover. Perlman flew to Switzerland in a vain effort to win backing of these stockholders. Meanwhile, in more merger maneuvering, the N&W announced plans to consolidate with the Nickel Plate Railroad and to lease the Wabash, which was 99.8 percent owned by the PRR. Frantically hunting for allies, the Central asked the Interstate Commerce Commission for permission to join the N&W–Nickel Plate–Wabash combine if not the Chessie-B&O. Years before, the Central had controlled the Nickel Plate only to divest itself of its interest under threat of Justice Department action. The latest development angered Perlman. "It is a bitter commentary on the nature of transportation regulation," he said, "to see the Nickel Plate, once virtually denied the Central, now proposed to be a part of the Pennsylvania system."

When the ICC held hearings on the C&O-B&O case, a surprise witness was Jim Symes. The Chessie asked him to support its takeover plan. He did. He also made clear that the PRR was ready to resume talks with the Central. If the Central knocked on the Pennsy's door, he said, "the door would not be closed."

The Central didn't have much choice. "They were out in left field," Symes, the ex-shortstop, told us, "without any sunglasses." On October 25, 1961, Perlman called on Symes and they agreed to take up where they had left off twenty-one months before. Agreement on key issues was quickly reached. The Central would sell its 20 percent interest in the B&O. The PRR would divest itself, over a period of years, of its one-third interest in the N&W. (More than $300 million realized from this divestiture supplied much of the money for the PRR's controversial diversification program.) The Central would be merged into the Pennsylvania. The Central would thus go out of business as a corporate entity while the corporate existence of the Pennsylvania would continue under a new name.

New York Central stockholders would receive 1.3 shares of the new stock for each Central share they held. Since the Central had fewer than half as many shares outstanding as did the PRR in 1961 — 6,521,838 to 13,167,754 — the merged company would be owned 60 percent by former PRR stockholders and 40 percent by ex-Central stockholders. The new board would consist of fourteen directors from the PRR and eleven from the Central. (Symes was asked at an ICC hearing if a fifteen-ten split of directors reflecting the 60–40 stock ownership would not have been a "more equitable division." "That is what we thought," he replied, "but the Central didn't.") No decisions were reached immediately on the location of the merged railroad's corporate headquarters or on the selection of its chief executive.

On January 12, 1962, the boards of both railroads unanimously approved the merger plan and in May their stockholders overwhelmingly endorsed it. In August 1962, the ICC began hearings which were to continue for fourteen months until 461 witnesses had been heard and 40,000 pages of testimony taken. In reading the transcripts nine years after the event, one is struck by the clairvoyance of the principals in some instances and their lack of it in others.

Regarding allegations that the Penn Central's size would "preclude manageability," Perlman snorted: "This is nonsense." Symes agreed. He pointed out that in number of employees, freight cars and locomotive units, the merged company would actually be smaller than the Pennsylvania alone had been in years past.[3] He also noted that in some previous years the PRR and Central had separately carried many more passengers than both together carried in 1961. "I think these figures clearly bring out that there is no need to be concerned over possible 'bigness' of the merged company," said Symes. He said the Penn Central would be the nation's largest railroad in miles of track and gross revenues but far down the list as regards net earnings and return on investment. The purpose of the merger, testified Symes, the first witness, was to "preserve and strengthen these railroads in the public interest and for the national defense, to arrest their physical deterioration of the last fifteen years, and to avert possible bankruptcy that could eventually lead to nationalization, not only of the Eastern lines, but of all railroads."

Neither Symes nor Perlman wanted any part of the New York, New Haven and Hartford Railroad, which asked to be included in the merger and, subsequently, was. Symes testified that if inclusion of the New Haven were made a condition of the merger he would recommend to his board that the merger not "go forward." Perlman was even more adamant, stating that "should this [New Haven] railroad, with all its inefficiencies and its liabilities today be taken over by systems that are still solvent, without first being made to help itself . . . it would be a grave mistake and a burden on interstate commerce and not in the public interest." He said

---

[3] At the end of 1961, the two railroads together counted 120,416 employees, 247,766 freight cars, 7,009 passenger cars and 4,805 locomotive units. In 1913, the PRR alone employed 241,388 workers. On December 31, 1968, after the merger was ten months old, the totals were: 94,453 employees, 187,362 freight cars, 4,976 passenger cars and 4,404 locomotive units. In other words: 21 percent drop in employees, 24 percent drop in freight cars and 29 percent drop in passenger cars. Employment rose to 103,325 on January 1, 1969, however, when the Penn Central took over the New Haven Railroad.

flatly that if the New Haven didn't do more to help itself, then "it deserves to go out of business."

Symes' solution and that of Perlman, too, was to have the New Haven combine with the Boston & Maine and the Central-affiliated Boston & Albany into a unified, efficient New England rail system. Perlman said that while the Boston & Albany was an asset to the Central, "I am willing to give up that asset to have balanced competition in New England." If one were to look this particular gift iron horse in the mouth, though, one would note, earlier in testimony by Perlman, that the Boston & Albany was a "marginal" operation that lost money regularly. The Boston & Maine was also deficit ridden and went bankrupt in 1970. That was the trouble with the plan of Symes and Perlman. They seemed to think it would be possible to combine three losers into a single winner. But Perlman had already told of New England's industrial decline, surely a big factor in the collapse of railroads there. In any event, the plea to exclude the New Haven from the Penn Central went unheeded. And some observers, Symes among them, believe that the addition of the New Haven to the trouble-beset Penn Central in 1969 was a major contributing factor in its subsequent collapse. Saunders, who accepted the New Haven at a cost of many millions, disagreed. In an interview with the authors, he said that while the New Haven was "a problem" for Penn Central, it was "not enough [of a problem] to make a difference."

The words that came back to haunt Perlman dealt with his conviction that electronics and cybernation would be the Penn Central's salvation. "We feel we are embarked on a second industrial revolution," he told the ICC. "In the first, human energy was replaced by machines. Today, in this second revolution, electronic thought and control functions can be substituted for the parallel human processes . . . Vastly improved communications and management techniques promise far greater control than ever before. In fact, with the proposed organization of the new company and the capital from savings available for investment in modernized electronically automated equipment, it is my judgment, based on my forty-five years of experience in railroading, that the merged company will be far more susceptible to efficient management than either company alone was only a few years ago."

Alas, when the merger finally began, the Penn Central discovered to its horror that its "modernized electronically automated equipment" didn't work worth a damn. Because the different computer systems of the Pennsylvania and Central were not made compatible in advance of February 1, 1968, they started off not talking to each other, electronically speaking. Data gathered along the old New York Central couldn't be transmitted directly to the PRR's — now the Penn Central's — brain center in Philadelphia. The merged railroad soon was confronted with lost waybills, missing freight cars, clogged yards, screaming shippers and a serious decline in business as freight customers quickly grew weary of Penn Central's modern methods and took their orders elsewhere.

In retrospect, the witness whose 1962 view of the merger seems most insightful was the official whom some now blame for the Penn Central's woes — David C. Bevan. Bevan, Haverford College graduate, former banker and insurance executive, was the PRR's lone-wolf financial expert. He ran his own shop and wielded tremendous power. To a considerable extent, he held the purse strings. And at the time of his testimony in October 1962, he seemed to be in the running as a candidate to succeed Symes, who had already reached the pension age of sixty-five but was staying on until the following year.

Bevan warned the ICC of the PRR's tremendous debt. More than $1 billion in debt would mature by 1982, he said. He specifically mentioned 1970 as a year with particularly heavy maturities.[4] "No other railroad has as much bonded debt coming due in the next fifteen years as we do," Bevan testified. He displayed little optimism over immediate gains from the merger.

"I don't see much in the way of profits, certainly, in the first five years," he said, "and if they [PRR and Central] go the way they are going there won't be any profits . . . I just am increasingly

---

[4] At the time it went broke, Penn Central's long-term debt, including obligations due in one year, was $2.6 billion. Of this, almost $1 billion was due in five years: $228 million in 1970, $156 million in 1971, $172 million in 1972, $270 million in 1973 and $160 million in 1974.

worried about the traffic trend more than anything else . . . We are going down a very tough shakedown period . . . With the ultimate savings to be realized [from the merger], it is going to be quite a while before we get them, because we will have a great many expenses prior thereto . . . And to come right down to the nub of the thing, if the Pennsylvania and the New York Central got into financial difficulties I can't think of anything that would be more disastrous to the Eastern railroad situation . . . I think that would be catastrophic . . . It would mean one thing, nationalization, and there would be no more merger movement."

Bevan was asked his views on possible government-guaranteed loans for Penn Central. Failure to obtain such loans in June 1970 precipitated the railroad's bankruptcy petition.[5] Back in 1962 loans for many needy railroads were guaranteed by the ICC. From 1958–1963, the commission backed nearly $250 million in loans to fourteen lines, including the Central. (Penn Central in 1971 still owed about $20 million of the $40 million Central debt.) Bevan said he hoped the new corporation "would not have to resort to government-guaranteed loans," but added: "I think each period of time is going to have to stand on its own."

Bevan said the PRR and other Eastern railroads could "cannibalize" — sell off their assets — to stay alive for quite a long time, but he thought such a policy would ultimately lead to liquidation. Opponents of the proposed merger refused to believe that the railroads' condition was as desperate as Bevan said.

Q: As a matter of fact, Mr. Bevan, a railroad such as the Central or the Pennsylvania or any railroad always has other income, do they not, of some sort?

BEVAN: You say always. We have had, but every time we sell off — we sold off nine water companies; every time we sell off a hotel we are getting near the end, so this slow liquidation cannot continue forever. I am not crying wolf and saying it is going to happen tomorrow, or the next day, but the railroad is not supporting itself, and we are living on past glories, and we are in slow liquidation. That will tend to accelerate as we keep losing other income.

---

[5] Early in 1971, $100 million in loans guaranteed by the government were obtained by Penn Central's court-appointed trustees to help pay bills during its reorganization.

The ICC hearings dragged on until October 2, 1963, and not for two and one-half years after that did the commission decide the case, which was then delayed nearly two years more by court litigation. But the day before the hearings ended, Symes stepped down as PRR board chairman. His successor had been recommended the previous June by Symes himself. In a confidential letter to C. Jared Ingersoll, chairman of the PRR directors' committee that was looking for a new chairman, Symes said the man he had in mind was "without question the outstanding railroad president in the Country today."

Symes ticked off the candidate's qualifications: a "young" (54) Virginian who had been educated at Roanoke College and Harvard Law and had practiced law privately for five years before joining the Norfolk & Western as assistant general solicitor in 1939. He moved up to assistant general counsel, general counsel, executive vice president and, in 1958, had been named president. With age, education and experience noted, Symes, in his letter to Ingersoll, then touched on the other abilities of the executive whom he thought should be given responsibility for putting together the largest business merger in the history of American capitalism:

4. An outstanding lawyer in the railroad industry. Served a term as President of the Virginia Bar Association.

5. Has done a wonderful job in merging the Norfolk and Western with the Virginian. He worked out a plan to merge the Norfolk and Western with the Nickel Plate and lease the Wabash. Also involved is the Pittsburgh & West Virginia and the Akron, Canton & Youngstown. The case is now before the Interstate Commerce Commission.

6. Highly respected by:
   (a) Railroad presidents throughout the industry.
   (b) The entire coal industry.
   (c) Heads of outside industry in general.
   (d) The financial world.
   (e) Senators, congressmen and various bureaus in Washington. Interstate Commerce Commission and Department of Commerce highly respect his opinions. He is an excellent witness.

7. His main hobby is hard work.

8. Keen sense of business judgment.

9. Firm, but nevertheless highly regarded and respected by railroad Labor leaders.

10. Some directors of the New York Central have indicated they would like to have [him] head up the merged company.

11. Good family life with charming and capable wife, who would fit into the Philadelphia picture quite well. He has four children.

Symes also argued that "bringing in a new face to head up our railroad would have a very sobering effect on the organization and provide a new leadership that is needed."

Acting on Symes' recommendation, the PRR board on June 26, 1963, unanimously elected Stuart Thomas Saunders chairman and chief executive officer, effective October 1, 1963. Saunders' salary was fixed at $130,000 plus $45,000 in deferred compensation for a total of $175,000. His N&W salary had been $110,000 plus $32,000 in deferred compensation. He was granted an option to purchase about 33,000 PRR shares at 21¾ (the closing price on the New York Stock Exchange the day he took office). His years at the N&W were to be counted in figuring his PRR pension, thus giving him thirty-five years' service for pension purposes upon reaching age sixty-five. The railroad agreed to buy his house in Roanoke "at its market value as determined by the Company's appraisals." There was no employment contract. The arrangement was as Symes set forth in his letter to Ingersoll: "Mr. Saunders could leave Pennsylvania at his will and Pennsylvania Railroad could dispense with his services at its will — without any further obligation on the part of either."

In leaving the N&W, Saunders was forfeiting his option on 3,800 shares of N&W stock on which there was a profit of about $132,000. He was to receive contingent compensation from the N&W amounting to about $20,000 a year for ten years. This added income would be subject to full tax — something over 80 percent. To compensate him for the tax loss and the forfeited N&W stock options, the PRR directors agreed not to deduct from Saunders' PRR pension the $20,000 annual pension he would get from N&W upon reaching sixty-five.

With his personal financial arrangements cleared away, the new PRR chairman could set to work on the business at hand: getting the merger off the siding and clickety clacking down the main line.

The ICC hadn't ruled yet but he faced formidable opposition. Already, the states of New Jersey and Pennsylvania and such cities as Chicago, Philadelphia and Pittsburgh, among scores of others, were arrayed against the merger. The New Haven Railroad was opposed unless it were counted in. The railroad brotherhoods were wary. There seemed to be no strong support for the consolidation.

And then, on the very day that Saunders took over, October 1, 1963, the Administration of President John F. Kennedy announced its opposition. The assistant attorney general for antitrust actions declared:

The Government's conclusion is that a Pennsylvania–New York Central merger would not be in the public interest. The combination would eliminate a vast amount of beneficial rail competition, depriving a number of important areas and traffic flows of satisfactory alternatives among roughly equal rival railroads . . . It would not only impose restraints on effective rail competition, but would also endanger the service capabilities, the prospects and even the continued existence of several smaller railroads which neither these applicants nor any other railroads have included in their merger or control proposals.

At the same time, the Kennedy Administration okayed the C&O-B&O combine which had won ICC approval the previous December 31, and the N&W–Nickel Plate–Wabash alignment, which the ICC was to approve the following July.

Saunders set to work. He drew on key men from both the PRR and Central for assistance but the job of winning over city, state and federal officials plus labor unions was essentially his. His performance was little short of sensational. Due largely to his amazingly effective politicking among both Republicans and Democrats, opposition melted.

In January 1964 Pennsylvania's Republican Governor William Scranton, reversing the previous stand of Democratic Governor David L. Lawrence, conditionally approved the merger. Scranton's conditions included protection for the Port of Philadelphia, job training for those workers laid off in the consolidation and guarantees for feeder railroads in Pennsylvania.

In February 1964 New Jersey's Deputy Attorney General William Gural, a Democrat, reversed the Garden State's stand. He said it would not oppose the merger if passenger and freight service were maintained and labor was protected.

In May 1964 the PRR and Central announced agreement with seventeen unions protecting the jobs of all those employed by the two railroads when the merger took effect, and promising to rehire thousands of employees furloughed before the merger. (About 2,400 of 5,000 eligible returned to work under this agreement even though they had been dropped earlier for causes unrelated to the merger.)

After reaching the labor agreement, for which he was later denounced for being overly generous, Saunders had no further trouble with the brotherhoods.

In June 1964 the city of Philadelphia protested that "no city, no state, and certainly no shipper can stand before this Leviathan." But two months later, in August, Mayor James H. J. Tate, a Democrat, after conferring with Democrat Saunders, said he would reconsider Philadelphia's opposition. He termed Saunders "very persuasive." And in July 1965 the city did in fact drop its objections after Saunders pledged that it would suffer no reduction in employment.

On April 27, 1966, the ICC, by unanimous 11–0 vote, authorized the merger on condition the Penn Central take in the New Haven. Despite Saunders' friendship with President Lyndon B. Johnson — autographed photos of Johnson lined the walls of the railroad executive's private office — the Justice Department continued to oppose the merger until November 1967. But with ICC approval and with most political subdivisions having been won over, Stuart Saunders' main job seemed almost done. In the final months and years before his dream was realized, however, Saunders faced constant harassment from a one-man wrecking crew who, believing the merger would merely line the pockets of fat cats, did everything in his power to derail it. This private citizen spent tens of thousands of dollars going from court to court and seeking to rally public opinion. Saunders never publicly criticized the man but his private opinion of him was unprintable. The Penn Central's fiercest critic didn't care what people said about him or thought of him. He was convinced of the rightness of his cause and he never ceased fighting the merger. Considering what happened to the Penn Central in less than thirty months of merged operation, it appears that the spunky little man may have been right all along, though possibly for the wrong reasons. He later became governor of Pennsylvania. His name: Milton J. Shapp.

4

Man against the Merger

The hand-lettered sign attached to the diesel engine said, "Penn Central Lamented." Milton J. Shapp, surrounded by two dozen reporters and assorted staff members and hangers-on, looked up at the sign and grinned.

It was September 21, 1970. In less than two months Milton Shapp would be elected governor of the state of Pennsylvania, the first Democratic governor in eight years and the first Jewish governor in the history of the state. But on this day he was still not certain that he would win, even though his polls showed him running far ahead. So Mr. Shapp, confident that the voters would respond favorably, did what he had been doing for the past ten years: He attacked the railroad.

The diesel engine was standing alongside a cobblestoned platform in Harrisburg's dreary train station, just a few short blocks from the green-domed state capitol building that obsessed Shapp. Attached to the engine was a special four-car train hired by the candidate for a whistle-stop tour through western Pennsylvania.

Shapp's plan was simple — and provocative: He would whistle-stop in a Penn Central train, along Penn Central tracks, through railroad towns dominated by the Penn Central. And he would blast the Penn Central at each of the thirty stops in twenty-one counties along the 800-mile route.

The Penn Central supervisory personnel assigned to the train watched nervously as Shapp and his entourage climbed aboard. They did not have to be told that their superiors considered Shapp

In a dig at the Penn Central, Milton Shapp, then the Democratic candidate for governor of Pennsylvania, called the train he was touring part of the state in "The Penn Central Lamented." (Wide World)

a dangerous character. Over the past decade, by his own estimate, he had spent nearly $200,000 to fight the merger of the Pennsylvania and New York Central railroads.

About 8:45 A.M., fifty minutes behind schedule, the Shapp Special pulled out on the first leg of the trip that would carry the next governor along the famed Horseshoe Curve and through the towns whose names had become familiar over the years to east-west railroad passengers — Lewistown, Huntington, Johnstown, Altoona, Latrobe and Greensburg. It was unseasonably hot; the temperature was reaching toward ninety, and the passengers were grateful for the air conditioning.

They were not grateful for long. Before the train reached Sunbury, the first stop, the air conditioning in the press car conked out. The toilet in Shapp's car backed up and overflowed on the candidate's luggage. Then the air conditioning in his car broke down. So did the cooling unit in the main sleeping car. There was no hot water for washing, and the drinking water was warm. In Pittsburgh the next day, as Shapp was about to address a large crowd gathered around the train, a hose coupling burst, showering him with steam.

Through it all, Shapp could barely conceal his glee. He clearly felt that the inability of the Penn Central, even with supervisors aboard, to keep a four-car train in reasonable working order provided first-hand evidence that his criticisms of the railroad were justified. He suffered cheerfully through the discomforts on the train. The railroad had savaged him far more bitterly, directly and indirectly, than any inconvenience caused by faulty plumbing or broken-down air conditioning.

Milton Jerrold Shapiro was born in Cleveland in 1912; his parents were immigrant Lithuanian Jews. In 1933, he received a degree in electrical engineering from Case Institute of Technology in Cleveland. Shortly after that, having discovered that employers, particularly in engineering, were reluctant to hire applicants with Jewish-sounding names, he changed his name from Shapiro to Shapp.

After World War II, in which he served as a captain in the Signal Corps, Shapp moved to Philadelphia. He was a small, aggressive man with an engaging grin that failed to disguise his restlessness and intensity, his enormous passion to succeed. In 1948, with an idea and $500, he formed the Jerrold Electronics Corporation, and with it the concept of community antenna television systems.

Community antenna television made Shapp a millionaire in less than ten years. When he retired as chairman of the board in 1966, he sold his interest in Jerrold for about $10 million. The firm then had 2,100 employees and the community antenna television industry, his brainchild, served 3,000 communities and employed 75,000 persons.

Like many men who have struck it rich relatively early in life, Shapp became dissatisfied with the world of business and began thinking seriously about the world of politics. He was drawn to the Democratic party because he was a political liberal and had contributed money to John F. Kennedy's 1960 presidential campaign. He also was at least partly responsible for the creation of the Peace Corps, a campaign idea that Kennedy relied upon heavily in the closing days of his quest for the presidency.

Some months before, Shapp had been in Moscow on a privately arranged people-to-people friendship program. It occurred to him that a similar program, supported by the government and aimed at countries that desperately needed technical, agricultural and educational assistance, would be well received around the world and could help shore up the sagging prestige of the United States.

Kennedy's brother Robert visited Philadelphia on October 25, 1960. Shapp was unable to see him because the younger Kennedy's schedule was drawn almost to the minute. Kennedy was leaving Philadelphia the same day to travel to Pittsburgh. Shapp bought a ticket for the same flight, sat next to Kennedy, and outlined his plan. He also gave Robert Kennedy a memo detailing his ideas on the subject. On November 2, 1960, John Kennedy made his first speech about the Peace Corps.

Shortly after Kennedy was elected, Shapp apparently determined to seek public office. If a Roman Catholic could become president of the United States, why couldn't a Jew become a senator from or a governor of Pennsylvania? At about the same time, he began to attack in earnest the proposed merger of the Pennsylvania and

New York Central railroads. After the boards of the two railroads approved the merger on January 12, 1962, Shapp mounted an offensive that never ceased until he was elected governor on November 3, 1970.

At first, the PRR considered Shapp a nuisance rather than a threat. In the eyes of the men who ran the railroad, Shapp was nothing more than a management-baiting hooligan out to make political capital of the largest merger ever contemplated in the United States. But when he persisted in his attacks, and began spending impressive sums of money to frustrate the merger, the railroad's attitude changed. Shapp had become a menace and he had to be stopped.

A formal application to have the merger approved was filed by the two roads with the Interstate Commerce Commission on March 9, 1962. It was not until January 16, 1963, that Shapp had an opportunity to officially tell the ICC hearing examiners, Henry C. Darmstadter and Jerome K. Lyle, that the merger should be disapproved. "Freight service throughout the state will be impaired seriously by the merger and this can only serve to accelerate the downward spiral of Pennsylvania's economy," Shapp told the examiners, at a hearing in Philadelphia's Bellevue Stratford Hotel. At that point, Shapp had plenty of support. In all, some 200 governmental units originally protested the merger. And much of this opposition was stirred up by Shapp.

The Pennsylvania Railroad began to get frightened. James M. Symes, the PRR board chairman and chief executive officer, had nurtured his dream of a merger with the Central for years, and he was not going to permit a nouveau riche Jew to defeat him. But Symes, in 1963, had reached the age of sixty-five; he would be sixty-six in July. He wanted to retire, but he also wanted the merger approved. On June 14, 1963, Symes believed he had found a means of achieving both his goals. He wrote the confidential letter referred to earlier recommending to the PRR board that Stuart Saunders be chosen as his successor. Among other things, it will be recalled, Symes wrote that Saunders was "highly respected by . . . *Senators, congressmen and various bureaus in Washington. Interstate Commerce Commission and Department of Commerce highly respect his operation. He is an excellent witness* [Emphasis added]."

The board agreed to hire Saunders on June 26, and he assumed office on October 1, 1963. At the time Saunders began working for the PRR, Shapp was preparing for his venture into active politics. He decided to seek the Democratic nomination for the senate seat held by Republican Hugh Doggett Scott.

Shapp's dream was short-lived. While he had money, he had no organization and very little experience. Besides, he was a trained administrator and executive, and he felt his natural goal should be the governorship. He withdrew from the senate race and continued to build for the 1966 gubernatorial contest. His principal issue was the proposed Penn Central merger. It served to keep his name before the public; it also served to mark him as a mortal enemy of Stuart Saunders, a Southern Democrat with close ties to Lyndon Johnson, another Southern Democrat who by this time had become president of the United States.

After Scranton reversed Lawrence by saying he would give "conditional approval" to the merger, Shapp attacked the governor.

"This is a classic case of putting private interest ahead of public interest," Shapp said. "In short, the Governor's proposal is a systematic sellout of Pennsylvania's future to the railroad interests."

Shapp was to make many statements like that in the months and years ahead. He compared the railroad interests to "robber barons." He warned that thousands of Pennsylvanians would be thrown out of jobs. He traveled the state like a circuit-riding preacher, carrying his warning to Renovo and Emporium and Moosic and New Castle. But his warnings began falling on deaf ears. The communities that had stood with him against the merger were caving in; and they began to support the railroads. In the end, only the city of Scranton and the borough of Moosic stayed aligned with Shapp against the merger.

As the railroads, led by Saunders, peeled away the opposition, Shapp realized what a truly formidable opponent the Pennsylvania Railroad was. He was a wealthy, intelligent man, but it soon became clear that he could never match the PRR in political muscle. Or ruthlessness. There was no way for him to prevent the local government units from defecting to the PRR.

Shapp did not give up. He hired Gordon P. MacDougall, a

Washington attorney, to represent him, and he told MacDougall to pull out all stops. Shapp said he was prepared to finance a blizzard of lawsuits and ICC actions to stop the merger. As it turned out, he was forced to.

The two ICC examiners, Henry Darmstadter and Jerome Lyle, recommended approval of the merger to the full, eleven-member commission on March 29, 1965. In the meantime, Saunders, President Johnson's friend, was hard at work persuading such men as Philadelphia's Democratic mayor James H. J. Tate that the merger was a good thing. On April 3, 1965, the Delaware River Port Authority, a joint New Jersey–Pennsylvania agency that oversees shipping activities in the Philadelphia area, reversed itself and approved the merger. Because of its size, Philadelphia was the dominant government represented on the Authority. Fredric R. Mann, Philadelphia's director of commerce at that time, was a member of the Authority; Mann used his influence within the agency to help the railroads. Two years later, he was named ambassador to Barbados by President Johnson.

Shapp, through MacDougall, filed objections to the examiners' report on August 18, 1965; on January 3, 1966, he asked the ICC to reopen the hearings. Both requests were rejected. Shapp had expected a bruising battle with financial and utility interests, but not with the executive branch of the United States government. He was becoming a very prominent Democrat, and he was fighting that most Republican of institutions, the Pennsylvania Railroad, but his fellow Democrats were preparing to destroy him on behalf of the railroad.

"He's a good friend of mine," Saunders told us, referring to Lyndon Johnson. "Oh, I had a good relationship with the White House, yes. A lot of these people are good friends of mine. I've known President Nixon for a long time and we have a lot of mutual friends. *That was no problem* [emphasis added]."

Dave Lawrence, when he left the governor's office in 1963, at the age of seventy-three, was appointed chairman of the President's Committee on Equal Opportunity in Housing by John F. Kennedy. He held the same position under Lyndon Johnson until his death on November 21, 1966. Lawrence was perhaps the canniest politician in Pennsylvania. He had attended his first

Democratic National Convention in 1912, as a page boy, and had been a delegate to every convention from 1924 on. He had served four terms as mayor of Pittsburgh before becoming governor and he had learned how to do business with every element of society. The chief example of his ability to get along was the relationship he developed with Richard King Mellon, Pittsburgh's billionaire industrialist, Republican party stalwart, and influential member of the board of the Pennsylvania Railroad. Lawrence and Mellon worked closely together to rebuild Pittsburgh, and the two men greatly respected each other.

Lawrence also knew Saunders and knew of Saunders' close relationship with Lyndon Johnson. Johnson had appointed Saunders to the National Alliance of Businessmen, a group designed to find jobs for the hard-core unemployed. He had also named Saunders to various other presidential panels, consulted him frequently on business matters, and entertained him at the White House.

After Lawrence began working under Johnson, he never mentioned his original opposition to the merger. In fact, he quietly reversed himself and began working *for* the merger. Democratic, and Republican, officials of towns that opposed the merger began receiving telephone calls from Lawrence, or were asked to visit him in his Pittsburgh office for friendly chats. To the Democrats, he talked of loyalty to the Johnson Administration, and of the future careers of local Democratic officeholders. To the Republicans, he talked of economic gains through the merger, of increased employment. And to both, he talked of federal subsidy payments that could be delayed, perhaps canceled, and of investigations into discrimination in housing against Negroes that could be started by his own agency.

Richard H. Biddle, a Democratic city councilman from New Castle, said that both Shapp and Saunders had applied pressure to his city on the question of the merger. New Castle, in 1963, formally voted to oppose the merger. In December 1965 the city council, three Republicans and two Democrats, reversed itself. "I just did what I thought was right," Biddle said. "I never sat down with Governor Lawrence. Now, some of the others may have gone to Pittsburgh to see Dave Lawrence, but I never did."

On April 27, 1966, the day the full ICC approved the merger,

Shapp stood virtually alone. The U.S. Justice Department, which had opposed the merger, showed signs that it was yielding, even though it would not publicly back away from the fight for seven more months. Nicholas Katzenbach was then attorney general, and was very sensitive to the wishes of the White House. He responded predictably when Myer (Mike) Feldman, the special White House counsel, called him to tell him that Lyndon Johnson favored the merger.

The ICC, in approving the merger, devoted four pages of its eighty-nine-page report to Shapp. It attempted to refute, almost point by point, the contentions Shapp had made.

"The contentions regarding the adverse effect of the merger on Pennsylvania's economy are not substantiated by the evidence," the ICC said. "On this record, the prospects clearly import that the merger will benefit rather than harm the Commonwealth.

"It will assist in attracting new industries through the applicants' increased ability to meet the needs for specialized equipment, more adequate car supply, new land for industrial development and expanded transit and stop-off privileges.

"The concentration of maintenance and construction operations in Pennsylvania should bring a net gain of employment to the Commonwealth."

"Today is one of the blackest days in Pennsylvania history," Shapp charged. "The merger will make it impossible for most areas to attract new industry and new jobs. I as an individual will take the case to the courts and, if necessary, follow the decision through to the Supreme Court of the United States."

Shapp was then engaged in a bitter primary fight with State Senator Robert P. Casey for the Democratic nomination for governor. Casey was the choice of the organization which included Dave Lawrence, and Shapp was relying on a massive television campaign, financed by himself, to carry him to victory. It cost Shapp 1.5 million, but he won the primary and became the party's nominee to oppose Republican Lieutenant Governor Raymond P. Shafer.

The Penn Central merger provided Shapp a constant flow of publicity, but it also required his attention. He filed suit in federal district courts in Scranton, New York and Roanoke. He twice filed appeals with the U.S. Supreme Court. All were unsuccessful.

After Shapp won the primary, and after the ICC had given its approval to the merger, the forces Shapp had been battling moved in for the kill. Shapp had to be stopped. Not only was he fighting the railroads, but he was promising that, as governor, he would force the utilities to pay property taxes, taxes they had escaped for years.

The first blow was not long in coming. On May 24, 1966, exactly one week after Shapp became the Democratic nominee by defeating Casey by 49,000 votes in the primary, Lyndon Johnson's secretary of commerce, John T. Connor, traveled to Philadelphia to speak at a Maritime Day luncheon in the Bellevue Stratford Hotel. "I disagree very sharply with Milton," Connor said. "I think the merger will result in a more efficient railroad transportation system."

Enraged at what he thought was a deliberate effort by a high Johnson Administration official to sabotage him, Shapp wrote a blistering letter to the president the next day. "I do not wish to be derogatory to top officials of your Administration," Shapp wrote, "yet it is obvious that Secretary Connor has not studied the railroad merger issue to the depth that I have, and that in making his statement he relied upon incorrect information furnished to him either by his own staff members or by railroad officials themselves."

Shapp told the president that it was "an extremely embarrassing situation" for the Democratic candidate for governor to be rebuked by a representative of a Democratic president, in his own state, and without prior warning. He repeated to Johnson his assertion that the merger was "a legalized multibillion-dollar swindle that would put the old robber barons to shame."

While Shapp was trying to repair the damage done to him by Connor's statement, another, far more devastating, attack on him was being planned in an elegant mansion on Llanfair Road in the Main Line community of Wynnewood, just a few miles from Shapp's much more modest home in Merion.

Walter Hubert Annenberg, who would become ambassador to England when Richard Nixon assumed the presidency, and his second wife, Leonore, lived amid staggering opulence. A multi-million-dollar art collection hung from his walls. Nixon and Spiro Agnew relaxed at his $5 million home in Palm Springs, and played golf on the private Annenberg course there.

In 1966, Annenberg was still editor, publisher and principal owner of the Philadelphia *Inquirer,* the second largest newspaper (behind the Philadelphia *Evening Bulletin*) in the state. Annenberg also owned the Philadelphia *Daily News, TV Guide,* the *Morning Telegraph, Seventeen,* a couple of detective magazines, and radio and television stations in Philadelphia, Altoona, New Haven, Binghamton, Lebanon (Pennsylvania) and Fresno. With all this, the *Inquirer* was still Annenberg's flagship. It provided him with a forum to air his conservative views; it was his membership card into power politics; it was the whip he used to flay his enemies.

Annenberg's "platform," which was printed on the editorial page each day, was that the news would be reported to the public "fearlessly." One bit of news that Annenberg did not prominently display to the readers of the *Inquirer* was that he was the largest individual stockholder in the Pennsylvania Railroad, with 177,000 shares, which were then valued at about $13.3 million. As such, he was vitally interested in seeing the merger of the PRR and Central approved.

Annenberg was also friendly with Stuart Saunders, another Main Line resident, and the two men frequently got together either in the publisher's mansion or in Saunders' mansion in Ardmore. While Annenberg, who joined the Pennsylvania Railroad's board in May 1967, was by far the wealthier, Saunders enjoyed something that the publisher never could find in the Philadelphia area — social acceptance. For years, Annenberg, a Jew, had lavished philanthropies on the city's colleges and museums but, unlike Saunders, he had never been invited to join the exclusive Philadelphia Club or the swank Merion Cricket Club. Even his enormous plunge into the most social of Philadelphia corporations, the Pennsylvania Railroad, had failed to open the doors of Proper Philadelphia Society to him.

But Annenberg was also a businessman and he did not intend to see his huge investment in the railroad damaged. He decided that

Walter Annenberg leaves the American Embassy in London on April 29, 1969 en route to Buckingham Palace to present his credentials as U.S. Ambassador to Queen Elizabeth II. (Wide World)

Shapp had to be defeated, and toward that end he involved his "independent" newspaper, the *Inquirer*, so deeply in politics that at times it resembled a campaign document for Shapp's Republican opponent, Ray Shafer.

In 1966, Harry J. Karafin, an *Inquirer* reporter, announced in the Philadelphia city hall press room that he had been ordered by Annenberg to assist in the anti-Shapp campaign. In May 1971, Karafin began a three-to-nine-year jail sentence after being convicted of using the *Inquirer*'s news columns for blackmail and unlawful solicitation, unconnected with the anti-Shapp campaign. His crimes were committed while Annenberg was still in control of the newspaper. Saul Kohler, the Harrisburg correspondent for the *Inquirer*, and others were given assignments similar to Karafin's during the 1966 Shapp campaign. Privately, Kohler later expressed revulsion at the work he was ordered to do and he subsequently resigned.

An *Inquirer* reporter covering Shapp asked him if he had ever been in a mental institution. Startled by the question, Shapp replied with some heat that he had not. The next day, the *Inquirer* prominently displayed a story reporting that Shapp denied ever being in an asylum, thus giving wide circulation to a patently false rumor.

The list of slanted and damaging stories the *Inquirer* printed about Shapp seemed endless, and they appeared throughout the 1966 campaign. In August, the newspaper said Shapp was paying a known criminal $125 a week for public relations work. The man was actually a $75-a-week messenger who had been fired in May when his background became known. Kohler researched and wrote a three-part series which was printed on the *Inquirer*'s front page purporting to link Shapp to an eccentric white supremacist, Harvey F. Johnston, a suburban Pittsburgh resident and president of the Pennsylvania National Association for the Advancement of White People. According to the *Inquirer*, Shapp had paid Johnston $15,000 to work for him.

In fact, Johnston was briefly on Shapp's payroll, having been hired by the candidate's western Pennsylvania staff, but had been dismissed as soon as Shapp discovered who he was. Nevertheless, the *Inquirer* wrote: "Who is Harvey Johnston? He is a white

supremacist, an anti-Semite, a political opportunist with whom
Milton Shapp entered an unholy alliance. . . . This, then, is
Harvey Johnston: racist political buddy of Milton Shapp. *Milton
Shapp knew the ideology and activity of the man with whom he
formed this unholy alliance, and if he didn't, he should have
known* [emphasis added]."

In attempting to paint Shapp as a racist, the *Inquirer* failed to
mention that he was probably the first Philadelphia executive to
have a Negro, Mrs. Katherine Boyd, as a personal secretary. Mrs.
Boyd also became the first Negro woman to serve as personal
secretary to a governor, after Shapp was elected in 1970. The
Inquirer also neglected to mention an earlier appraisal it made of
Shapp, in May 1966, before Annenberg decided to destroy Shapp.
At that time, the newspaper said: "Shapp has been doing something about unemployment, particularly among Negroes. He has
actively supported the job training programs for Negroes and
Puerto Ricans at the Berean Institute here and has served as
chairman of the city's Manpower Utilization Commission."

Having tried to damage Shapp with the Negro voters through
this series, the *Inquirer* tried to alarm white voters by accusing
Shapp of buying the campaign services of 100 Negro ministers.
These attacks continued almost on a daily basis and, despite the
fact that Shapp spent $2 million in his general election campaign,
he was powerless to effectively combat them. "The *Inquirer* smear
campaign cost me a minimum of 125,000 votes," Shapp told us.
"We would have won if it hadn't been for Annenberg." Shapp lost
the election to Ray Shafer by 240,000 votes.

The only explanation Annenberg ever gave for his attack on
Shapp was in a rare interview with *Philadelphia Magazine* two
years later: "I had a sympathetic view towards Mr. Shapp long
before the campaign but then he used the Pennsylvania Railroad
as his *schtick*. Do you know what a *schtick* is? It's a show business
term, a device to call attention to yourself. The Pennsylvania Railroad was Mr. Shapp's *schtick,* a publicity gimmick he used for
political purposes. I've always been tremendously interested in the
Pennsylvania Railroad; it is one of the great American corporations and has played an important role in the history and growth of
our country and this community. Stuart Saunders, the chairman of

the board and chief executive officer, is a personal friend of mine and we've had a warm and stimulating relationship serving the Pennsylvania."

Annenberg never saw fit to use the *Inquirer*'s news columns to discuss his relationship with Saunders or the railroad while he was systematically harassing Shapp. About the only step Annenberg failed to take was to contribute to Shafer's campaign, since he had publicly taken the position that a newspaperman who made cash contributions to candidates compromised himself. Four years later, as ambassador to the Court of St. James's, he contributed $2,500 to Shapp's second opponent, Raymond J. Broderick.

In 1966 and in 1970, persons with strong ties to the railroad made contributions to Shapp's opponents. Shapp charged in 1966 that Shafer had received, directly and indirectly, $81,250 from Richard King Mellon, the PRR director, and Mellon's family. These contributions, Shapp said, were made as a result of Governor Scranton's decision not to oppose the merger. Official campaign records only disclose $21,000 in GOP donations directly from the Mellons, still a substantial sum. Shafer also received $3,000 from Philadelphia stockbroker Howard Butcher III, second only to Annenberg as an individual stockholder at the time, with 147,000 shares, and a PRR director from 1962 to 1968. John Dorrance, a director of two PRR subsidiary railroads, gave Shafer $5,500. In 1970, the Mellons gave $10,000 to defeat Shapp. Dorrance, who was elected to the Penn Central board in March 1968, gave Broderick $4,000. Interestingly, Dorrance was also a codirector with Annenberg of Campbell Soup Company.

Shapp said he made one attempt, through a mutual friend, to have Annenberg call off the attacks. "We were at a garden party [in the summer of 1966] and my friend, who is not connected with the railroad, called Annenberg on the telephone while I was there," Shapp recalled. "I got on the extension. Annenberg's wife also got on the phone. They were both very adamant. Annenberg's wife [Leonore] shouted that she would never forget that I called her good friend Stuart Saunders a robber baron."

Shapp, anticipating another run for the governorship, tried to lessen Annenberg's influence in July 1969, when the license of WFIL-TV, owned by Annenberg's Triangle Publications, Inc., came up for renewal. In a letter to the Federal Communications Commission, Shapp urged that the license renewal be denied: "This company exercises a near news monopoly in the Philadelphia area. Over the years, the record shows that the company's handling of the news is distinctly not in the public interest. The Philadelphia *Inquirer* conducted a vendetta against me in the 1966 Pennsylvania gubernatorial campaign which reached a low in character assassination. While I was the victim of the *Inquirer* smear, much more than any personal matter is involved. The Philadelphia *Inquirer* and other publications controlled by Walter Annenberg are and often have been used to poison the political life of Pennsylvania and to attack the fabric of the democratic process. The news has been censored, omitted, twisted and distorted and used for personal vengeance and other personal purposes."

The FCC refused to deny WFIL-TV[1] a renewal, but, in any case Shapp was relieved of his tormentor. Annenberg, confirmed as ambassador to England on March 13, 1969, disclosed on October 28, 1969, that he was selling the *Inquirer* and *Daily News* to Knight Newspapers, Inc., for $55 million. The Knight chain had no connection with the Penn Central and, in Shapp's 1970 primary and general election campaigns, he received fair, if superficial, coverage from the *Inquirer*. "There's all the difference in the world between Knight and Annenberg," Shapp said, after he won the election by 500,000 votes.

While Annenberg was harassing Shapp, the railroad was at work on another level. Every Monday morning, when the Pennsylvania legislature was meeting, a tall man with thinning white hair, invariably dressed in somber dark blue, would step onto the platform at the North Philadelphia station to board *The Duquesne,* the PRR's 9:01 train to Harrisburg and Pittsburgh. His name was William Reiter and his destination was the state capitol. He was a PRR executive, but he worked full time as the railroad's lobbyist.

While the legislature was in session, Reiter and Harry Davis, the Sun Oil lobbyist, took up their positions in the chamber of the state senate, a few feet from the desks of the fifty state senators. Confident and unembarrassed, they buttonholed legislators on the

---

[1] In May 1971, WFIL-TV became WPVI-TV.

floor itself, giving them "the word" in full view of spectators and the press. So pervasive was their influence, and so constant their presence, that they earned the nicknames "the fifty-first and fifty-second Senators." Reiter was the fifty-first.

Many of the legislators had no well-defined concept of their roles or responsibilities. They found Reiter's room in the Penn Harris Hotel, and his expense account, always accessible. He played cards with them, bought drinks for them, picked up their dinner checks, and purchased tickets for them to testimonial dinners at which they honored each other. When it came time to do Shapp in, Reiter was assigned to the task. The legislators were his province, all 253 of them, the Democratic house and the Republican senate.

Shapp, always a maverick, was not counting on too much support from the regular Democratic organization. But he was not expecting treachery from organization Democrats. In the end, however, several Democratic legislators quietly crossed over and worked against Shapp. Shapp was convinced that he could detect Reiter's hand in this.

It was left to Saunders to make the most daring move. After Shapp won the 1966 primary, Saunders became increasingly worried about his opposition to the merger. Shapp said Saunders twice tried to arrange meetings to discuss the matter. Shapp refused.

Shapp had talked with Saunders before that time and felt there was no point in having such a meeting. "There's no doubt Saunders wanted to get out of the railroad business even during the merger controversy," Shapp said. "I've been at several parties with him where he had a few drinks and he was always talking about Litton Industries and how Litton and these other conglomerates had cash coming in and were putting it to good use, getting good returns. He said he wanted to keep the money for real estate investments instead of putting it in the fucking railroad. That's what he said, the fucking railroad."

Faced with his refusal to meet with him, Shapp said, Saunders turned to the White House. Shapp said Saunders appealed to Lyndon Johnson for help in arranging the meeting. Arthur B. Krim, who had been elected finance chairman of the Democratic

National Committee on April 20, 1966, was selected to help Johnson's friend Stuart Saunders.

Krim was the former boy wonder who, at the age of forty-one, had saved United Artists Corporation from going under in 1951. He was a dapper and urbane New Yorker, and a lawyer with sensitive political antennae. He was chief fund raiser for New York City mayor Robert F. Wagner, and he headed Johnson's $1,000-a-membership President's Club in New York. The president had frequently invited Krim to his Texas ranch and came to rely on his financial genius. In 1966, he wanted Krim to wipe out the Democratic party's $2.4 million debt.

In June 1966 Krim called Shapp. Shapp, in discussing the call, refused to disclose Krim's name, saying only that the caller was "an official of the Democratic National Committee." Saunders, in an interview with the authors, admitted the meeting had taken place and supplied Krim's name. "The meeting was arranged by the Democratic National Committee," Shapp said. "Two others had called to try to set up a meeting with Saunders but I rejected them.

"Saunders was very close to Johnson. I remember when I was fighting the merger Saunders told me that Johnson favored the merger. The first call that Saunders got after the merger was approved, he said, was from Johnson. Johnson put him on the NAB (National Alliance of Businessmen). And he used Johnson and the White House to get political leverage to work for the merger. *Johnson brought the Democratic National Committee in to work for Saunders* [emphasis added]."

After receiving Krim's call, Shapp agreed to meet with Saunders. The meeting was set for the first week in July. They would meet for breakfast in the Warwick Hotel, at 17th and Locust streets in Philadelphia. Shapp went to the meeting alone. Saunders showed up with Krim.

"In July 1966, when I was running for Governor, Saunders came to see me with an official of the Democratic National Committee," Shapp recalled, picking up the story. "Saunders said he wanted me to drop my opposition to the merger, or at least modify it. He said it would be 'politically advantageous' to me if I did so. I

Milton J. Shapp, elected governor of Pennsylvania in 1970, campaigns in shirtsleeves. He was the most vocal opponent of the PRR-NYC merger and one of Stuart Saunders' most bitter enemies. (Philadelphia *Bulletin* photo)

was in the middle of a campaign, remember, and the other party had far more money.

"Then the Democratic National Committee official told me pointedly that the President favored the merger. At my meeting with Saunders, he told me the White House wanted the merger approved and he left no doubt that he was talking about the President. He turned to the official from the Democratic National Committee, and the official confirmed what he had said.

"Saunders told me that if I dropped my opposition or softened it, my campaign would receive a large contribution. He said a similarly large contribution would be made to the Democratic National Committee and that's what the party official was interested in.

"I could have used the money. Shafer outspent me by three or four to one. I called my attorney in Washington, Gordon Mac-Dougall, and asked him if there was any way we could moderate our opposition without damaging our case. He said there was no way. So I didn't drop my opposition or modify it."

MacDougall had a different recollection of the event. He said Shapp telephoned him and directed him not to modify Shapp's case against the merger in any way. MacDougall said he did not recall Shapp ever indicating any willingness to accept Saunders' offer.

In discussing his meeting with Saunders, Shapp said he and the PRR chief engaged in some wary chit-chat before getting down to specifics. During this conversation, said Shapp, he remarked that he was leaving for a European holiday the next day. "Saunders wanted this merger so badly, he was ready to do anything," Shapp said. "He offered to put on his private railroad car to take me and Muriel and my daughter and a friend up to New York to catch our plane."

Saunders, while acknowledging the meeting took place, told the authors he at no time offered to make a contribution to Shapp's campaign in return for Shapp's dropping or modifying his opposition to the merger.

In the end, Saunders appeared to have won all around. Shapp was defeated by Shafer. The merger was approved and sustained in the courts, after Lyndon Johnson's Justice Department reversed itself and supported the merger.

But during this time, when Saunders was fighting Shapp and marshaling political support for the merger, there was apparently very little attention being paid to the results of the merger. Two giant railroads were about to become one in name, but would they actually become one in operation?

Saunders was to learn that Shapp, far from being the end of his, and Penn Central's, troubles, was only the beginning.

5

The Red and the Green

On Merger Day, February 1, 1968, three kinds of internal problems confronted the Penn Central: operational, financial and "people." These problems were interrelated, but of the three the most disruptive were the "people" problems.

When two railroads that had been bitter rivals for 100 years combined, human conflicts were inevitable. Yet they were never dealt with openly and honestly. They weren't even anticipated. One could read 40,000 pages of merger testimony before the ICC without encountering a hint of impending trouble in meshing "red" PRR people with "green" Central people.[1] Even after the collapse, Stuart Saunders considered reports of red-green feuding "greatly exaggerated." The reports, if anything, were understated. The differences were excruciatingly real. And the failure of Saunders, Alfred Perlman and David Bevan to work as a team and to inspire their subordinates to do so hastened Penn Central's collapse.

James Symes to the contrary, the PRR and Central were not like "two peas in a pod." In operating style, in marketing philosophy, in personnel, they differed sharply. The Pennsylvania, stolid, steady and traditional, carried ore over mountains. It was "volume oriented," and its operations were highly decentralized. It generally promoted from within its own ranks. The Central was smaller, scrappier, hungrier, more inclined to abandon the book and innovate. Perlman once said: "After you've done a thing the

---

[1] So designated because of the color of their respective boxcars. The Pennsylvania's were red and the Central's were green.

same way for two years, look it over carefully. After five years, look at it with suspicion. After ten years, throw it away and start all over again." The Central carried manufactured goods along its "water-level route." It was profit oriented and centralized. PRR critics conveyed the impression that the Central was run "out of Al Perlman's hat." But Perlman often went outside the company for promising executive talent.

In addition to major stylistic differences between the two rival railroads there were many minor operational ones. The Central, for example, used in-cab locomotive signals; the Pennsylvania used visual signals along its right-of-way. Central locomotives came equipped with cushioned armrests for engineers; Pennsylvania locomotives didn't. (Central engineers refused to operate PRR locomotives until the armrests were installed.) The two railroads even used different kinds of railroad spikes. And then there were the incompatible computers . . .

Not one of these operational problems was insuperable. But the problem of incompatible executives proved to be just that. "The most difficult part of the merger," William A. Lashley, Penn Central's perceptive vice president for public relations and advertising, said in an interview nine months before the bankruptcy, "is the human personality. You can combine tracks and stations but getting people together is something else." Another executive said it was "human nature" for the reds and the greens to fight it out. "Not that you'll find blood an inch thick on the floor. It's all been fairly gentlemanly. But I don't see the rivalry as having lessened at all lately. It's surprisingly deeprooted in the human psyche." And he was talking at a point seventeen months after the merger began.

The consolidation of any two longtime competitors would cause a certain amount of anxiety, insecurity and undercutting in the newly merged executive suite. Corporate loyalties die slowly. In Penn Central's case, these natural animosities were intensified by differences between such remarkably dissimilar cities as Philadelphia and New York and such remarkably dissimilar people as Stuart Saunders, Alfred Perlman and David Bevan.

In the Philadelphia suburbs, set in an autumnal landscape so ripe and misty that it might have been painted by Constable . . . lives an oligarchy more compact, more tightly and more complacently entrenched than any in the United States, with the possible exception of that along the north shore of Long Island . . . The Main Line lives on the Main Line all year around . . . It is one of the few places in the country where it doesn't matter on what side of the tracks you are. These are very superior tracks . . . What does the whole Main Line believe in most? Privilege.

— John Gunther, *Inside U.S.A.*

On his appointment as Pennsylvania Railroad board chairman in 1963, Stuart T. Saunders had moved to the Main Line. Where else? After virtually creating the Main Line in the 1870's and eighties, the PRR had more or less required its presidents, says Nathaniel Burt, the social historian, to "plunk their estates out there." Whether under duress or not and whether or not they rode the renowned Paoli Local commuter trains to work — Saunders never did — all PRR chief executives in the twentieth century lived in Philadelphia's plush western suburbs. The trains didn't always run on time — after World War II the service got plain awful — but a real estate mystique continued to hang over those tracks. "Nothing was so holy," rhymed Christopher Morley, "as the local to Paoli." And out in Oklahoma, people named three towns after the Main Line stations of Ardmore, Wynnewood and Wayne.[2]

Past PRR presidents had owned Main Line showplaces. A. J. Cassatt's "Cheswold" was in Haverford, W. W. Atterbury's "Bou-

---

[2] If the Pennsylvania Railroad could lend a certain enchantment to an appropriately named station, it could also take away — both the name and the station. In the last century there was a Main Line stop between Radnor and Villanova called Upton. One night the oligarch on whose property Upton Station stood gave a fancy-dress party that continued until dawn. Still in their formal attire, his guests then were driven to the station to catch the train to town. But the train, when it came, passed Upton without as much as slowing down. The outraged oligarch, so the story goes, stormed into the office of the PRR president, A. J. Cassatt, protesting the incident and demanding a promise that it would never happen again. Cassatt gave his word. And no train ever again did pass Upton Station without stopping — because Cassatt had the station torn down that very day. Though possibly apocryphal, the story illustrates a point made by Nathaniel Burt, that no other railroad "was more sublimely ruthless if still respectable" than the PRR in its great years.

dinot Farms" in Radnor, and Martin W. Clement's "Crefeld," in Rosemont. Saunders chose a $195,000, Norman-style mansion on 7.7 acres in Ardmore, not far from Bevan's estate, "Treverigge," in Gladwyne. Saunders' property ran alongside the swank Merion Golf Club, which he soon joined. Many of his railroad colleagues belonged to Merion, too, which was not surprising. For, by tradition, Pennsylvania Railroad executives not only lived close to one another on the Main Line; they also clubbed together.

"The Club," according to Burt, "is Philadelphia's most characteristic form of organization." Since Proper Philadelphia has always been clubby and since "The Railroad" — in the right circles it was never the "Pennsy" or the "PRR" — was always such an important part of Proper Philadelphia, it was perhaps inevitable that Pennsylvania Railroad men would be clubmen. They belonged to social clubs, golf clubs, cricket clubs, business clubs, hunt clubs, cooking clubs, patriotic clubs. Most of these clubs were exclusive, i.e. open only to white Protestants.

In the annual edition of Philadelphia's Social Register, vernacularly known as the "stud book," some railroad types would list a dozen or more club affiliations. Martin Withington Clement's entry, by no means the longest, listed "Ul. R. Rb. Ph. Me. Gm. Cp. Rv. Cw. Wt. San."[3] To this imposing list R. (for Rudolph) Stewart Rauch, president of the Philadelphia Saving Fund Society and a longtime PRR director, could add: "Cts. Pkg. Rd."[4] And David Bevan and his wife, the former Mary Heist, listed "Cp. Dar. Mfy."[5]

Club-conscious Proper Philadelphia warmly welcomed Stuart Saunders. Within a few weeks of his arrival he was guest of honor at a gourmet dinner given by — and cooked by — members of the Rabbit, a very exclusive gentlemen's cooking club. Saunders quickly joined the Merion Cricket Club, the Racquet Club and the Gulph Mills Golf Club, as well as Merion Golf, and in two years

---

[3] Union League, Rittenhouse Club, Rabbit, Philadelphia Club, Merion Cricket, Gulph Mills Golf, Colonial Society of Pennsylvania, Sons of Revolution, Society of Colonial Wars, Society of the War of 1812, St. Anthony–New York.

[4] The Courts, Pickering Hunt Club, Radnor Hunt Club.

[5] Colonial Society of Pennsylvania, Daughters of the American Revolution, Society of Mayflower Descendants. Mrs. Bevan died in 1970.

Stuart Saunders and his wife, Dorothy, spend an evening at Philadelphia's venerable Academy of Music on January 23, 1968, a week
before the Pennsylvania merged with the Central. (Philadelphia
Bulletin photo)

he was taken into the city's most prestigious club, the Philadelphia Club. The Philadelphia Club, which claims to be the oldest private men's club in the country (founded in 1834), generally limits its membership to Old Philadelphians with impeccable social credentials and others who, over a period of years, have made major contributions to the community. While Saunders' early admission might not impress New Yorkers or Chicagoans, Proper Philadelphians considered it quite a feat. Even some eminently qualified citizens long resident in Philadelphia have had the devil of a time getting into this "Gibraltar of Social Order."[6]

Not long after Saunders joined the Philadelphia Club another PRR executive was inducted. He was A. Paul Funkhouser, one of the so-called "Virginia Mafia" whom Saunders had brought with him from the Norfolk & Western to help run the Pennsylvania. Funkhouser, a vice president, was little known in the city. His admission into the "holy of holies" gave some people the idea that Virginians were taking over Philadelphia's best clubs. Not everybody liked it. "Don't you think Philadelphians are inclined to overdo it when a stranger comes?" once grumbled Bevan, a native Main Liner, an Episcopalian (like Saunders), but a member of the Rittenhouse Club, which is rated a distant second to the Philadelphia Club. "They wouldn't do this for a [native] Philadelphian."

The fact was that Saunders, both personally and professionally, had much to recommend him to the best clubs. After hours, he enjoyed martinis, fine wines, dancing (although his one social setback came when a select "Dancing Class" of couples at the Gulph Mills Golf Club blackballed him), poker (often with publisher Walter Annenberg) and the company of women. The "right people" found him a most attractive companion. But if he played hard he also worked hard. In the late 1960's, he drove Pennsyl-

---

6 Richardson Dilworth, former Philadelphia mayor who is widely regarded as the city's outstanding citizen of this century, was made to wait many years before being taken into the Philadelphia Club. His membership became a political issue in Pennsylvania's 1962 gubernatorial election. His opponent, William W. Scranton, said the Philadelphia Club had no Jewish or Negro members (which was true). Dilworth delights in recalling that Scranton, shortly after winning the election, joined the Philadelphia Club himself.

vania Railroad stock up, up, up, and in three years boosted its annual dividend payments from $6.8 million to nearly $32 million. For his fellow club members as well as for "widows and orphans" and Pennsylvania Railroad stockholders generally, these results meant money in the bank — literally. It was to put money in their banks and in their personal accounts that the bankers and other Establishment representatives on the PRR's board recruited Saunders in the first place. And for quite a while the short, bald, bouncy man in the vest with the watch chain of gold and the cigarette holder produced remarkable results — while also joining George and Peggy Cheston (he being president of the Philadelphia Art Museum board and she an heiress to the Dodge millions) at the opera, keeping up his memberships in Pittsburgh's Duquesne Club, New York's Links and Washington's Metropolitan Club, and engaging in cross-country high-stake poker with Walter Annenberg, John (Jackie) Dorrance of Campbell Soup and PRR's board, and a few other well-placed cronies.

With all that, Saunders somehow found time for outside directorships — U.S. Steel, Chase Manhattan Bank, Bell Telephone Company of Pennsylvania, First Pennsylvania Banking and Trust Company, among many others — and for corporate good works. He served on the high-level Business Council, the John F. Kennedy Library Corporation and the Philadelphia Bicentennial Commission. He advised President Lyndon B. Johnson on labor-management policy. He was vice chairman of the National Coal Policy Conference and Philadelphia metropolitan area chairman of the National Alliance of Businessmen. He was also chairman of the board of trustees at his alma mater, Roanoke College, in Virginia. And back home in Ardmore, the *Essays of Montaigne* was on his library shelf.

Small wonder that the *Saturday Review,* after a national poll of 300 business leaders, economists, business writers and others, picked Saunders as its "Businessman of the Year" for 1968. It hailed him as a hard-nosed, profits-oriented executive and as a railroad innovator. The PRR's consolidated earnings had tripled — from $31 million to $90 million — in Saunders' first three years in Philadelphia, said *SR,* and the railroad had spent nearly $600 million on capital improvements. *Saturday Review* termed

Saunders "the best-known innovator and initiator of the modern railroad merger movement." It credited him with launching "a program of diversification to free the company from the cyclical swings and low rate of return, which unfortunately characterize the railroad industry."[7]

Despite all the publicity given Saunders, the PRR's record in the five years before the merger was almost identical to that of Alfred E. Perlman's New York Central. Penn Central reports to the ICC show that between 1963–1967 the PRR lost a total of $32.9 million from rail operations while the Central lost $48.8 million. From nonrail operations in that five-year period the Central made $175.6 million to the Pennsylvania's $164.3 million. Overall, the Pennsylvania showed earnings of $131.4 million and the Central $126.8 million, or just $4.6 million less. The PRR's capital spending for railroad improvements was more than double that of the Central, and its debt retirement was almost twice as great. Since the PRR was half again as large as the Central, these results were not far out of line.

But if the performances of Saunders' railroad and Perlman's railroad were not very different, the contrasts between the men themselves were great. "Personally, I like Perlman," Saunders was to say after the Penn Central's collapse. "I really do. And he's got a lovely wife. She's a nice woman. A real lady. And he's got nice children. I like Perlman. I really do."

Saunders may have liked Perlman but they weren't friends, really. They were never close. Perlman was, in the view of PRR executives, "a complicated fellow." Certainly, he was a rarity — a Jew who made it to the top in the railroad industry. Before the merger the highest-ranked Jew in the 60,000-employee Pennsylvania Railroad was an accountant. Roman Catholics also were notably absent from its upper echelons. The Central had a broader ethnic mix. An Irish executive at the Central was said to have complained: "I was brought up to hate Protestants and the Penn-

---

[7] Although the diversification program began just after Saunders' arrival, Bevan was the driving force behind it. Since he is now blamed for its failure he should have been more closely identified with its bright beginning.

sylvania Railroad. After this [merger], I've got to love them both."[8]

Perlman's railroad experience differed sharply from Saunders'. Saunders had spent most of his career with the prosperous N&W. Perlman worked the other side of the tracks. In testimony in Washington after the bankruptcy, Perlman put it this way:

I went through the depression of the 1930's, and all my experience has been with railroads that were in trouble. Mr. Saunders came from one of the wealthiest railroads in the country and his outlook on these railroad problems may be entirely different from mine. A lot of people say, "Well, here the two men have different philosophies." Well, sure, a man that comes from one side of the tracks may have a different philosophy than the other. I have always had to help out, every time a railroad got into trouble . . . This has been my whole experience. Mr. Saunders had an entirely different experience, you see. So we looked at things from different ways.

It seems clear that Perlman and Saunders were simply on different wavelengths. This was true professionally and it was also true socially. New York society was neither as compact nor as homogeneous as Philadelphia's but, in any event, Alfred Edward Perlman wasn't a part of it. He and other New York Central executives lived in posh Westchester County but they didn't "occupy" it as PRR executives did the Main Line. Few Central men had had time to sink their roots as deeply in the New York area as many PRR men had sunk theirs in Philadelphia. The Minnesota-born Perlman had moved around a good deal and J. R. Sullivan, his marketing vice president, to cite one example, had moved twenty-four times in his first thirty years as a railroader. (His twenty-fifth move was to Wayne, Pennsylvania, after the merger.)

Perlman's thirty lines (compared to Saunders' fifty-three) in the 1970 *Who's Who* listed membership in four clubs: the M.I.T. Club, the Economic Club of New York, the Sky Club (a businessmen's luncheon club in New York's Pan Am Building) and the Westchester Country Club. He wasn't a joiner. "My father," said

---

[8] Largely because of Saunders' involvement in the National Alliance of Businessmen, the PRR employed many more Negroes than the Central. On both railroads blacks were employed only at the lower work levels.

Lee Perlman, one of Perlman's three children, a partner in a Philadelphia public-relations firm, "is not a big socialite. He liked to stay around home by the pool. He joined the Westchester Country Club — finally — when he took up golf. They wanted to put him on the [club's] board of directors but he wouldn't do it."

Perlman didn't pal around with New York's bluebloods but, as a railroad executive, he had close and continuing relations with some of the leaders of corporate finance. They never awed him. When he and Robert R. Young once disagreed on a major policy issue at the Central, Perlman recalled, "I put on my hat and coat and walked to the door." Whereupon his boss called him back and made him a director.

At an ICC hearing many years ago, Perlman was asked to identify A. P. Kirby, who was then on the Central's board. "Mr. A. P. Kirby," said Perlman, "is an industrialist or a financier or whatever the heck you want to call him. I don't know, he has got a lot of money anyway."

He was asked about another wealthy Central director, John Murchison, son of Clint, the late Texas oil tycoon. To commissioners who were trying to decide whether or not the PRR and Central should be merged, Perlman proceeded to tick off John Murchison's social graces: "He is a good fisherman. I have hunted with him. He is a good shot. He has a very nice-looking wife. He dances well." One can't imagine Saunders — or many executives — publicly discussing individual board members so flippantly.

At still another point, Perlman was asked if it were true that while heading the Central he was also president of a dozen or more affiliated railroads. He said it was. Each railroad was named; most were Toonerville trolley lines like the Indiana Harbor Belt Railroad Company and the Peoria and Eastern. The interrogation bored Perlman.

Q: You are president and director of the Troy Union Railroad?
PERLMAN: That is right. I don't know whether that is defunct yet, but I guess I am.

Not that Perlman was self-effacing or overly modest. Neither his friends nor his detractors accused him of that. "A man of sublime self-confidence." "Hard-headed." "A very personable, cultured, intelligent, persuasive guy of whom a lot of people are awfully afraid." "A fearsome antagonist." "Temperamental." "He's got human frailties." "His sarcasm slices like a frozen scalpel."

Did Saunders' social-club connections, the whole Philadelphia Social Register syndrome, poison his relations with Perlman? Perlman may have been privately contemptuous of such socializing but it's unlikely that he ever took offense at not being invited for drinks at the Racquet Club or dinner at the Philadelphia Club or to one of the special gourmet meals at the Rabbit, where toasts are offered to "Mr. Washington" and to the president of the United States. He never moved to Philadelphia, so the Philadelphia social clubs never rejected him. In a sense, he rejected the clubs and the Main Line and the entire PRR-Protestant Establishment. And in so doing, he worsened the chances of the railroad merger's success. Distance lends enchantment, but not to a company whose two top executives rarely see each other and rarely speak.

Perlman's son, Lee, did move to the Philadelphia area and he soon became aware of the realities of its social-club life. "It's so subtle — who can say that [discrimination] is the reason [for the absence of Jews in clubs]? For instance, for me and the Racquet Club, I won't even try. You can get paranoid about these things. That's Philadelphia," said Lee Perlman. "That's the way it is. It would be nice if it changed but I don't think it's going to change overnight."

Penn Central's "people" problems were explained only in part — perhaps only in very small part — by religious, ethnic and social differences. More important were the ages of the red and green team members, their differing attitudes toward railroading and their different perceptions of each other. Also, there is reason to believe that the two railroads blundered seriously in the way they went about planning the meshing of executives in the merged operation.

Shortly after Perlman and James Symes agreed to resume merger talks in October 1961, joint meetings of key staff officers of the two railroads began. The purpose of the meetings was to anticipate merger problems and prepare an organization that could deal with them. These talks continued on a regular basis for more than six years — right up to Merger Day.

Time magazine, in a February 1968 cover story on Saunders, said of these meetings: "The first sessions were stiffly formal, but even though some Central executives fear that they will be frozen out of key jobs by their opposite numbers at the dominant Pennsylvania, the atmosphere soon thawed. More than 3,000 major merger problems have been discussed . . ."

Actually, the atmosphere never did thaw. And while merger problems were discussed, they weren't dealt with. Nothing was really dealt with. Until the final U.S. Supreme Court approval on January 15, 1968, the two railroads were never sure that the planned merger would in fact take place. Lacking such assurance, neither side was prepared to make its operations conform with the other. It was largely for this reason that nothing was done about the incompatible computers. "I had no power to tell Perlman he was going to have to accept our system," Saunders said later, "and I wasn't about to let him tell me we had to accept the Central's."

Even more important, because of the uncertainty, department heads and other key personnel of the merged railroad weren't named until the last minute. There was a reason for the long delay. If a "green" executive were chosen over his "red" counterpart to head, say, the new traffic department and the merger didn't go through — always a possibility — then the "red" executive's effectiveness in his own company would be seriously impaired. Everybody would know that he had been passed over for a top job in the merger that didn't come off.

Rather than place men in that position, Saunders and Perlman decided to delay picking men for the top posts until the merger was sure. "The decision was made not to pick the top people," said a former PRR executive who attended the talks. "That situation lasted for more than six years. Then, all of a sudden, the merger was on the track. Here sat these same people six and seven years older, sticking to their ways. You had people with their horns locked — on computerization, on finance, on operations, on traffic. It went right through Saunders and Perlman, too."

At the Central, Perlman had built a staff of bright Harvard Business School graduates and other outsiders with fresh ideas on railroad freight marketing. They had few contacts with shippers and not much experience but they were full of creative notions on rail shipping for maximum profits. Using operations research, systems analysis and other scientific management tools, they revolutionized the Central's marketing department and were starting to work on its operating department just before the merger. To many of Perlman's young Turks the merger was bad news. They reckoned that the PRR would control the merged operation, and they had little or no respect for the PRR. Even before the merger many of them began to bail out. Harvey A. Levine, a former Central marketing analyst, gave the views of many of his colleagues when he wrote to *Business Week* magazine explaining why he quit to join a Washington, D.C., management consulting firm:

The NYC's [New York Central's] young, ambitious and well-educated nonrailroad staff hoped to run a profit-oriented business. The PRR takeover meant a retreat to the old, conservative, up-from-the-ranks management whose objective was increased volume. It was bad enough convincing NYC railroad traditionalists that marketing was the key to increased profits, but having to fight a real estate empire presented too much of a challenge.

An important premerger departure from the Central was that of its number two man, a vice president named Wayne Hoffman. A six-foot-five-inch lawyer with a Phi Beta Kappa key from the University of Illinois and a Silver Star won as an infantry captain in World War II, Hoffman was considered by many as Perlman's heir apparent. But he quit the Central in September 1967, five months before the merger took effect, to become chairman of the Flying Tiger Corporation, in Los Angeles. "I had a lot of faith in the merger," Hoffman said later, in an interview. "I didn't have faith in the way they were handling matters, primarily from the Pennsylvania side. I had no regard for the PRR management or their philosophy. I felt they had to be changed."

Hoffman said he thought the Pennsylvania had been "going downhill" while the Central was "getting ahead." The record does not bear him out, but the feeling Hoffman expressed permeated Central staff headquarters. Perlman himself encouraged it. After the Central's 1966 income from rail and nonrail operations together topped $50 million (to the Pennsylvania's $45.1 million),

Perlman announced that his railroad was "depression proof." Following this declaration, said a PRR executive, "Perlman became impossible to live with" in the merger talks. He didn't break them off, however, and in 1967 the Central's income skidded to just $1.2 million. After that, there was never any doubt of his going ahead with the consolidation if the courts would allow it.

Not until Merger Day was the Penn Central's organization chart made public. Then a company press release identified the men chosen for the top jobs and gave their previous railroad affiliation. It read as though the red and green were neatly dovetailed. Beneath Saunders, Perlman and Bevan were three executive vice presidents — two from the old PRR and one from the Central — and two senior vice presidents — one from each of the former rivals. Beneath these officers were twenty vice presidents — eleven from the PRR and nine from the Central. Throughout the organization reds and greens seemed intermingled. An ex-PRR man, Richard Davis, was named Perlman's personal secretary in New York and an ex-Central man, Robert Lawson, was chosen as head of Penn Central's Philadelphia division. Of the nine newly named general managers, five were from the Pennsylvania and four from the Central. At Cleveland and Chicago, green (Central) assistants worked under red (PRR) general managers. At Indianapolis and Detroit, the reverse was true, with red assistants to green GMs.

In theory, this meshing of staff was fine. But an artist who mixes red and green gets brown. And that's what the corporate artists who blended Central's green and Pennsylvania's red got — a brownish, gooey mess. It was a mixture that pleased no one. Perlman's reaction has been widely publicized. To him, the Penn Central amalgamation "was not a merger, it was a [PRR] takeover." What is less well known is that the new table of organization enraged David Bevan. Actually, Bevan had been unhappy for a long time. He had hoped to succeed Symes as board chairman of the PRR. When the selection of Saunders was announced in 1963, Bevan threatened to resign. He made such a fuss that the press release announcing Saunders' appointment was delayed.

Even Bevan's foes — and they are legion — concede that he had done an impressive job tidying up the PRR's chaotic financial structure in the 1950's and reducing its debt. A graduate of Haverford College and the Harvard Business School, he had been junior officer of a Philadelphia bank and then treasurer of the New York Life Insurance Company before being named vice president–finance of the PRR in 1951. Under his direction, the railroad's debt was cut from $765 million in 1952 to $531 million in 1964. The number of subsidiary and affiliated companies was cut from 171 to a low of eighty-nine. Because of diversification, the number rose to 102 by 1968 and the merger itself brought in another eighty-four companies, making a new high of 186, but Bevan had begun reducing that total, too. With Bevan putting a brake on spending of all kinds, the PRR employment force tumbled from 137,765 in 1951 to 67,242 ten years later. All of these developments, coupled with what was for quite a while an extremely successful diversification program, suggested that Bevan, as chief financial officer of a railroad that didn't really want to run railroad trains, knew his job and did it well. And he also served as director and finance committee chairman of Saunders' Norfolk & Western, from 1952–1964.

But Bevan had this problem: Outside his own staff, nobody seemed to like him. "Very bright, egocentric, very difficult to work for, power hungry" is the way one PRR officer described Bevan. Another said: "He is his own worst enemy. He has an unfortunate manner. He's a centipede for putting his foot in his mouth." The head of one of Philadelphia's top-drawer banks rated Stuart Saunders "a genius" in putting the merger together and a man whom "I would hire tomorrow and give him the next job to mine." But for Bevan, this banker had nothing but contempt. "The favorite villain in the banking community," he said after the Penn Central's bankruptcy, "is Bevan."

Bevan and Saunders never seemed to have gotten along. Though their homes were only a few miles apart they never entertained one another. And at the office their relations were correct but cool. Bevan had less authority under Saunders than he had enjoyed under Symes. Tension between the two mounted as the merger time approached. "It was common talk before the merger," said a Saunders supporter, "that there were two Pennsylvania Railroads. There was Bevan's railroad and there was our railroad. Bevan wouldn't let his men talk to officers of other [PRR] departments."

Whatever Saunders may have thought of Bevan before the merger, he took no overt action against him. And in the merger shuffle Bevan retained his high-salaried post as finance committee chairman. But Bevan's wings were clipped. He'd been a director of the PRR; he was left off the twenty-five-member merged board of directors. This was a shattering blow to a proud man. And it created an anomalous situation: Penn Central's finance committee consisted of seven members, six of whom were members of the policy-making board of directors. The seventh was not a director — yet he was the committee chairman. Penn Central's news release made no mention of the decision to drop Bevan from the board. Instead, it played up his appointment to the finance committee chairmanship. But Bevan knew very well that his wings had been clipped. And he resented it. Furthermore, he resented the entire organization chart. He had three vice presidents reporting to him. But Perlman had ten — three executive vice presidents, two senior vice presidents, five vice presidents. And Bevan lost responsibility for the merged railroad's critical accounting system. It was turned over to a former Central man.

In an interview early in 1971, Bevan poured out his bitterness over the organizational setup:

> Perlman had ten people reporting to him, far too many. And seven of them were New York Central men. They gave Perlman Budget Administration, Data Processing, Accounting, Taxes and Insurance. I got Accounting in 1958 [with the PRR] and had it until the time of the merger.
>
> Practically everything was taken away from me. I said, "The hell with this." I called Dick Mellon, our senior director, and said, "I don't want anything, I can't live with this, I want out." He said, "The whole thing may blow up if you walk out. You've got an obligation to the stockholders and to the company." This was in January 1968, a couple of weeks before the merger. Mellon said he had been up till four o'clock that morning working on the organization chart. He said, "I want to ask you as a personal favor, and I've never asked you for anything, to stay on, grit your teeth and bear. I will change everything I can." He did change some things, but then he got sick.[9] I wasn't even going to have charge of the bank account.

---

[9] Mellon died in June 1970, a week before Bevan was fired.

This was the Penn Central's board of directors as it gathered for its first meeting on February 1, 1968. From left to right, they are: first row — Stuart T. Saunders, Alfred E. Perlman; second row — James M. Symes, Walter H. Annenberg, Howard Butcher III, Fred M. Kirby, Daniel E. Taylor; third row — Seymore H. Knox, Isaac B. Grainger, Edward Hanley, Franklin J. Lunding, Carlos Routh;

standing — Thomas L. Perkins, R. Walter Graham, Joseph H. Thompson, James S. Hunt, R. Stewart Rauch, John M. Seabrook, Otto N. Frenzel, Robert S. Odell, William L. Day, William G. Rabe, Gaylord P. Harnwell. Missing from photo: Richard King Mellon, R. George Rincliffe. (Philadelphia *Bulletin* photo)

Richard King Mellon, Pittsburgh industrialist, served on the board of the Pennsylvania Railroad and then the Penn Central for thirty-five years. He died in June 1970. (Wide World)

Bevan left no doubt that the celebrated red-green feuding was actually a tricolor — red, green and Bevan. He attacked both Perlman and Saunders with equal ferocity.

Perlman could ride around a small railroad like the D&RGW [Denver & Rio Grande Western] and keep on top of things. He wanted accounting done his way, not our way. I wanted an income budget where we would know what was coming in and where it was going. He said, "You can't run a railroad on an income budget." His budget was just a bunch of statistics. He had no budget.[10] He put his budget chief in over my budget chief. He put Mike Flannery,[11] a damn good operating guy, in charge of data processing. He didn't know a damn thing about it . . . We lost ten or twelve of the best young guys we had. They didn't want to work under Perlman or under people they thought were inferior, and they were.

All Perlman wanted to do was build classification yards. He spent money like it was going out of style. At a meeting in June 1969, he was madder than hell. "I'm not a harbinger of gloom," he said. I remember that phrase, "harbinger of gloom." "I don't care if we lose X dollars this year and X dollars next year. I'm building for the future."

On the subject of Saunders, Bevan had this to say:

When Symes went out the railroad was in very sound condition. Symes took my advice on financial matters. After Saunders came in . . . (Bevan shook his head.) Saunders said, "As soon as the merger takes place, I'll be the boss." But he never exercised authority. He seemed to be afraid of Perlman. Some of us thought he wanted to be in a position to say, "I'm not an operating man," if anything went wrong.

One board member came up to me and wanted to know what was

---

[10] Bevan wasn't the first to express surprise at some of Perlman's operating methods. Back in 1962, an ICC lawyer was shocked at the way in which Perlman went about studying the proposed merger.

Q: And so, from November 1957 to January 8, 1958, you had under active exploration the possibility of merger between the Pennsylvania and the New York Central and you never got a written report on it?

PERLMAN: That is just what I said three times before.

Q: Mr. Perlman, I must apologize. I don't like to ask questions over again. The statement is so amazing that I must admit I have some very great difficulties believing it.

[11] Robert G. Flannery, ex-Central.

going on. I told him Accounting and Budget Administration had been taken away from me. He said, "Well, they didn't let the word back to the board. The board didn't know anything about it." I said the board voted on it at the first meeting and he was there and had voted on it.

I had no control over expenditures. At every board meeting, I said, "Cash is tight, we've stretched this rubber band as far as it will stretch." In June 1969 I submitted my resignation to Saunders. I said, "You've got to accept it." Finally, Saunders got nervous. He said he wanted me back on the board. I said I wanted no part of it. I was electing early retirement and I wanted to be out no later than March 1, 1970. I said I would leave at the convenience of the board, that I would not embarrass anybody . . .

Saunders said, "You can't do this. You've got a responsibility to the banks and to the stockholders. You're the best man we've got." You'd never know we had a disagreement, the way he talked. He said he wanted me to keep it [the job] until after he got back from Europe. He was going on vacation. When he came back from Europe, he asked me to go on the board and I said, no. He went through an intermediary, a friend of mine, and my friend said, "Won't you at least talk to Stuart?" I said okay. Saunders said, "We've got to get a new president and I want you to help me find one." . . . He said, "What do you want in compensation?" I said I didn't want to talk about that, that wasn't my aim in life. I helped him look for a new president. I got involved in that. Some of the directors were after me to stay. One director said, "If you walk out, the banks walk in."

Bevan never did walk out; he was pushed out, along with Perlman and Saunders. But the Penn Central tragedy is much like *Rashomon;* each witness has a different view of what happened. Who was running the railroad? Saunders is firm on this point. He told the subcommittee on surface transportation of the Senate Commerce Committee:

When Mr. Perlman was president, he was in charge of railroad operations and he had full authority. He may not agree completely with this, but he was given complete responsibility.

Saunders also told us:

I have the highest regard for Mr. Perlman and he had complete responsibility for running the railroad. That was his job and I believe in giving responsibility. He had authority . . . Never once was he denied any authority of any consequence. I can't recall a single instance where he was ever turned down.

We never had any disagreements to my knowledge about any officer. I gave no consideration, and I don't think Mr. Perlman did, to whether a man was a Pennsylvania man or a New York Central man. Considering the relative size of the two railroads the management was pretty well balanced and today a lot of your top officers are New York Central people.

Perlman is equally firm that he was *not* running the railroad. In his testimony before the same Senate subcommittee, he engaged in this exchange with Sen. Vance A. Hartke, Democrat, of Indiana, the subcommittee chairman:

SEN. HARTKE: Mr. Saunders . . . left the impression at least with this Senator that you had the complete authority to run the operation and you were given everything you needed to run it. Is that true or not?

PERLMAN: It was not true.

SEN. HARTKE: In other words, it was not true in personnel, was it?

PERLMAN: No, sir.

SEN. HARTKE: Was it true in regard to money for these projects you were talking about?

PERLMAN: No, sir.

SEN. HARTKE: Why not?

PERLMAN: Well, as an example, that budget never even was seen by the board of directors.

SEN. HARTKE: Why not?

PERLMAN: Well, it was held on his desk.

SEN. HARTKE: On Mr. Saunders' desk?

PERLMAN: Yes.

SEN. HARTKE: Why did he hold it?

PERLMAN: He said we had no money, so why show it to them.

On the subject of staff selection, Saunders had testified: "Mr. Perlman and I agreed at the outset of the merger that we would put the best man in every job that we thought was qualified for it regardless of whether he was a Pennsylvania or New York Central man." In an interview he insisted that this was done. Again, Perlman saw matters differently. He and Senator Hartke had this exchange:

SEN. HARTKE: As I gather it, you would have instituted, if you had
had the authority to have done so, the same basic marketing concept
that you used for the Penn Central.

PERLMAN: Yes, sir.

SEN. HARTKE: But you could not get that done; why not?

PERLMAN: If you notice the people at the heads of the departments
of the merged company, everyone was from the Pennsylvania Railroad
except myself. To me it was not a merger, it was a takeover, frankly.

SEN. HARTKE: It was not a merger, it was a takeover. I think that is
at the heart of this. I think this really is why to a great extent, going
back into the merger from the very beginning, it has been one that
required just a little more concern than has heretofore been given to
this. Now in this what you call takeover, was it a requirement that you
retain those people at the heads of departments?

PERLMAN: Yes, sir; unless I got permission from the chairman to
replace them.

SEN. HARTKE: In your opinion, without being disrespectful to any
of these people, was the best man put in the best job?

PERLMAN: No, sir.

SEN. HARTKE: Now you see this is at the heart of what I am talking
about.

Senator Hartke clearly accepted Perlman's version of history
and, indeed, sometimes seemed to put words in the witness's
mouth. Perlman's version also won wide acceptance in the news
media and the railroad industry press. Robert E. Bedingfield, of
the *New York Times,* a highly respected transportation writer,
thought that President Perlman was "pretty much ignored." In his
post-mortem one week after Penn Central's bankruptcy petition
was filed, Bedingfield wrote:

Not only did many Pennsylvania-trained operating employees belittle
many of Mr. Perlman's ideas so long as their overall "chief" was their
old boss, but also Mr. Saunders turned his attention more to an aggressive diversification program than to reviewing Mr. Perlman's sugges-
tions for spending large sums to upgrade the consolidated company's
transportation plant and expanding the railroad's marketing activities.

Fortune magazine writer Rush Loving, Jr., in describing Penn
Central's unhappy executive suite, wrote that "Perlman, who was
used to exercising complete authority over his railroad, was frustrated by his lack of authority over finances." Loving continued:

Although Perlman made up his budgets, the outlays and other key financial data were controlled by Bevan, who was suspected of favoring land investments over the railroad. Perlman wanted more money for car repairs and modernization, but Bevan offered too little to suit him. Saunders presided over all this like the mediator he was, trying to bring the two to an accommodation and only frustrating Perlman's love for decisions that were hard and binding.

Finally, Nancy Ford, columnist for *Modern Railroads* magazine, made clear where her sympathies were:

Again, every one who knows Al Perlman's ability concedes that if he had been permitted to run the property instead of being frustrated at every turn, it might not have wound up the biggest bankrupt in U.S. corporate history.

What are the facts in the Saunders-Perlman-Bevan tug-of-war? The facts concerning control over and responsibility for financial outlays will be developed in later chapters. Regarding red-green rivalries, the facts are that the "people" problems centered primarily on two departments: marketing and operations. Of the Penn Central's twenty-five top officers immediately below Saunders, Perlman and Bevan, eleven, as indicated earlier, came from the Central and fourteen from the PRR. But veteran PRR executives were named to head both operations and marketing. Perlman didn't like either one of them. They were two big reasons why he answered "no" to the Senate subcommittee's question whether he thought the best men were placed in the best jobs. What was not disclosed is that Saunders also was dissatisfied with the performance of these two officers. And he joined Perlman in working to replace them.

At the time of the merger, the Central's operating vice president was a restless, hard-driving executive named Robert G. (Mike) Flannery. Flannery, a Presbyterian and a Mason, was a Purdue graduate and a twenty-year man at the Central. He was one of its bright stars. But he was young — just forty-three. And he had been moved into the operations hot seat only shortly before merger when John C. Kenefec, who had the job, quit the Central to join the Union Pacific. By contrast, the PRR's vice president for operations, David E. Smucker, looked back on almost forty years of

David E. Smucker, Penn Central's vice president for operations, was one of Alfred E. Perlman's targets. (Storer-Spellman photo)

Henry W. Large, vice president traffic, was another. (Courtesy of the Penn Central)

railroading. Smucker had joined the PRR in 1929, following his graduation from Ohio State. In the succeeding years he moved gradually up the ladder. He was, his associates said, tough, autocratic, articulate. He could swear like a yardhand but he also enjoyed opera. (Stuart Saunders much later helped bring the opera to Philadelphia, but he was a lawyer who never pretended to be a railroad operator.)

After many years Smucker moved over to the PRR's deficit-ridden Long Island Rail Road. In 1950 the Long Island was undergoing reorganization. Smucker was one of its two trustees and chief operating officer when twin tragedies struck. In February 1950 a train wreck took thirty-three lives. Nine months later, on Thanksgiving Eve, another, more terrible crash killed seventy-eight persons and injured 332. Following this second wreck, Governor Thomas E. Dewey of New York demanded the resignations of Smucker and the other trustee, Hunter L. Delatour.

Both men subsequently quit. For the next two years Smucker served out of the public eye as the Pennsylvania's assistant chief engineer. In January 1953 he was named president of its Detroit, Toledo & Ironton Railroad, a kind of farm club for aspiring PRR executives. After ten years there, he was brought back into the home office as vice president of operations. Smucker held this post throughout the years of the PRR-Central premerger meetings. He held it when the Penn Central's table of organization was finally prepared. He was sixty years old and nearing retirement. But he still had a few years left. He was the senior operating man, and when Penn Central's key executive vice presidency for operations was filled, he got it. Mike Flannery was named vice president for systems development, reporting directly to Perlman.

In Penn Central's marketing department a similar situation developed. The Central's flashy marketing setup had been headed by the much-traveled, widely respected James R. Sullivan. Sullivan was fifty-two. The PRR's more traditional traffic department had been headed by Henry W. Large, who was ten years older than Sullivan. Large was a quintessential Proper Philadelphian. Good family, good education (Princeton '28), good clubs and good jobs with the biggest club in town, The Railroad. Large was a member of the Philadelphia Club and had used his influence to get A. Paul

Funkhouser, a fellow Princeton alumnus, in after Saunders made it on his own.

Large was no dilettante. He joined the PRR immediately after graduating from Princeton and worked his way up in the railroad freight business. After twenty-five years he was made assistant vice president–traffic. Six years later he became vice president and northwestern regional manager. In 1963, he went out to the Wabash farm club for executive seasoning as president of that railroad, returning one year later as the PRR's vice president–sales, and then traffic. He was well liked. "A real gentleman." "A sweet guy." "A lovely guy but not a hard-driving railroader." "Very bright but not aggressive or imaginative." At merger time, he was even closer to retirement than Smucker was but he, too, had a few years left. He also had seniority over Sullivan. So he got the big traffic job, nominally reporting to Perlman. (Perlman later complained to Hartke's subcommittee that Large bypassed him and went "directly to the chairman.") Sullivan and J. G. Patten, of the Central, and the PRR's Funkhouser were named vice presidents in Large's department.

The upshot of these developments was that the two highest-ranked and best-paid[12] officers under Perlman — the numbers four and five men in the entire 100,000-employee organization — were ex-Pennsylvania executives for whom the president had very little regard. Even before the merger, the sharp-tongued Perlman had been openly disdainful of both Smucker and Large. "You run a wooden-wheeled railroad!" he once roared at the former, known to his men as "Mother Smucker." Nothing that happened in the first days and months after merger caused Perlman to change his opinion of either officer. Large's job was to get the freight business; Smucker's was to see that shipments moved on time. Each was soon overwhelmed with unforeseen problems.

Yet the basic weakness was one for which neither Smucker nor Large could be entirely blamed. Saunders and Perlman had taken a calculated risk in seeking to consolidate virtually overnight all of the operations of their two huge railroads. They could have gone

---

[12] A salary schedule filed with the ICC put Smucker's 1969 pay at $78,000 and said he received $6,590 in "other compensation." Large's salary was $73,000 and he got $4,050 additional.

about it much more slowly. The C&O-B&O merger was a case in point. Though technically merged, the C&O and B&O continued to function essentially separately but with a single top management. Penn Central's planners decided to accept all the headaches and heavy costs of quick consolidation for anticipated major gains once the fully merged railroad was running smoothly. They originally thought it might take eight years to recover all of the start-up losses. Saunders later cut the estimate to five years.

"We took our medicine early," said William A. Lashley, reviewing what had happened eighteen months after Merger Day. He conceded that the sudden switchover was "drastic surgery," but he believed it had worked. If so, this was another case of a successful operation killing the patient. Penn Central, from the very beginning, was beset with woes caused by instantaneous merger. And the most serious problems tied up its crucially important freight business, for which Smucker and Large had such heavy responsibilities.

In railroad freight handling, the trick is to collect as quickly as possible all of the boxcars that are going to the same place and get them rolling over the rails. If an entire train of freight cars loaded with shipments to the same destination can be assembled, that's wonderful. It means the train can run past all intermediate classification yards to the final delivery point. More often, blocks of cars must be left off at specific points for rerouting. Under the best of conditions, this is time consuming. It requires careful classification of cars so that yard dispatchers know what is to go where.[13]

When the PRR and Central merged, the freight classification system went *pfutt*. Thousands of employees didn't know the new system; dispatchers for connecting railroads didn't know it; shippers didn't know it. Cars piled up at yards where they weren't expected or wanted. Cars got separated from waybills — the papers supposedly accompanying them giving routes and destinations. Harassed yard superintendents sent out whole trains of no-waybill cars just to get rid of them. Full freight trains sat idle on main-line tracks, delaying other shipments and creating shortages of yard locomotives needed to move them. In one case, a coal

---

[13] Perlman was a pioneer in developing fully automated, computerized classification yards.

train of more than 100 cars was said to have been lost for ten days outside Syracuse.

Confusion was greatest in such cities as Chicago, Cincinnati and Cleveland, where the PRR and Central both had had freight yards. In Chicago, for example, the Pennsylvania yard was at 59th Street and the Central yard at nearby Elkhart, Indiana. When the merger began, Penn Central asked shippers whose freight was to be routed through 59th street to show "PCP" (Penn Central–Pennsylvania) on their waybills. Those using Elkhart were to show "PCN" (Penn Central–New York Central). "Time went by," explained a Penn Central executive, "and shippers began routing just 'PC.' Suddenly, we discovered a flood of misdirected cars. Cars were going to 59th Street and their waybills to Elkhart. Congestion grew. And as the cars moved to Columbus or Fort Wayne, the problems moved with them. Soon it was all over the map."

A good computer system might have helped untangle the mess of freight cars strung out all over, but Penn Central's computer system wasn't any good — not at this point. That was because there were two systems. Each road used a different method of generating freight-car movement information — the basis for car tracings. Both had used IBM computers to record freight movements, but while the PRR fed printouts and punched tapes to its computers the Central used IBM punch cards. The PRR used a Teletype inquiry system, the Central a cathode-ray TV setup. Like virtually everything else on the two railroads, the computers also differed. The Central's "random access disc file" updated car information quickly. The PRR's, though a disc file, was not "random access" and it updated information only periodically.

The Central's system proved to have less flexibility in handling the combined volume of the merged railroad. So the decision was made to depend on the PRR's $10 million electronic nerve center in Philadelphia. This meant that data gathered along the old Central had to be sent to New York, where it was retransmitted to Philadelphia, where it was reformulated and fed into the big computers. In the case of each transmission, at least an hour was lost. With the Penn Central getting 50,000 daily requests for car tracings at the height of the freight-movement fiasco, the computer delays compounded an already chaotic situation.

For many shippers, the Penn Central's birth pains were pure torture. One traffic manager reported that a rail shipment of his took twenty-six days to get from Yonkers, New York, to Brighton, Massachusetts. The car spent eighteen days at the Alfred E. Perlman Yard, Penn Central's newest electronic classification yard at Selkirk, New York, and one in which its namesake had taken personal pride. Nobody, not even "Iron Mike," the yard's computer, knew the car was sitting there. Another shipper, Keith Ramsden, of International Salt Company, told *Business Week* magazine: "I'm convinced they've taken the worst service of the two lines and combined them . . . The service has deteriorated to the point where it is completely unlivable." A Penn Central executive agreed. "We started mixing up the people, and problems were inevitable," he said. "All of a sudden dispatchers were getting orders to run trains to West Jockstrap."

Perlman himself never minimized the extent of the freight problem. "All we were getting," he said, "was feathers and guts." Yet the railroad's chief administrative officer was nowhere near the scene of most of the action. Except for trips once or twice a week to Philadelphia, President Perlman remained in New York, 100 miles from the computers, the car-tracing gear, the wall charts with coded designations for every train and every freight route, and most of the operating staff charged with responsibility for correcting the mess.

There was the public Perlman and the private Perlman. The public Perlman, addressing Penn Central's annual stockholders' meeting in May 1969, conveyed the impression that the red and the green were working in perfect harmony. For two formerly bitter competitors, Perlman told the stockholders, agreement upon merged management philosophies required "a full understanding of divergent viewpoints. And I am happy to say," Perlman said, "that our Transportation, Marketing, Sales and all other departments are imbued with a spirit that is rapidly welding the whole group into a dynamic team."

But while waxing euphoric to the stockholders, Perlman, in the executive suite, was going after Smucker and Large with sledge-hammer blows. *Fortune* magazine's Rush Loving, in an article published in August 1970, said that "Smucker did not get out on the road very often and he failed to show enthusiasm for Perlman's attempts to streamline the company." Loving wrote:

Time after time, as the railroad's operations descended into an ever gooier mire, Perlman pleaded with Saunders to let him dump Smucker, but each time Saunders refused. Finally, early last year [1969], Perlman asked one last time, and when Saunders turned him down, Perlman announced that he was through. A day or so later, Saunders gave in and Smucker was replaced with . . . Flannery.

With Smucker out, Perlman turned his attention to getting rid of Henry Large, according to the *Fortune* account. It described a conversation between Perlman and Saunders over lunch at the Sky Club — one of the few clubs that nonjoiner Perlman belonged to — in New York in August 1969. Loving must have gotten the story from Perlman because it certainly didn't come from Saunders, and they were the only two mentioned as being present:

Perlman is said to have presented Saunders with statistics proving that Large's policies were costing the railroad money.

"You just don't like Henry Large," snapped Saunders.

"I do like Henry Large," said Perlman. "He's a great big lovable St. Bernard. No one can help but like him. But he's giving away the railroad."

"But the shippers like him," countered Saunders.

"Well, who doesn't like Santa Claus?" Perlman replied, and Saunders proceeded to tell Perlman that he was being negative.

Saunders later insisted the *Fortune* story was dead wrong. After the article appeared, he wrote Louis Banks, the magazine's managing editor. His letter was not published. It said:

I disagree strongly with many of the statements and conclusions contained in the August 1970 *Fortune* magazine article entitled, "The Penn Central Bankruptcy Express." I say flatly that many of these statements and conclusions are inaccurate and untrue.

Inasmuch as there are a number of pending lawsuits relating to the matters covered by this article, I think it inappropriate for me to comment further on them at this time. The true facts will undoubtedly be developed in these legal proceedings.

When we interviewed him five months and again nine months after the bankruptcy, Saunders remained unwilling to put his story on the record. He did say that, in his opinion, reports of differences between Perlman and himself had been "greatly exaggerated. I don't pretend that we didn't have some differences of opinion," he said, "but I never had any feeling that that was a basic reason for the merger not operating or succeeding as it should."

On the selection of Penn Central's top officers, Saunders said:

Mr. Perlman and I made them together and there was not any disagreement. Now it did develop later on, some of the officers, for instance Smucker, whom we put in as chief operating officer under Perlman, didn't do the job. And Mr. Perlman and I agreed. And we got rid of him.

Saunders would say no more. Perlman refused our request for an interview. But he did testify in Washington that the merger was, in fact, a "takeover" and that he couldn't replace department heads such as Smucker and Large without Saunders' approval.

Our investigation suggests the following timetable of events:

Almost from the opening day, Perlman was out to get his two executive vice presidents. He considered them incompetent and told them so. At a meeting of executive staff in Tarrytown, New York, he delivered a two-hour diatribe against Large that stunned the ex-PRR witnesses. They had never heard anything like it. Large, by birth, breeding and career, was a pillar of the Philadelphia Establishment; he was such a decent fellow that it was hard to imagine anybody wanting to throw him out, and Perlman's brass-knuckles methods simply weren't those of the old Pennsy. Beyond all that, Henry Large had spent decades building up contacts and he was a close friend of more big shippers than anyone else in railroading.

Saunders' initial inclination was to mediate the differences between the green president and the red executive vice presidents. He sought to "work things out" through compromise. Trying to "work things out" was a mark of the chairman. One of Saunders' closest associates at Penn Central said: "Perlman had been after Saunders to let him get rid of Smucker. Saunders wouldn't do it. He wanted a compromise. The feud between Perlman and Smucker did more than anything else to set up the red-green rivalry." This official, viewing the contretemps from a vantagepoint of almost two years, said that Perlman "could never adjust to being number two," suffered from megalomania and conducted a "personal vendetta" to oust both Smucker and Large. Saunders, faced with Perlman's demands, vacillated and compromised and didn't make the tough decisions that were needed, said this observer, himself a member of Penn Central's executive suite.

Despite these delays, not too many months passed before Saunders concluded that Perlman was right: Smucker and Large had to go. Indeed, Saunders actually wanted Perlman to replace Smucker with Mike Flannery when the merger was less than one year old. But Flannery was gradually making sense of the nightmarish computer operations, and Perlman delayed the switch. Finally, on February 23, 1969, Penn Central announced that Smucker was being "freed from his day-to-day administrative duties in order to fill . . . [a] position on the chairman's staff and will handle special projects for the chief executive officer." Smucker soon retired to his home, "Green Meadows," in Villanova, on the Main Line. Mike Flannery took over operations.

Saunders and Perlman also agreed to seek a replacement for Henry Large. And the agreement was reached early in 1969 — long before their celebrated lunch at the Sky Club. To help them find candidates, Saunders and Perlman hired an executive "head-hunting" firm, Spencer Stuart and Associates, of Chicago. The firm was retained on June 26, 1969. In its search for Large's successor, it looked in the Penn Central organization, in other railroads and in industry generally. Its choice, Edward G. Kreyling, vice president–traffic, of the Illinois Central Railroad, was named in January 1970 to replace Large, who took early retirement. By this time, the third of Penn Central's original executive vice presidents had long since left. He was Walter R. Grant, who had worked with Perlman for thirteen years at the Central and was his financial expert. In the merger he played second fiddle to Bevan in a setup that pleased neither man. Grant was an independent-minded executive who, in his Central days, had been known to shout back at Perlman when his boss gave him a dressing down. (Perlman was famous for his rough dressing down of subordinates.) Grant quit

Penn Central in less than a year to become executive vice president of Consolidated Edison in New York. Although his explanation for leaving was that "I just didn't want to move to Philadelphia," few doubted that his dissatisfaction with the organization and disagreements with Bevan were more significant reasons. (A former PRR executive who knew both men said: "Grant and Bevan hated each other's guts.")

While these major changes were taking place in Penn Central's badly divided executive suite, Stuart Saunders was doing something that Alfred Perlman knew nothing about: Saunders was secretly hunting for a man to replace Perlman. Perlman had reached sixty-five, the normal retirement age, in December 1967, three months before the merger. His contract with Penn Central continued him in office as president until December 1, 1970, when he would be sixty-eight.

Saunders believed the railroad could not afford Perlman's leadership for that length of time. It would be cheaper to force his retirement, even though it meant Perlman, whose salary had been raised to $220,000 a year on February 1, 1968, would receive at least $170,000 until November 30, 1970, and would be paid $50,000 annually for ten years and eight months after that by the Penn Central.

One of the things that bothered Saunders and several board members was that Perlman, despite his advanced years, had groomed no one to succeed him.[14]

Late in 1968 or early in 1969, Saunders quietly obtained the approval of key board members to purge Perlman. Then he searched for a successor. The hunt was top secret. It appears that none of Penn Central's other officers knew of it and possibly only two or three of the directors closest to Saunders did. Saunders first approached Louis W. Menk, who was chief executive of the Northern Pacific Railroad. Menk, dynamic, aggressive, occasionally volatile, was one of the nation's most respected railroad execu-

---

[14] Under the original merger agreement of 1962, Perlman was to become vice chairman of Penn Central's board and serve in only an advisory capacity. When the merger finally came, six years later, the board decided that the New York Central had no one else capable of assuming the presidency and so gave it to Perlman.

tives. At Saunders' invitation, the fifty-year-old Menk flew to Philadelphia early in 1969 for talks with the chairman. His wife accompanied him. They were entertained by Saunders and his wife, Dorothy, at the Saunders' Ardmore home. The Menks even did some preliminary house hunting — along the Main Line, of course.

Under the offer by Saunders, Menk apparently would have joined Penn Central as chief executive officer or as president with the promise of prompt elevation to the top post. In March 1969, Menk turned down the offer. He wrote Saunders that he was bound by contract to the Northern Pacific and to leave would impugn his integrity.[15] Saunders next sought to recruit a General Motors vice president but he couldn't match that officer's salary. Then in June another executive problem fell into Saunders' lap. Bevan, as he explained in the interview with us, wrote the chairman an angry, emotional letter of resignation. Bevan said, in effect, that he was sick and tired of playing second fiddle to Perlman and wanted out. He then knew nothing, of course, of the move to oust Perlman.

Saunders had no love for Bevan, and in fact considered Bevan and Perlman his two biggest headaches. But if he had to choose between the man who raised the money and the man who spent the money, there was really no choice at all. Perlman had to go; Bevan had to stay. Costs had to be cut. Saunders placated Bevan with a deal which the finance committee chairman accepted: Perlman was to be removed as president and kicked upstairs into the meaningless position of vice chairman. Bevan would gain control of Penn Central's accounting department and its budget. A Bevan protégé, Jonathan O'Herron, then executive vice president of Buckeye Pipeline Company, a profitable subsidiary owned by the Pennsylvania Company, would become Bevan's vice president for finance. And Bevan would be invited to sit on Penn Central's board of directors.

---

[15] In March 1970, the Northern Pacific and the Great Northern Railway combined with their jointly owned Chicago, Burlington & Quincy Railroad to form Burlington Northern, Inc., the nation's biggest railroad in terms of route miles. On May 1, 1971, Menk became the Burlington Northern's chairman and chief executive.

Finally, in September 1969, Saunders found the man to succeed Perlman: Paul A. Gorman, just retired as president of the Western Electric Co. Gorman, though a stranger to railroading, knew how to run a big corporation. At this critical moment, Saunders thought, maybe a hard-nosed businessman could turn the railroad around. Gorman's appointment, at $250,000 a year, took effect in December. When Perlman was informed of the decision just before the September meeting at which Gorman was named, he was very unhappy. He had not intended to quit and did not want to step down. But lacking the votes on Penn Central's board of directors, he could not fight back. However, he insisted that his contract, which provided that he should remain as a top officer for three years beyond the normal retirement age of sixty-five, be honored. He also insisted that all the incidental benefits specified in his contract, such as office space in both New York and Philadelphia, a secretary and a car, continue in force. And this was done. But when Perlman became vice chairman his influence in decision making diminished. After that, he was relatively inactive for the final seven months until he was finally dropped, along with Saunders and Bevan.[16]

When Gorman arrived in December 1969, the eastern United States was engulfed in its most severe winter in decades. With switches frozen, yards frozen, snow and ice causing delays everywhere, railroad expenses rose calamitously and revenues sank. Mike Flannery's rescue mission suffered a fatal blow.[17]

Saunders and Bevan were in a race against time. As Penn Central's outside investments went sour, they borrowed desperately for what one of their associates termed "this money-consuming monster, the railroad." Nothing seemed to work. Service slipped, deficits grew and morale worsened. Making matters even more chaotic was the fact that, by this time, these two men, who bore such heavy responsibility for keeping the nation's largest rail-

---

[16] In December 1970, Perlman became president of the Western Pacific Railroad, with headquarters in San Francisco. The Western Pacific gave up its last passenger train several months before Perlman took over. It now carries only freight.

[17] Flannery, after being named Penn Central's executive vice president for operations, left at the end of 1970 to work under Perlman at the Western Pacific.

road running, were barely on speaking terms. Bevan jealously guarded information concerning his own activities and swore his staff to secrecy. For a long time, Saunders, for example, was unaware of the existence of Penphil, Bevan's private investment company which later was to draw such heavy criticism.[18] Penn Central's chairman also knew very little of what was happening in the railroad's accounting department, which had been returned to Bevan's control in the fall of 1969. He apparently was equally uninformed about other phases of Bevan's operations. Even as the Penn Central careened toward bankruptcy, Bevan kept "his railroad" implacably apart from the railroad proper. He demanded absolute loyalty from his employees and forbade them to talk to Saunders or members of the chairman's staff. Occasionally, though, one would talk. In March 1970, word concerning a development at Executive Jet Aviation, a firm in which Penn Central had invested heavily, leaked out.[19] The word was that money was being diverted from Executive Jet to another enterprise in which Executive Jet's flamboyant founder and head, retired Air Force Brigadier General Olbert F. Lassiter, had an interest. Basil Cole, a Penn Central vice president who reported directly to Saunders, heard of the development. He told his boss. Bevan discovered the leak. In a subsequent memo to Saunders, Cole reported that Bevan was "said to be furious" and had "already accused three people in the Financial and Legal Departments of leaking this to me."

"This incident is not in itself important," Cole wrote Saunders on March 13, 1970, "because there is little chance Mr. Bevan will learn how I obtained the information. But the lesson is not lost on anyone who might in the future be tempted to pass anything to you through me. Doors in this building have been slamming ever since the Accounting Department was returned to Mr. Bevan's jurisdiction. Now all the cracks are sealed."

Infighting at the top permeated the entire railroad organization. High-salaried executives, both red and green, left in a steady stream. In two years, all five principal associates of Saunders, Perlman and Bevan either had been eased out or had quit. Eight of

---

[18] Penphil's operations are analyzed in detail in Chapter 7.

[19] Penn Central's costly plunge into Executive Jet Aviation is discussed in Chapter 8.

the original twenty vice presidents were gone. Gone, too, were more than 100 of the Central's former marketing staff. With Perlman out of the picture, the shift of railroad operations to Philadelphia was accelerated.[20] In this sense, the City of Brotherly Love won out over its bigger, richer, more aggressive rival metropolis. But considering the railroad's declining health, this was a dubious triumph. And even some Philadelphians weren't sure it was wise for Penn Central to establish its headquarters in their city. Some still thought Perlman should have been running the show in New York.

"With all of its inferiority complexes," John Bunting, president of the First Pennsylvania Banking & Trust Company, Philadelphia's biggest bank, was to say much later, "it would be impossible to imagine that Philadelphia would let the head of the New York Central do what he was best at, which was run that complex. It would be asking a great deal of Philadelphia board members to give over control of the company to Perlman. Everything would have gone to New York."

As the end drew near, Stuart Thomas Saunders, the man in charge of the entire $6.5 billion conglomerate — the railroad, the hotels, the real estate, the pipelines, the trucks, and on and on — withdrew into himself. "In his last months in office," said a close associate, "Saunders changed from an outgoing, self-confident man to a frightened man. He ceased communicating with everybody. I wouldn't see him for weeks at a time, where before we had been in touch almost daily. He knew the countdown was on. The question was whether he could keep borrowing until the railroad started making money."

He couldn't. Nobody could. Time and money ran out. How the mighty fell: Stuart Saunders, businessman of the year in 1968, business bankrupt of the year in 1970. Hailed as a genius for getting the merger on the track, he couldn't make it run. A great advocate of "working things out," he never really worked anything out. Of the three top executives, he had the greatest faith in the

---

[20] At the time of the merger, the Penn Central employed 4,101 in its New York offices and 2,929 in Philadelphia. Eighteen months later, with Perlman still the nominal operating head, the Philadelphia staff had grown to 3,391 employees while New York's had shrunk to 832 (including Perlman).

merger even though he had nothing to do with the original concept. Unlike so many of his associates, he never gave up on it. And when the crash came he lost the most — close to $1 million in Penn Central stock which he had purchased on options and then held until the bitter end while Bevan and other executives were unloading theirs through insider trading that was later questioned. The end came on June 8, 1970, when Saunders, his dream shattered, was thrown out.

His manicurist was one of those who noticed a change in the chairman after he was fired. In the weeks before June 8, when Saunders went downtown for his manicure, his hands shook as though they were palsied. But shortly after that terrible day he went back. And now his hands were firm and steady and he seemed self-assured again. Only Stuart Saunders would know how much of a relief it was to have the nightmare end.

6

"If You Don't Like It, Walk!"

It was the evening of February 4, 1970, two years after the merger. Stuart Saunders was preparing to go in to dinner with his wife, Dorothy, when the telephone rang. Saunders did not ordinarily answer the telephone; there were servants in the French-Norman mansion in Ardmore, on Philadelphia's Main Line, to take care of such details. But on this night, for whatever reason, he picked up the telephone. And he regretted it instantly.

The caller was Harold E. Kohn, a law partner of former Philadelphia mayor Richardson Dilworth. Kohn, tall and slim, was a transportation expert in his own right, and he was a commuter on the Paoli Local. He was also enraged. The 5:53 train had been a half hour late leaving Thirtieth Street Station. When it had finally got underway, it wheezed and puffed and halted periodically to catch its breath. Kohn had arrived at the Devon Station at 7:30, instead of at 6:25, and had found his wife waiting for him, chilled and anxious.

Kohn had served as special transit counsel to the city of Philadelphia and to the Southeastern Pennsylvania Transportation Authority. He told Saunders the Penn Central's service on its six Philadelphia area commuter lines was abominable. He said he was sick and tired of late trains, filthy stations and slave-ship conditions.

Saunders had heard it all before. Wearily, he recited the railroad man's litany: The commuter operation cost the Penn Central millions in losses, the equipment was old, more government help was needed. Then he went a step farther.

The station that Stuart Saunders never used. The Ardmore Station, on the route of the Paoli Local, was just a short distance from the home of the head of the Penn Central, who preferred a chauffeur-driven limousine to his own trains. (Philadelphia *Bulletin* photo)

"I would be delighted to give it to you lock, stock and barrel," Saunders said, referring to the 219 red coaches, the sixty-four stainless-steel cars, the several dozen stations and other facilities that comprised the commuter service. Startled, Kohn asked if Saunders really meant what he said. "Of course I mean it," Saunders replied. "It's a drag and a drain."

The next day, Saunders was chagrined to read the details of his telephone conversation with Kohn in the Philadelphia *Evening Bulletin*. He quickly backed away from his hasty offer. He had "no authority" to give away the railroad's rolling stock and commuter stations, he said. Only the board of directors could do that. And the railroad would have to be paid in full for its facilities. "The shocking thing is that I can't have a private telephone conversation without having it in the paper," Saunders complained. "I was not speaking for publication last night."

Whether he was speaking for publication or not, Saunders quite clearly meant what he said. He would have liked nothing better than to have the Penn Central relieved of the burden of all passenger operations.

When the merger took effect, Saunders had grand plans. Not the least of these was getting rid of the passenger service. The federal government could take over the long-haul trains. Local authorities could take over commuter lines. The railroad would be excused from the crushing costs of maintaining the service and could quite possibly turn a neat profit by operating the passenger trains under contract with the governments involved, who would have to subsidize the service.

With the passenger service gone, the Penn Central would be relieved of its biggest cash drain. Carrying riders became unprofitable for the railroads about 1950, and the history of passenger service had been written in red ink ever since. From 1963 through 1966, the Pennsylvania and the Central reported combined losses of about $210 million on these operations.

In 1967, the year before the merger, the two railroads spent one dollar and twenty-four cents for every dollar that a passenger spent for his ticket. The loss that year was $85 million. In 1968 and 1969, passenger losses were $100 million and $105 million. For every one dollar spent in dining cars, the railroads were spending one dollar and forty-four cents. The passenger loss in 1970 totaled $131 million.

If these losses were eliminated, Saunders believed, the profits would come quickly. There would be money to expand, to move into other, nonrailroad, enterprises. The conglomerates were doing it. Saunders was already sitting atop an enormous empire but, at the time of the merger, that appeared to be just the beginning.

The Penn Central had a considerable investment in its passenger service, but this investment was not paying off. The burden, in fact, was growing heavier. The commuter operation was particularly onerous, accounting for some 46 percent of passenger losses, according to the railroad's figures. While all passenger traffic appeared to be unprofitable, commuter traffic was even more so.

Commuters traveled during short periods of time, in the mornings and in the evenings. But the Penn Central could not require its trainmen to divide their working day in this fashion. The result was that some employees sat for long hours with nothing to do. And it cost the railroad $12,500 annually, in salary and fringe benefits, for each employee.

The inclusion in the system of the bankrupt New Haven Railroad dramatically increased the Penn Central's responsibilities in the commuter field. In 1968, the year before the New Haven was taken in, the Penn Central carried 36,514,274 commutation passengers, realizing revenues of $27.4 million. In 1969, after the New Haven came in, commuters totaled 54,001,358 with revenues of $45.4 million.[1]

To service these passengers, Penn Central owned or leased 896 coaches, 222 sleeping and parlor cars, 122 dining and club cars (all but a handful were club cars, since the diners were being phased out), thirteen other cars that could be used for passengers, 853 self-propelled electric cars and sixty-four self-propelled diesel cars.

---

[1] Penn Central passenger statistics:

	1969	1968
Coach	36,735,110	28,998,815
Sleepers and Parlor	701,305	601,467
Commuters	54,001,358	36,514,274
TOTAL PASSENGERS	91,437,773	66,114,556

The passenger dilemma was underscored when the railroad's board, at the June 1968 meeting, enthusiastically filched an idea from the Chesapeake & Ohio, which had been giving shareholder parties at its Greenbrier Hotel in White Sulphur Springs for years. The Penn Central did not have a Greenbrier Hotel but, through a subsidiary, Arvida Corporation, it had the Boca Raton Hotel and Club. The board scheduled two parties there, from October 23 to 27, and from November 27 to December 1. A special brochure offered a package at 20 percent off regular rates and promised "superb accommodations, meals, tea dances, cabanas, free golf and golf carts, baby-sitting and an exciting program of activities."

About 300 of the company's 118,000 shareholders signed up for each party. The railroad offered three alternative, all-inclusive packages — rail travel (about $300 for a roomette, $200 for a coach seat from the New York–Philadelphia area), air travel via Eastern Airlines ($298 first class, $264 coach), or get there on your own by auto, with individually adjusted rates.

For the first party, fifty railroad shareholders said they would travel by train. Sixty said they would travel by Eastern's jets. The rest said they would drive.

The reluctance of even railroad stockholders to ride the trains illustrated the Penn Central's difficulties in its passenger operations. Passenger revenue throughout the decade of the sixties steadily decreased. The only exception was 1969. Revenue showed an increase that year, but only because the bankrupt New Haven Railroad was brought into the Penn Central system at the direction of the Interstate Commerce Commission. The inclusion of the New Haven's passenger receipts gave the appearance of an upturn in revenue but, compared to combined revenue figures for earlier years, there was actually a decrease. The 1969 revenue picture was also brightened somewhat by the inauguration of Metroliner service on January 16.[2]

---

[2] Combined passenger revenue of the Pennsylvania and New York Central 1960 through 1969:

1960 — $167,785,995	1965 — $134,494,269
1961 — $160,443,354	1966 — $129,661,193
1962 — $152,519,899	1967 — $114,961,837
1963 — $146,588,654	1968 — $105,087,068
1964 — $142,576,667	1969 — $147,111,527

The Metroliner was the only serious attempt by the railroad in more than a generation to do something positive about improving passenger service. And, if it did nothing else, it proved that travelers *will* patronize trains that are clean and modern, that keep to schedule and are convenient. It also proved that this type of service can make a profit, which was the railroad's basic concern.

The principal attraction of the Metroliner, at the outset, was its speed. It could make the 226-mile trip from New York to Washington in two hours and fifty-five minutes, compared to the four hours conventional trains required. But there were attractions in addition to the 120-mile-per-hour speed the Metroliner was capable of achieving in two minutes.

The stainless-steel cars were *clean.* The seats were padded with foam rubber and reclined like seats on a jetliner, slowly and smoothly, not like the old reclining seats that reacted like berserk barbers' chairs, flinging you backwards at the slightest touch or refusing to budge at all. The heating and the air conditioning worked the way they were supposed to. There was carpeting on the floor. Riders could make or receive telephone calls. The windows were large, free of grime, and you could see the boats and the water as you traveled through Delaware and Maryland. Best of all, the Metroliner was usually on time.

For all this, the passenger paid two dollars more than a regular coach seat would cost. One-way fare from New York to Washington was seventeen dollars instead of fifteen dollars on a conventional train. For sixteen years, ridership in the New York to Washington corridor had been decreasing. The Metroliner reversed that trend. It carried more than two million passengers in its first two years of operation. In the first year of its operation, ridership on this route increased by 8 percent.

But, if it hadn't been for President Lyndon Johnson and his Secretary of Transportation, Alan Boyd, the Metroliner might never have been installed. As always, the railroad was extremely reluctant to embark on any project that involved spending money for passenger service. Not even the highly successful Tokaido Line built by the Japanese, which operated at 120 miles per hour, could persuade the railroad that modern, efficient service could pay off. Railroad officials just weren't interested.

The Metroliner was started by the Penn Central on its New York to Washington run in January 1969. It made the trip at speeds up to 120 miles per hour, covering the 226 miles in less than three hours, a full hour faster than conventional trains. (Courtesy of the Penn Central)

What they were interested in was approval of the Pennsylvania-Central merger. Stuart Saunders knew that President Johnson wanted the high-speed service. Saunders also knew that if Johnson actively opposed the merger, the long-planned union of the two railroads would be seriously jeopardized, despite the supposed independence of the ICC. Johnson always had recourse to his Justice Department, which could have, if he wanted it to, fought the case through the courts. But, in the end, the government did not oppose the merger and Saunders saw to it that Johnson got his Metroliner.

Even then, Saunders had internal problems. Perlman opposed the project. Asked about Perlman's attitude toward the Metroliner, Saunders said it was "lukewarm."

"Still is," Saunders added. "Mr. Perlman, he doesn't — he's always been very critical of the Tokaido Line. And he quotes a lot of figures to show they lose money; actually, they don't, I don't think. They lose a lot of money on their railroads as a whole but it's not the Tokaido Line. But Mr. Perlman was never sympathetic toward the Metroliner project."

Saunders said there was "no relationship" between the government's approval of the merger and the railroad's agreement to provide the Metroliner service.

Under the agreement, Penn Central was to put up $44.5 million and the federal government $11.5 million. Of this, $21 million went to the Budd Company for fifty stainless-steel electric cars. The railroad's investment eventually mounted to $70 million, although the increase in costs was hidden and charged to other items. The federal government, however, shaved its participation to about $10 million and did not start paying Penn Central until almost two years after service was begun.

Most of the railroad's expenditures went to upgrade the roadbed and rails between New York and Washington. This maintenance, at some time in the future, would have been necessary anyway. Because of the Metroliner, the railroad accelerated its maintenance program.

Despite its success, the Metroliner encountered serious mechanical problems. At any one time during the first two years, 25 to 30 percent of the equipment was in the shop for repairs. Saunders blamed these problems on the federal government. He felt the Metroliner was put into service before it had been fully tested out.

"Well, they operated test cars for six or eight months," Saunders said. "Up here on this test track before the cars were actually built — to get experience. And as the cars were being built. Beyond that, we had such pressure on us from the government to put these damn things in operation. And we put them in operation before we should have. Because the politicians were hollering so and then Alan Boyd was putting the pressure on us."

Despite the problems, Saunders thought the Metroliner was bound to make money for the railroad. "I think it's a great thing and I think it's going to make money," he said. "Even on the full investment the Metroliner I think is going to make money — assuming they'll ever get the damn things so they'll run. I gather they're making progress in that regard but that's been a terrible headache. The builders, suppliers greatly underestimated the job they were undertaking, and didn't do proper engineering. And also government has some of the blame, and Penn Central as well. But it's primarily their responsibility. When you have 25 or 30 percent of your cars sitting idle every day — but the Metroliner is making money now, I think."

The success of the Metroliner did not, however, cause the railroad to undertake any other projects to improve passenger service. An experimental turbo-train demonstration project between New York and Boston was started on April 8, 1969, and carried 60,000 passengers in its first year. This was sponsored by the Department of Transportation and was not the Penn Central's idea. The railroad acted as operator in the project.

The reluctance of the Penn Central to spend money on passenger service was, to a large extent, understandable. For years, the Pennsylvania and the Central had neglected their passenger operations. Rolling stock was old and unreliable, stations were in ramshackle condition, labor costs were high. Because of generations of neglect, Saunders and Perlman were faced with spending incredible sums of money if they were ever to bring passenger service back to where it should be.

Both men were businessmen, and their first allegiance was to the stockholders, not to the riding public. If they spent huge sums, and reduced the dividends in doing so, new managers would be found, managers who didn't care so much about passengers. They had produced the Metroliner, they had satisfied their obligation to the public, so they set about persuading the ICC to permit them to reduce the number of passenger trains they were required to run. Shortly after the merger, they petitioned the ICC for permission to terminate fourteen long-distance trains running west of Harrisburg, Pennsylvania, and Buffalo. The railroad followed this petition up with another one in January 1970, seeking to eliminate another thirty-four trains along the same routes. The Penn Central claimed it could save $23 million annually if these trains were eliminated. But it would have meant the end of long-distance service west of Harrisburg and Buffalo.

Before the Penn Central's petitions were finally disposed of, the federal government made them unnecessary. On May 1, 1971, the National Railroad Passenger Corporation (Amtrak), a quasi-public agency set up by Congress, took over the running of intercity train service. Ironically, the first thing Amtrak did was to cut almost in half the intercity service which the private railroads were compelled to maintain because of the ICC's refusal to permit their elimination.

In the face of continuing passenger losses, Saunders looked with covetous eyes toward other business investments for the railroad. Although the railroad itself made possible Saunders' dream empire, it became in his eyes, and the eyes of finance chairman David C. Bevan, an anchor that was preventing the Penn Central from moving on to more profitable ventures. Perlman, though he was later to proclaim that money should have been plowed back into the railroad to maintain and upgrade equipment and service, went along willingly with the philosophy that the railroad, and its assets, should be used to make money in other fields.

When the moguls thought of profit, they did not think of the Penn Central or the other railroads the company owned, like the Lehigh Valley, or the Pittsburgh & Lake Erie or the Detroit, Toledo & Ironton. They thought of the rich parcels of land the railroad owned in Chicago and Cleveland and Detroit and Pittsburgh, land that made the railroad the largest real estate company in the nation. Countless hours were spent by Penn Central executives drafting plans to sell air rights to eighty-seven acres over the railroad's Thirtieth Street and North Philadelphia stations in Philadelphia. The air rights were to be sold for millions to the Philadelphia Bicentennial Corporation, which would then construct appropriate buildings above the stations as part of the nation's 1976 Bicentennial celebration. Like so many other railroad projects, the air rights sale proved to be just a pleasant illusion.

The search for profits to offset the passenger losses never stopped. While commuters suffered, Penn Central chased a wild dream of establishing a worldwide air freight system, complete with a passenger charter service and a domestic air taxi service. The company acquired 58 percent of Executive Jet Aviation, Inc., before the Civil Aeronautics Board ordered it out of the air travel business and directed it to divest itself of its holdings in the firm. The net loss to Penn Central: nearly $21 million, which was the total cost of the original fleet of fifty Metroliner cars.

Every weekday, the Penn Central transported some 300,000 passengers. The company's responsibility in this area was enormous. It moved 65 percent of all rail passengers east of the Mississippi, and 35 percent of all rail travelers in the nation.

In statements to the government, to the public and to stockholders, Penn Central emphasized the weight of the burden of operating 1,280 passenger trains a day, but it also attempted to convey how seriously it took its responsibilities in this area. Without Penn Central, the northeast quadrant of the United States would be paralyzed.

Commuters in the New York City area made 175,000 trips a day on Penn Central equipment. There were 75,000 commuter trips on Penn Central trains in Philadelphia daily, and 15,000 in Boston. Between Baltimore and Washington, there were 1,000 commuter trips a day. Conventional trains between New York and Washington carried 13,675 passengers each day, and the Metroliner, which started its runs on January 16, 1969, added another 3,450 riders.

But with the exception of the Metroliner there is little evidence that the railroad did anything but talk about improving passenger service. There is a great deal of evidence that it deliberately permitted passenger service to deteriorate, hoping to pressure governmental agencies into providing ever larger subsidies to Penn Central. The railroad consistently pressed for higher payments from transit authorities in Pennsylvania, New Jersey, New York and Connecticut, with whom it had contracts to operate commuter lines. It also consistently pressed these agencies to buy new equipment to be used by Penn Central on its runs.

"We are experiencing severe difficulties with the New York and Philadelphia service, and we are deeply concerned about the seriousness of this problem," Penn Central said, in its 1969 annual report. "Much of our commuter equipment is fifty to sixty years old and is simply wearing out. Some of it is beyond repair, and some of it is approaching that state. Most of it is virtually impossible to maintain in reliable operating condition.

"This problem cannot be corrected by our railroad alone. The solution lies in a partnership between government and private enterprise, in recognition that commuter operations are a public service dependent on public support."

The Penn Central's complaints were valid to a large degree. And because of the importance of rail travel, the governments involved did make efforts to help the railroad absorb its passenger losses. New York and Connecticut, for example, agreed to spend $104 million to buy 144 new commuter cars and to rehabilitate stations, shops and trackage along the railroad's New Haven route. New Jersey purchased thirty-five new commuter cars and promised to deliver an additional forty-five cars. It also committed itself to building with state funds a new passenger station at Trenton for the railroad. The Southeastern Pennsylvania Transportation Authority (SEPTA) agreed to acquire, over a period of years, 116 new cars, costing about $250,000 each. Penn Central's major expenditure in return for this governmental largesse was $4.4 million toward the SEPTA cars.

The disdain for passenger traffic even carried over into the railroad's accounting practices. It was widely suspected that Penn Central, and before that, the Pennsylvania and the Central, charged off a disproportionate share of maintenance-of-way, taxes and administrative expenses to the passenger operation. Freight trains ran over the same tracks commuter cars did, so who could say that the heavier, rail-grinding freights caused so little need for maintenance while the lighter commuter and passenger cars caused so much? Only the railroad. And, when a petition was sent to the ICC to discontinue a passenger train, or when a presentation was made to a regional transit authority, the passenger losses looked that much more impressive.

From 1962 to 1969, the railroad, on a combined basis, paid out more than $297 million in dividends. In the four years prior to the merger, the Pennsylvania, in making four acquisitions outside the railroad business, spent another $144 million in cash. But, when asked if the Penn Central couldn't have spent some money to improve passenger operations, Stuart Saunders replied: "Oh, we couldn't possibly do it. Didn't have the money in the first place. But how can you justify — you can't borrow money on a project that you're not going to get a cent of it back. Nobody's going to lend you any money for anything like that."

Saunders lived just minutes away from the Ardmore Station on the Penn Central's Main Line. A dozen trains, many of them sections of the Paoli Local, stopped at Ardmore during the morning rush hour. The trains terminated at Penn Center Station, a block from Saunders' office at Six Penn Center Plaza. But Saunders refused to ride the train, preferring instead a chauffeur-driven limousine, one of ten the railroad maintained for its executives, in addition to its private plane and its private railroad cars.

"At least a third of the days I would go I wouldn't even go to the office," Saunders explained. "I was going to New York. Or I was going to Chicago or Detroit. I had suitcases, briefcases — I always had four or five briefcases. How the hell could I get on a Paoli Local with all that? And I wasn't even going to town. I was going the back way to the airport. I traveled at least 50 percent of my time and I wasn't even going to town."

Saunders discussed his traveling habits several months after he "retired" from the Penn Central. Seated in his imposing library, in which were hung various memorabilia of his career in railroading, including a miniature locomotive with the inscription "Chief" on it, Saunders acknowledged that his preference for his limousine might have been bad public relations, might have angered the thousands of commuters who daily suffered indignities on his trains.

"I agree that from a psychological standpoint it's important but

I was willing to take that criticism," he said. "Maybe I shouldn't have. But I don't live that way and I wasn't going to do it. It wasn't practical. It wouldn't have changed the service any. But you've got a point. I wouldn't deny that. But the other side is that it was wholly impractical from my standpoint. To do that, I would have just been wasting my time. Although from a public relations standpoint it might have been a good thing. I ride the trains a lot now."

Saunders said the heavy passenger costs destroyed the Penn Central's overall performance record. In handling freight, he said, the Penn Central's operating expenses as opposed to its revenues compared favorably with most other railroads. But the passenger burden started out each month with a built-in loss of at least $6 million.

"I've never pretended the [commuter] service is good," Saunders said. "But basically you're never going to get good service until you get new equipment. This equipment is fifty to sixty years old and there's no way in God's world you can operate it dependably. I mean particularly in bad weather. It just won't run."

The ancient equipment, Saunders said, was responsible for the abandonment, at least temporarily, of a plan to link the Penn Central's Penn Center Station with the Reading Railroad's Reading Terminal, six blocks away in central Philadelphia, with an underground tunnel. Finally, after city and civic leaders persisted in pushing the plan for the tunnel, Saunders said he was forced to spell out just why the scheme wouldn't work. He invited Philadelphia mayor James H. J. Tate, Penn Central director R. Stewart Rauch, Richard C. Bond, the head of the Wanamaker department stores (and later a trustee for the Penn Central), and Philadelphia Electric Company head R. George Rincliffe, who was also a railroad director, to lunch in his office.

"They were always pushing this center city tunnel thing," Saunders said. "I have no objection to that but I told them this thing is wholly unrealistic. You've got the cart before the horse. I said if you get the money and build the center city tunnel you're not going to have anything to operate in it. I said eighty percent or more of this equipment can't operate in that tunnel. Because it'll have over a two percent grade and they won't go up the hill. Empty."

The railroad publicly kept up the fiction that it was truly concerned about the Penn Central's riders long after it became clear that the opposite was true. Equipment broke down, stations fell into disrepair, and the railroad, while making sympathetic pronouncements, did very little about it.

Only occasionally did the railroad tycoons slip and reveal their real feelings about passenger service, and the riders. One occasion came after the merger, and the witness to it was Perlman's son, Lee.

Young Perlman was living in Bucks County, Pennsylvania, at the time. Each day, he drove to Trenton, where he boarded a Penn Central train to Manhattan. In the evening, he commuted back home. Like so many others, Perlman grew dissatisfied with the arrangement. The trains were always late, they were dirty, they were too hot or too cold. One day he complained to his father. The elder Perlman, autocratic and domineering, did not take kindly to complaints from his son or anyone else. "If you don't like it, *walk*," the president of the railroad told his son.

At times, Perlman's advice seemed eminently wise. Perhaps walking *would* get you there faster than the Penn Central could. Tales of the abuse of commuters grew, rather than decreased, after the merger. On July 9, 1969, many eastern newspapers carried this news item:

"Approximately 16,000 commuters homeward bound from New York had to find other means of transportation at the height of the evening rush hour when all electrified service was stopped.

"Police were called to New York's Penn Station to control crowds of disgruntled commuters. No trains left the station for two and a half hours during the evening rush."

The next month, when the railroad announced it wanted to increase fares on its New Haven line, a group of prosperous-looking commuters picketed the Penn Central. Max Berking, an advertising executive from Rye, New York, told why he was picketing: "There have been many delays, a failure to announce delays, and the running time of the trains has not changed since 1899. I have an 1899 schedule to prove it."

On a cold winter day in 1968, the Media Local left Philadelphia's Thirtieth Street Station about fifteen minutes late. The conductor made his way through the car collecting tickets when a loud voice broke through the normal low-level chatter:

"You come back in eleven minutes and I'll give you my ticket. You kept me waiting eleven minutes, now you can wait eleven minutes." The conductor muttered something, and the voice responded:

"This is the third time this week you've made me late. I want to know why these trains are late. Why is this train late?"

"Someone on the train had a heart attack in Suburban [Penn Center] Station and had to be taken off," the conductor answered. "And if you got sick, we'd hold the train and take you off, too."

"Well, how about all those other times?" the voice said, "You come back in eleven minutes and you'll get my ticket and if you don't like it report me to Stuart Saunders."

"You are the most miserable bastard I've ever seen," the conductor shouted back.

One week in January 1970 was particularly ghastly for New York area commuters. On Monday morning, the railroad's Harlem Division had trains delayed for an hour because of an engine failure, which resulted in the tracks being blocked. The same morning, the New Haven line was delayed by more than a half hour because a traction motor caught fire. To round it out, faulty signals on the Hudson Division line delayed commuters by as much as forty-five minutes.

On Tuesday evening, an electrical fire in the tunnel leading out of Grand Central halted all outbound traffic. A fireman, attempting to put the blaze out, was killed by an inbound train, bringing all traffic to a halt. By the time commuters got home, more than an hour late, snow was falling.

The snow forced many motorists to take the train on Wednesday morning. The trains were more jammed than usual, and service, as a result, was slower. On Wednesday evening, a faulty rail was discovered in a tunnel. Two of the four tracks leading out of the tunnel were closed to traffic and commuters were delayed by as much as four hours.

The temperature fell close to zero on Thursday morning. One of the tracks in the tunnel was still not repaired. Switches froze, brakes failed, power failed, and delays were routine.

By Friday, railroad personnel and commuters alike, conditioned to disaster, were waiting for the latest misfortune to overtake them. They were not disappointed. An overhead power line on the New York–Washington run snapped, reducing traffic between Manhattan and Newark to a single track. A local freight going south on the Hudson Division turned north at the Harlem Division junction, and ripped out a large section of the power-laden third rail, bringing everything on the two divisions to a halt.

On an ordinary day, the Penn Central operated 903 trains into and out of New York, including the trains to Trenton, Philadelphia, Wilmington, Baltimore and Washington. The on-time performance that week would have made the Pony Express look good by comparison. And, on that disastrous Friday, 108 trains, including four Metroliners, were "annulled," a railroad euphemism for canceled. Paul A. Gorman, the former president of Western Electric, had succeeded Perlman as president of the Penn Central on December 1, 1969. On that Friday, Gorman had reserved a parlor car seat on one of the Metroliners that had been annulled.

During that same month, Alan Casnoff, a young lawyer, was waiting for the two-car 8:34 A.M. Penn Central train from Wynnefield, a section of Philadelphia. The train came at 9:20, and it was a one-car train jammed with passengers. The conductor refused to let Casnoff board, saying the car was too crowded. Casnoff ran to the middle of the tracks and refused to budge until he was assured he could get on the train. The conductor found room for him.

The commuters who had hoped the merger would bring better service soon found out differently. While the railroad was preoccupied with other matters, service got worse. Inevitably, pressure was brought to bear on the public regulatory agencies and the Penn Central found its commuter operations subjected to a series of investigations.

"The Penn Central management is either unwilling or incapable of undertaking the type of supervision required to provide a reasonably satisfactory passenger service," said New Jersey Transportation Commissioner David J. Goldberg. "The simple fact is that with a concerned railroad management much can be accomplished. Without such concern, service will continue to deteriorate."

On June 5, 1969, the New York State Public Service Commission ordered the Penn Central to make substantial improvements in service and equipment or face court action. Among the steps it ordered was that trains on the Harlem and Hudson divisions, which serviced 40,000 passengers traveling between Manhattan and Dutchess, Westchester and Putnam counties, run on schedule at least 80 percent of the time. The railroad consistently missed this goal, before and after the order, by a wide margin even though a train was considered "on time" if it was five minutes behind schedule. The commission also ordered stepped-up maintenance programs, the installation of two-way radios on all locomotive-drawn trains to summon help when one of the frequent failures of equipment occurred, and the installation of loudspeaker systems at suburban stations to inform commuters of deviations from schedule.

The most scathing criticism of the Penn Central came from an ordinarily genial Irish lawyer from Philadelphia, James McGirr Kelly. Kelly was also a member of the Pennsylvania Public Utility Commission and a commuter himself.

"Due to the inadequate number of cars many commuters must not only stand during the rush hours but are forced onto the platforms between trains, sometimes with the car doors open to the extreme hazard of the passengers," Kelly wrote, in a special report on the Penn Central. "Such conditions are intolerable for senior citizens, mothers with small children or persons who have physical or medical impairment. How is a man with a serious heart condition supposed to get to work? Does he drive the crowded highways endangering himself and others or does he stand in a crowded, late and dirty train to the aggravation of his health? Sometimes Americans are considered by other nations as being soft. It is suggested to such critics that they ride the Penn Central commuter lines."

Commuters, Kelly said, very often "stand like sheep on a cold platform in the dead of winter waiting for trains that never arrive" because the railroad failed to tell them that trains have been canceled. "A cursory review of the testimony regarding the trains and station facilities discloses a pattern of neglect bordering on contempt for the public," Kelly said.

In his investigation, Kelly learned that, of four transit lines studied, Penn Central had the highest per-car maintenance cost annually,[3] yet it was consistently outperformed by other lines. Kelly found that the Penn Central was able to use its cars about 26,000 miles a year, while the much smaller Reading, which had a far superior "on-time" performance record, used its cars 38,000 miles a year. Part of this, Kelly said, was attributable to the railroad's lack of interest in passenger business, which was reflected in its shoddy maintenance practices.

In 1958, the Pennsylvania received its first "Silverliner" commuter car. By 1970, the Penn Central had sixty-four of the cars, which by that time cost $250,000 each, most of the purchase price coming from the government. It was not until 1970, twelve years after receipt of the first Silverliner, that Penn Central maintenance personnel were given any instructions, either on-site or through the manufacturer's manual, on repairing the Silverliner. The decision to finally provide these instructions came only after Kelly had started his probe.

"If the attitude of management is so fixed that it believes the only future of rail passenger service is government ownership then it would appear that any increased subsidy may be a waste of the taxpayers' money," Kelly stated. "If management is convinced that it must get out of the rail passenger service, then increased subsidy can never be a panacea for the problems of rail passenger service."

Kelly's words came late, on June 3, 1970. But harsh words had come earlier, with no discernible effect. To the railroad, the issue was simply profit, quick and neat. Passenger service wasn't profitable, at least it wasn't in the foreseeable future, even with an enormous outlay for equipment and maintenance, an outlay that should have been made over the years but wasn't.

---

[3] Maintenance cost per car per year, prepared by Edson L. Tennyson, city of Philadelphia transit official:

Penn Central	$18,640
Long Island Railroad	$14,800
Reading	$12,200
Staten Island Rapid Transit	$ 8,550

7

A Very Small Affair

The letter was addressed to the board of directors of the Penn Central Company and it was marked, "Attention: Mr. Stuart T. Saunders, Chairman." It was dated February 23, 1970.

As head of the nation's largest railroad, a railroad plagued by misdirected freight shipments and passenger train breakdowns, Saunders was accustomed to receiving large quantities of mail, most of it critical. This letter, however, was unlike anything he had ever received before.

It was written by Marion E. Sibley, a Miami Beach attorney, on behalf of George J. Franks, a Penn Central stockholder. Sibley demanded that the board of directors "institute an action for discovery against (and, if necessary, for an accounting and recovery from) Penphil Co., a Pennsylvania corporation, and any of its stockholders who are officers or directors of Penn Central Co. or any of Penn Central's subsidiary corporations."

The action, Sibley wrote, should ascertain:

(a) whether the stockholders [of Penphil] have profited at the expense of Penn Central and its stockholders;

(b) whether the purchase or sale of securities or other activities of Penphil involves a conflict of interest, trading of insider or confidential information, or other similar conduct on the part of any of the stockholders, including but not limited to investments by Penphil in the stock of Great Southwest Corporation, Holiday International Tours, Inc., Continental Mortgage Investors (a Massachusetts business trust), First National Bank & Trust Co. of Boca Raton, N.A., University

National Bank of Boca Raton, N.A., and National Homes Corporation; and

(c) whether the financial resources or other assets of Penn Central or any of its subsidiary corporations including but not limited to Arvida Corp., Great Southwest Corp., Buckeye Pipeline Co., Penn Company, and American Contract Co. have been utilized for the benefit of any unaffiliated corporation including but not limited to Kaneb Pipeline Co., Tropical Gas Co., Inc., Executive Jet Aviation, Inc., and National Homes Corporation, in which Penphil, or the stockholders have a direct or indirect interest as stockholders, directors or officers of such unaffiliated corporations.

Saunders had been expecting the letter, but he was nevertheless stunned by its implications. A few weeks earlier, he had heard disquieting rumors about Penphil and he had sent his chief troubleshooter, Basil Cole, vice president of the executive department, to Florida to interview Sibley. Cole met with the attorney on February 1 and February 3. On February 5, Cole wrote a memo to Saunders which alarmed the chairman even more. Penphil's activities did indeed seem to be tied closely to the railroad. What was worse, railroad executives were deeply involved in Penphil.

"There were fifteen initial shareholders of Penphil including David C. Bevan and the four senior officers in the Financial Department of the Pennsylvania Railroad, all of whom then reported directly to Mr. Bevan," Cole's memo stated.

"Now this Penphil thing, I never heard of it," Saunders subsequently told us. "It was apparently organized in 1962 or something like that — before I came here. I don't know whether they did anything wrong or not. I'm not passing judgment on that."

Until he heard the rumors, and received the letter from Sibley, Saunders said, he was not aware of the existence of Penphil. In view of the nature of Penphil, which its organizers claimed was a "private investment club," and the composition of its membership, Saunders' lack of knowledge about it bordered on the amazing. As much as anything else, this situation reflected the total lack of communication at the very top of the Penn Central.

The organizers of Penphil were David C. Bevan, the railroad's chief finance officer, and Charles J. Hodge, a partner in the Wall Street investment banking firm of Glore Forgan, Wm. R. Staats,

Inc.[1] Hodge was one of Bevan's closest friends and he was the Penn Central's principal outside investment advisor.

The president of Penphil was Thomas R. Bevan, a prominent Philadelphia lawyer with the firm of Duane Morris & Hecksher and David Bevan's brother. Investors in the club included five other Penn Central officers, all from the finance department, all part of "Bevan's railroad." Four officers and directors of Penn Central subsidiaries were also shareholders in Penphil.[2]

---

[1] Glore Forgan later became F. I. duPont–Glore Forgan, Inc.

[2] Penphil was incorporated in Pennsylvania on July 10, 1962. Of the original members, five were connected with the railroad. Its membership at one point numbered twenty-six. A complete list of members, and their holdings, follows:

Stockholders in Penphil Corporation

Name	Title	No. of Shares and Date Acquired	
David C. Bevan	Finance Chmn., Penn Central	3,300	9- 7-62
Thomas R. Bevan	Lawyer, brother of David	3,300	9- 7-62
Warren H. Bodman	Partner, Yarnall Biddle & Co.	3,300	9- 7-62
Francis A. Cannon	V.P., First Boston Corp.	3,300	9- 7-62
Paul D. Fox	V.P. (ret.), Penn Central	3,100	9- 7-62
Wm. R. Gerstnecker	V.P., Treasurer Penn Central	3,300	9- 7-62
Robert Haslett	V.P., Penn Central	3,300	9- 7-62
Mrs. Marie L. Hodge	Wife of Charles J. Hodge	3,300	9- 7-62
Frederick B. Holmes	V.P., Gladfelter Paper Co.	3,300	9- 7-62
Benjamin F. Sawin	Chmn., Provident Intern'l Corp.	3,300	9- 7-62
Mrs. Dorothy B. Stevens	Wife of Lawrence M. Stevens, Partner, Hornblower & Weeks–Hemphill, Noyes	3,300	9- 7-62
Mrs. Dorothy H. Warner	Wife of Penn Central V.P. Theodore K. Warner	3,300	9- 7-62
Angus G. Wynne, Jr.	Pres., Great Southwest Corp.	3,300	9-21-62
Fred H. Billups	Pres., Tropical Gas Co.	3,000	7- 1-63
Herbert E. Fisher	Chmn., Kaneb Pipe Line Co.	3,300	7- 1-63
Edwin B. Horner	First Colony Life Insurance Co.	3,300	7- 1-63
Hobart C. Ramsey	V.P., Glore Forgan	3,300	7- 1-63
Samuel A. Breene	Lawyer, Oil City, Pa.	3,300	6- 1-67
Joseph W. Davin	V.P., Arvida Corp.	577	2-19-68
O. F. Lassiter	Pres., Executive Jet	408	2-19-68
Alfonso Manero	Retired Partner, Glore Forgan	407	2-19-68
Harry F. Ortlip	Pres., Box Hill Realty	1,323	2-19-68
Brown L. Whatley	Pres., Arvida Corp.	1,323	2-19-68
Cornelius A. Dorsey	V.P., Penn Central	715	Aug. '68
Thomas F. Fleming, Jr.	Chmn., First Bank Boca Raton	2,285	Aug. '68
Vincent G. Kling	Architect	3,300	2-26-69

The potential for conflicts of interest was enormous. Bevan and Hodge, to a large extent, controlled Penphil's investments; they decided what stock the club would buy. Bevan, with Hodge's advice, controlled the investments of the Pennsylvania Railroad and, after the merger, of the Penn Central. If they chose to use their unique positions, these men would have tremendous advantages in stock-dealing. They knew, indeed they decided, what stocks the railroad would buy. They also decided what stocks Penphil would buy. The possibilities were obvious.

The operations of Penphil, when they were finally exposed, served to discredit Bevan and mark him as the chief villain in the collapse of the Penn Central. Bevan found this incomprehensible. He could not get over the injustice of it all. How could anyone accuse him of contributing to the failure of a $4.5 billion railroad just because he was a member of a private investment club? His total investment in Penphil was only $16,500. The railroad paid him $132,000 a year. And he received more in deferred compensation in a single year from the Penn Central than the entire amount of his investment in Penphil.[3] How could anyone question his true loyalty?

Democratic Congressman Wright Patman, the seventy-six-year-old banker-baiting Populist from Texas could — and did. In a letter to the members of the House Committee on Banking and Currency, which he headed, Patman said the Penphil story "consti-

---

The following, at one time or another, owned shares in Penphil:

Edward D. Meanor	Investment Banker	3,300	9- 7-62 to Dec. 1966
John K. Acuff	Brooke, Sheridan, Bogan & Co.	3,300	9- 7-62 to Dec. 1964
C. Carroll Seward	Yarnall Biddle & Co.	3,000	9- 7-62 to 1- 6-69
Leslie M. Cassidy	Former Chmn., Johns-Manville	3,300	9- 7-62 to 2- 7-67

[3] Deferred compensation was a tax device established by the railroad for its executives. Under various optional arrangements, the railroad paid into a Contingent Compensation Fund sums of money in behalf of the executives. These sums, and whatever appreciation accrued, were to be paid to the executives when they retired or left the company, usually when they were past their peak earning years, thus reducing their tax liability. In 1969, Bevan received more than $22,000 in deferred compensation in addition to his $132,000 salary.

Rep. Wright Patman, Texas Democrat, Populist and chairman of
the House Banking and Currency Committee. (Courtesy of the
Democratic National Congressional Committee)

tutes a classic example of the use of corporate power for personal profit."

"In effect, it is the chronicle of how two men, David C. Bevan, the former chief financial officer of the Penn Central, and Charles J. Hodge, the former chief investment adviser of the railroad, manipulated the financial resources, the assets and the credit of the nation's sixth largest corporation for the benefit of an investment company, Penphil, which they established and directed," Patman wrote, on February 15, 1971, to his committee.

"The ultimate goal of Bevan and Hodge was to create a large conglomerate operating and holding company while orchestrating Penn Central investments in a way that would serve the interests of Penphil," Patman added. "In an overall sense, the history of Penphil is not only the story of monumental disservice to the Penn Central, the nation's largest transportation system; it is a detailed record of activities which distorts the concept of the democratic free enterprise system."

David Bevan did not agree. Testifying before the Senate Commerce Committee on August 6, 1970, he gave this description of his investment club: "The Penphil Corporation was a small, informal investment company set up by a number of us who were linked by friendship to invest for capital appreciation. It was a very small affair and run quite informally. I was a stockholder."

As a result of investments that paralleled, or were closely related to, investments made by the Penn Central, Penphil, Bevan's "very small affair," was able to realize profits, in cash and on paper, of about $1,750,000 in eight years.

When David Crumley Bevan returned home to the Main Line in 1951, he was not yet forty-five years old but he had already built for himself a reputation as one of America's budding financial geniuses. He had traveled the world over and, despite his dour disposition, had made hundreds of contacts among the men who counted in national and international finance.

Bevan was born in Wayne, on the Main Line, on August 5, 1906. He graduated from Haverford College in 1929, with a major in economics, and went on to the Harvard Graduate School of Business, receiving his MBA in 1931. After leaving Harvard, Bevan worked for eleven years in the Provident National Bank in

Philadelphia, putting in long hours and acquiring a thorough knowledge of every operating department.

During World War II, Bevan served on the War Production Board and later went to Australia as a member of the United States Lend Lease Mission. He was promoted to Deputy Chief of the Economic Mission in London in 1945. After the war, Bevan returned to the Provident briefly, but he resigned to become treasurer of the New York Life Insurance Company in October 1946.

Bevan was still treasurer of New York Life in 1951, when the Pennsylvania Railroad decided it needed somebody to overhaul its cumbersome debt structure and bring some sort of financial sense to its operations. It was not an easy job. Earnings in 1951 fell off by $12 million. Debt was at an all-time high. The plant was rapidly wearing out as a result of the around-the-clock use it had received during the booming war years. The railroad concluded that if anyone could do the job, it was Bevan.

Besides his obvious professional qualifications, Bevan had other necessary attributes — old Philadelphia–Main Line background, a wife who could trace her American ancestry back as far as any member of the Union League could, an Ivy League education. Coming from that background, Bevan knew better than most just what the railroad had to offer. Instant respect. Vast power. Big money. And, at his age, a clear shot at becoming the railroad's chairman. In May 1951, Bevan quit New York Life to become chief financial officer, vice president and a director of the Pennsylvania Railroad.

Bevan moved his wife, the former Mary Heist, and his two sons back to Philadelphia. Eventually he established them in Gladwyne, on the Main Line, in a huge home he named "Treverigge." With a zest for work that pleased his superiors, Bevan set about restoring fiscal stability to the railroad. But he ran his own shop. Anybody not part of "Bevan's railroad" was considered, and treated like, an intruder. He mingled with railroad employees on his own terms or not at all.[4]

---

[4] Stuart Saunders said that in six years and eight months of working with Bevan he had never been invited to the finance chairman's home, although it was only a few miles west of his own Main Line mansion.

By 1962, it was clear to Bevan that, despite all his hard work, he would not be chosen as the successor to James M. Symes, the chairman of the railroad, when Symes reached retirement age in July 1962. At the age of fifty-five, Bevan began to develop other interests, interests that the chairman of the railroad would not have been expected to consider.

Charles Joseph Hodge was not tall, dark, broad-shouldered and handsome like his friend Bevan. He was not cold and distant in his personal relationships, as Bevan was. He was "Charlie" Hodge to his friends, and there seemed to be many of them. He preferred that everybody else address him as "General."

Hodge was born just a year after Bevan, on August 30, 1907, in Washington, D.C. His educational accomplishments did not match Bevan's. Hodge attended Georgetown University's Foreign Service School in 1928 and 1929, and he attended New York University in 1939.

Hodge had moved from Washington to Short Hills, New Jersey, and, with the signs of war growing unmistakable, he joined the New Jersey National Guard in 1940. The following year, he went to Europe with a motorized cavalry division, serving with distinction (the Bronze Star, the Croix de Guerre twice, the Medaille Militaire Volontaire) until 1945. When he retired from the National Guard in 1955, Hodge had earned the permanent rank of Brigadier General. He was a Wall Street figure of some note when Bevan became acquainted with him after the war.

Although Hodge was not an official of the railroad, he exerted a curiously strong influence on the Penn Central's operations. In the summer of 1969, when Stuart Saunders was searching for someone to replace Alfred E. Perlman as president of the railroad, Hodge somehow became involved in the recruiting effort. One director, who managed to get along with all factions inside the railroad, told us Hodge was responsible for finding Paul A. Gorman, who had retired as head of Western Electric, and helping persuade Gorman to become president of the Penn Central. Another director, E. Clayton Gengras, said that Hodge's banking house, Glore Forgan, made a feasibility study of the merger for the PRR and the Central. "When you talk about mergers, the first thing you do is discuss it with your board," Gengras said. "Then you go out and get a good bank or investment firm to analyze it for you. You go over earnings, you look at the debts. What happened here? Did anybody analyze it? Charlie Hodge's firm looked at it for them. Hodge was a good friend of Bevan's. Glore Forgan bought Great Southwest and Arvida and the pipelines for the Penn Central."

Saunders said he had never heard of Hodge's report, nor did he know that Glore Forgan had been asked to make such a study. "Not to my knowledge," Saunders said. "If he did, I don't know anything about it. Well, he may have made it for the board, but I never saw it. I don't know anything about it. But he had no official or unofficial connection with the railroad at all, to my knowledge. He was a good friend of Bevan's, I think. And still is, as far as I know. Although I'm not even sure of that. I don't know."

Hodge may very well have had no "official or unofficial connection with the railroad." But, from May 1965 to May 1970, the railroad paid out at least $20,835.94 in charter airline fees billed to the Penn Central by Hodge.

After Bevan learned he would not be chosen to succeed Symes, and after he decided to develop interests outside the railroad, it was only natural that he should talk it over with his good friend Charlie Hodge. Hodge was chairman of the executive committee of Glore Forgan, the railroad's principal investment banker, he knew his way around Wall Street, and he was always interested in making good investments.

David Bevan was not a private club enthusiast like Saunders. But he did like to sip a vodka martini and, when time permitted, he enjoyed fishing. He was part of an informal fishing group that called itself "The Silverfish." The members of "The Silverfish" were men who were prominent in finance and business with whom Bevan felt comfortable. Not surprisingly, most of the original investors in Penphil were members of "The Silverfish."

William R. Gerstnecker was not a fisherman. But he was the railroad's treasurer and corporate vice president.[5] And he was

---

[5] Gerstnecker left the railroad in 1969 to become vice chairman of the Provident National Bank in Philadelphia, Bevan's old bank. On January 19, 1971, he resigned from Provident after disclosures were made about his role in Penphil and in the railroad's attempt to enter the air carrier business illegally by acquiring Executive Jet Aviation, Inc. Executive Jet is discussed in the next chapter.

very close to his boss, David Bevan. Gerstnecker told investigators from the Patman committee that Bevan, during the first part of 1962, asked him if he would like to join a group of "good investment people" who would "have good advice." Gerstnecker joined without hesitation.

Robert Haslett was the railroad's vice president for investments. Like Gerstnecker, his boss was Bevan, and like Gerstnecker, he invested $16,500 in Penphil. He told the Patman investigators that Bevan informed him about "a little investment club" in which the members would "put some money to work and try and make some money."

Bevan and Hodge had no trouble getting investors to join Penphil. By the summer of 1962, when the ICC was beginning hearings on the PRR-Central merger application, Bevan's "little investment club" was ready to go. On July 25, just fifteen days after it was incorporated, Penphil made its first stock purchase.

Excluding its investment in Holiday International Tours, Inc., Penphil invested about $1,208,000 in seven separate transactions over the subsequent six-year period. During that period, Penphil borrowed $1,810,209 from Chemical Bank New York Trust Company, a creditor of the Penn Central.

The Chemical Bank loans to Penphil, according to the Patman committee staff report, were made primarily because of Bevan's key position with the railroad — Bevan, among other things, determined the volume of Penn Central business each bank received. The Chemical Bank naturally was interested in the railroad's business.[6]

"It is clear, therefore, that the $1.8 million in loans to Penphil were not made by Chemical Bank on the soundness of the line of credit," the Patman staff report found. "They were made on preferential terms, as compared to loans of a similar nature, because of the value to Chemical Bank of Penn Central's loan and deposit business. In effect, it was Penn Central's compensating balances, interest payments and deposits that were subsidizing the Penphil line of credit for the personal profit of Penphil members."

---

[6] In May 1970, Chemical Bank was owed $34 million by the Penn Central — $15 million it had advanced through a revolving credit plan and $19 million in conditional sales agreements. It also held, for two nominees, 721,119 shares of railroad stock, about 3 percent of the total.

A Chemical Bank interoffice memo, summarizing a telephone conversation between Bevan and C. A. McLeod, vice president of Chemical's international division, lent weight to the Patman staff's findings. The memo, written by McLeod in the summer of 1962 and sent to W. S. Renchard, Chemical Bank chairman, and Melville A. Chamberlain, vice president of the metropolitan division, stated:

David Bevan, financial vice president of the Pennsylvania Railroad Company, called me on the telephone today and said that he and a group of friends, totaling about fifteen, are planning to organize a corporation to purchase a substantial block of common stock of Kaneb Pipe Line Company. The group will include Charlie Hodge of Glore Forgan and Company, Benjamin F. Sawin, president of Provident Tradesmen's Bank and Trust Company [subsequently changed to Provident National Bank], Messrs. Gerstnecker and Haslett of the Pennsylvania Railroad's financial staff and others.

Frankly the rate on the proposed loan is too low, but in view of the size of the deal and the fact that it has such good friends connected with it, WSR (W. S. Renchard, Chemical's chairman) felt it was preferable not to quibble with Mr. Bevan over the rate. He indicated that George Bartlett of Glore Forgan and Company would probably be the one to negotiate the purchase of the stock and very likely Charlie Hodge would be the one to work out the mechanics of the loan arrangement.

The loan arrangement was unusual in that interest was fixed at the prime rate, instead of at one or two points above, which would have been normal for loans of this type. Chemical also did not require Penphil to maintain a compensating balance of at least 20 percent of the loan outstanding, which again would have been normal. Penphil's checking account with Chemical averaged about $4,000, less than one percent of the usual outstanding balance on its loans.

Melville Chamberlain, Chemical's vice president, told the Patman investigators that normal loan requirements were not applied in the Penphil case because of "other considerations." He listed these "other considerations":

— Penn Central was a major client of the bank.
— David Bevan was well known to senior Chemical officers.

Bevan had a personal line of credit with the bank and had established to the bank's satisfaction that he was worth one million dollars. "All of Bevan's personal loans from Chemical were at the prime rate, a situation enjoyed by few individuals in the nation, no matter how wealthy or powerful they are," the Patman staff report noted.

— Chamberlain had a long professional relationship with Charlie Hodge. In November 1968, Chemical loans outstanding to Hodge and his wife, Marie, totaled $950,000.

— Other Penphil stockholders had professional relationships with Chemical.

— All the Penphil stockholders were "responsible people."

— The Penphil loans were "fully and properly secured."

There was other evidence of the intermingling of Penn Central and Penphil business. On September 6, 1968, Robert W. Loder, a Penn Central assistant vice president under Bevan, wrote a letter to John N. Page, vice president and senior investment officer of the National Newark & Essex Bank.[7] Loder was not a member of Penphil, although the letter dealt with a Penphil transaction and was written on Penn Central stationery.

Loder's letter to Page stated:

Your bank has agreed to purchase *from us* [emphasis added] on September 10, $750,000 principal amount of Kaneb Pipeline Company six and seven-eighths percent Subordinated Notes dated December 19, 1967. These notes are being sold to you at par together with accrued interest at six and seven-eighths percent from March 18, 1968, to September 9, 1968, inclusive, amounting to $24,645.43.

The Notes are presently in possession of the Manufacturers Hanover Trust Company, Transfer Agent, and are being reregistered in the name of George & Co. for delivery to you.

Will you please arrange to bank wire the sum of $516,423.62 to the Chemical Bank New York Trust Company, (Attn Melville Chamberlain, Vice President), Church Street Post Office Station, for credit of the account of Penphil, account number 066-106-397. . . .

---

[7] National Newark & Essex Bank was part of a consortium of banks that loaned $300 million to Penn Central. National Newark's share was $3 million.

Once Chemical Bank agreed to turn on the money valve for Penphil, the investment club was in business. Its investments proved profitable. But when the railroad collapsed, Penphil, more than anything else, was to bring about Bevan's downfall.

Upon receiving Marion Sibley's letter, Stuart Saunders immediately placed the matter before the Committee on Information, Disclosure and Conflict of Interest of the board of directors of the Penn Central. The chairman of the committee was Edward J. Hanley, chairman of the Allegheny Ludlum Steel Corporation.[8]

Hanley's committee was formed on September 24, 1968, the day that Philadelphia stockbroker Howard Butcher III resigned from the Penn Central board. Butcher had been accused of using "secret information" to sell off 81,700 shares of Penn Central stock on July 12, 1968. His accuser was a railroad stockholder, Simon Kaminsky, who filed suit in the U.S. District Court in New York. The lawsuit caused an uproar in the railroad's board room and, within three weeks, Butcher resigned.

On February 25, 1970, Hanley's committee met to discuss Penphil. Other Penn Central directors who sat on the committee were Seymour H. Knox, of Buffalo, chairman of Marine Midland Trust Company of Western New York; John M. Seabrook, of Salem, New Jersey, president of International Utilities Corporation; Thomas L. Perkins, of Rye, New York, counsel to Perkins, Daniels & McCormack; Franklin J. Lunding, of Oak Park, Illinois, finance chairman of Jewel Companies, Inc., and Walter A. Marting, of Cleveland, president of the Hanna Mining Company.

Two decisions were reached at that meeting. One was to have Saunders write a soothing letter to Sibley, assuring the attorney that the board was investigating. The other was to retain Leslie H. Arps, of the New York City law firm of Skadden, Arps, Slate, Meagher & Flom, to do the investigating. Arps filed his report with the committee on September 4, 1970. By then, the Penn Central was in reorganization and four trustees had taken over the functions of the board of directors.

From the Arps report, from government and other sources, and

---

[8] Bevan served on the Allegheny Ludlum board at that time.

from an independent investigation, we have pieced together the following picture of Penphil's operations:

GREAT SOUTHWEST CORPORATION

Great Southwest was formed in 1956 to develop an industrial park outside Dallas. It was reincorporated in Texas on October 2, 1959, with control vested in the Rockefeller and Wynne families. The Wynnes were Texans with huge oil interests, including American Liberty Oil Company.

Penphil became involved with Great Southwest on July 18, 1963, when it purchased 10,000 shares of stock for $165,000. On that same day, the Pennsylvania Railroad bought 4,000 shares of Great Southwest stock for $66,000, increasing its holdings to 5,200 shares.

Penphil sat on its shares, but the railroad steadily sought to enlarge its holdings. From December 12, 1963, to June 26, 1964, the railroad bought an additional 7,300 shares for $144,337.50. Almost one year to the day that Penphil bought into Great Southwest, the PRR acquired control of the real estate company. In two days of massive buying, on July 15 and 16, 1964, the railroad purchased 520,367 shares of Great Southwest at a cost of $11,633,257.50, or $22.41 a share. In the ensuing fifteen months, after having acquired control, the railroad bought an additional 275,095 shares for $6,381,087.35, or $22.59 a share.

It was not until December 7, 1965, seventeen months after the PRR took over the company, that Penphil sold its interest in Great Southwest. The investment club, which paid $16.50 a share for its stock, sold its 10,000 shares for $37.75 a share, or a total of $377,500. This meant a profit to Penphil of $212,500 on an original investment of $165,000 in less than two and a half years.

Another interesting aspect was the fact that Charlie Hodge's firm, Glore Forgan, acted as broker in all the Great Southwest transactions. When Penphil bought, it was through Charlie Hodge's firm. When the PRR bought, it was through Charlie Hodge's firm. When Penphil sold out, Charlie Hodge handled it. And to make sure there were no loose ends, the railroad purchased an additional 10,100 shares of Great Southwest stock through Glore Forgan on December 7, 1965, the very day that Penphil sold its 10,000 shares. In effect, Glore Forgan sold Penphil's shares to the Pennsylvania Railroad.

Throughout this period, Hodge was a vice president of Glore Forgan. He was a director of Great Southwest and, through his wife, he was a stockholder in Penphil. He recommended to the PRR that it buy Great Southwest.

Hodge's recommendations were made to David Bevan, who controlled the railroad's investments. Bevan, while buying Great Southwest for the railroad, was also buying for Penphil.

To complete the circle, the president and chief executive officer of Great Southwest was Angus Gilchrist Wynne, Jr. On September 21, 1962, Wynne had become a member of Penphil by purchasing 3,000 shares.

The Arps report stated: "Thomas Bevan, president of Penphil, stated in an interview with committee's counsel that Penphil's investment in Great Southwest was made upon the recommendation of General Hodge, David C. Bevan and Robert Haslett [Bevan's assistant at the PRR], among others.

"The question therefore arises whether at the time of the Penphil acquisition both Messrs. Bevan and Hodge knew or had reason to believe or suspect that Penn Central would subsequently seek to acquire control of Great Southwest. If they knew of this possibility, then they would be open to the charge that they were availing themselves of inside information."

In a letter to Edward Hanley, dated July 21, 1970, Bevan denied there was anything improper about the parallel PRR–Penphil investments in Great Southwest. "At that point [when the railroad and Penphil first bought into Great Southwest], control of Great Southwest was tightly centered in the Rockefeller and Wynne families," Bevan wrote. "No one had any possible way of knowing that at a later date a rift would occur in the Wynne family. However, this occurred in the following year [1964] and as a result Toddie Wynne, Angus Wynne's uncle, thereupon expressed a desire to dispose of the family's interest in Great Southwest. Since the understanding between the Rockefellers and the Wynnes was that they would act in consort, control of the com-

pany became available and it was offered to us through Glore
Forgan and, of course, as you know we purchased controlling
interest."

Bevan elaborated on the Great Southwest transactions in an
interview. The railroad's purchases, he said, had been made by
Bob Haslett, his assistant. Haslett was also a member of Penphil.

"We bought 1,200 shares for the Contingent Compensation
Fund in January 1963," Bevan said. "It was probably offered as a
good go-go stock to Haslett. Twelve hundred shares is nothing. It
was an odd lot. Bob bought it as an interesting speculation.

"In the summer of 1963, he bought 5,000 or 6,000 more shares
for one of the railroad's funds. About that time we [Penphil]
made our only purchase of Great Southwest. In December or
January 1964, there was a public offering and the railroad bought a
little more. Penphil didn't buy any.

"The inference in the Arps report is that Hodge and I knew in
1963 that control would have been offered. If that were true, it
would have made sense for Penphil and the railroad to buy a lot
[of shares] in the public offering.

"The truth of the matter is that the rift in the Wynne family
didn't occur until 1964, so we couldn't know. Chances are nine
out of ten that I didn't have anything to do with it.

"Toddie Wynne said, 'There is a rift between my son and my
nephew and I can't tolerate that. It's a good company. If you don't
like the investment in a couple of years, we'll buy it back from
you.' "

What Bevan did not mention in his letter to Hanley or in the
interview was the fact that one of the two parties involved in the
rift in the Wynne family was Angus Wynne, the head of Great
Southwest and Toddie's nephew, the man who became a Penphil
stockholder on September 21, 1962. If any person knew of trouble
in the Wynne family, it would surely be Angus Wynne.

In his letter to Hanley, Bevan acknowledged that Penphil's
ownership of Great Southwest stock could be construed as a conflict of interest because of the railroad's control of the company.
"A few months later I expressed a desire that Penphil sell its Great
Southwest stock so that we would be sure to avoid any future
possible conflict of interest," Bevan wrote. "My wishes were re-

spected and the stock was sold at a price of thirty-eight dollars. All members of Penphil made a sacrifice in this connection as the price of $38 compares with even today's (July 21, 1970) very low price of approximately $60 a share since the stock was later split ten for one."

Bevan, however, never explained why, if he were worried about a possible conflict of interest, Penphil didn't sell its shares of Great Southwest when the railroad acquired control. "I can't tell you why the time elapsed between the time the railroad got control and we sold," Bevan said. "I had a lot of things on my mind."

One possible answer is that when the railroad acquired control, Great Southwest was selling for $22.41 a share. When Penphil finally sold out, *seventeen months later,* Great Southwest was selling for $37.75 a share. And it was the railroad that paid Penphil $37.75 for each of its 10,000 shares.

Great Southwest was, for a time, the most attractive of Penn Central's subsidiaries. By December 1969, the merged railroad had acquired 90 percent of the company and had invested $92 million in it. In January 1971, however, after a continuing series of setbacks that saw Angus Wynne ousted as president, Great Southwest wrote down its book value from $157 million to $50 million.

"In light of the above [writedown in book value], Penphil's sale of GSC stock in December 1965 appears even more lucrative," the Patman staff report stated. "Had David Bevan exercised the same business acumen on behalf of the Penn Central regarding its investment in GSC, Penn Central would not find itself in its current position of holding a $92 million investment in a $50 million corporation."

The Great Southwest story also touched on another friend of Charlie Hodge's — Maurice H. Stans, Secretary of Commerce in the Nixon Administration. Stans was head of Glore Forgan before he joined the Cabinet in 1969. While associated with Glore Forgan, Stans acquired options to buy shares in Macco Corporation. Macco was another real estate subsidiary of the railroad and it was subsequently merged into Great Southwest. Through these options, Stans ended up with 38,000 shares of Great Southwest. Although he pledged that he would put all his holdings in a so-called "blind trust," from which he would receive no information,

Stans did not specifically inform the Senate Commerce Committee of his interest in Great Southwest when he was confirmed to the Cabinet post in January 1969. At that time, his stock in the company was worth, on paper, $570,000.

On June 12, 1970, Stans was still listed as the owner of the 38,000 shares, which by that time had decreased in value to $318,000. The date is crucial because the Penn Central was then negotiating with the Nixon Administration for special government guarantees of $200 million in emergency short-term loans. If the loans did not come through, the railroad could very well collapse. If the railroad, the parent of Great Southwest, collapsed, the effect on Great Southwest would be tremendously harmful.

Stans, representing the Commerce Department, participated in one meeting on the loan guarantees. He subsequently disqualified himself from further participation because "of the circumstances." A Commerce Department lawyer, however, was involved in the negotiations from start to finish.

KANEB PIPELINE COMPANY

Kaneb was the first purchase made by Penphil. From July 25, 1962, to February 7, 1963, Penphil bought 30,488 shares of Kaneb for $153,247. All but 5,000 of these shares were purchased for amounts from $5 to $5.25 a share. The last 5,000 cost $8 a share.

The PRR owned 25,000 shares of Kaneb before Penphil started buying into the company. On April 9, 1963, two months after Penphil had completed its purchases, the railroad began increasing its holdings. By December 3, 1968, Penn Central had bought an additional 101,473 shares. On April 9, 1963, the railroad paid $9.16 each for four hundred shares. By December 3, 1968, it was paying $22 a share for 24,000 shares, four times more than the $5.20-a-share average paid by Penphil.

Late in 1970, Penphil's original investment in Kaneb was worth about $579,000, or a paper profit of some $426,000.

The Kaneb transaction also contained an element that was to be found in most Penphil deals. The president and chairman of Kaneb during this period was Herbert E. Fisher. On July 1, 1963, after

Penphil had completed its purchases and while the railroad was buying, Fisher became a Penphil stockholder by acquiring 3,300 shares. During 1963, David Bevan became a member of the Kaneb board of directors. While Glore Forgan had no members on Kaneb's board, the investment banking firm and its partners owned 107,000 shares of Kaneb.

CONTINENTAL MORTGAGE INVESTORS

On May 26, 1964, Penphil purchased 10,000 shares of this investment trust, paying $19.68 a share, or $196,800. At this time, the railroad owned 12,500 shares. Beginning on June 18, 1964, through February 24, 1970, the PRR bought an additional 40,500 shares of Continental. The stock split three-for-one on July 22, 1968, and two-for-one on February 15, 1970.

Late in 1970, Penphil's investment was worth, on paper, $491,-250, or a profit of about $294,000. There were no corporate interlocks between Penphil and Continental. Glore Forgan was not involved in any of these transactions.

NATIONAL HOMES CORPORATION

Penphil acquired 5,000 shares of National Homes on June 5, 1968, for $74,370.53, or slightly less than $15 a share. In three separate purchases in September 1968, Penn Central acquired 10,000 shares of National Homes for $282,044, or about $28.20 a share. Penn Central subsequently sold off 8,700 of its shares for $24.20 a share, suffering a loss of about $33,000.

In October 1970, Penphil sold its shares for $82,407, or a profit of a little more than $8,000.

There were no corporate interlocks between Penphil and National Homes, and Glore Forgan was not involved as a broker in these transactions.

TROPICAL GAS COMPANY, INC.

From August 1 to August 29, 1963, Penphil bought 10,000 shares of Tropical Gas for $191,495, or slightly more than $19 a share. All but 200 of these were acquired through Glore Forgan.

Prior   to   Penphil's   purchases,   the   PRR   owned   40,403 shares, for which it paid $955,736, or more than $22 a share. After Penphil bought in, the railroad purchased an additional 52,697 shares, at a total cost of $1,353,797, at prices ranging from $21.79 to $32.59 a share. Glore Forgan was the broker for all but 13,400 of these shares.

On October 2, 1968, a firm called Mapco, Inc., made a public announcement that it intended to acquire control of Tropical through an exchange offer — nine-tenths of a share of Mapco, which was selling for $37, for each share of Tropical, which was selling for $32. Nine days later, the management of Tropical advised the company's stockholders to resist Mapco's blandishments.

The president of Tropical at the time was Fred H. Billups. On July 1, 1963, in accordance with the pattern established by Penphil, Billups became a Penphil stockholder by purchasing 3,000 shares. Sitting on Tropical's board with Billups were four other Penphil stockholders — David Bevan, Charlie Hodge, Alfonso Manero, a retired partner in Glore Forgan, and Hobart Ramsey, a former Glore Forgan vice president.

In the summer of 1968, before Mapco publicly announced its intention to take over Tropical, Tropical's management entered into discussions with Glore Forgan for a new common stock issue of 230,000 shares to raise an additional $7 million in capital. On October 16, Tropical made a public announcement of its new stock issue, and Mapco subsequently filed suit to block the issue, claiming the proceeds would be used to perpetuate control of the company by "the present officers and directors."

The natural result of such a massive new stock issue would be a dilution in earning power of each share outstanding. From Penn Central's point of view, it would mean that each share of Tropical stock it held would be reduced in value, at least at the outset. During this period, Bevan and Hodge, in addition to being directors of Tropical, also served on Tropical's executive committee. They held these positions, which enabled them to know months in advance of the proposed stock issue, while they were still functioning as Penn Central's chief investment advisors, Bevan on the inside, Charlie Hodge on the outside.

Despite these circumstances, Penn Central continued to increase its holdings in Tropical. From September 20 until October 15, 1968, the very day before the public announcement of the new stock issue, the railroad bought 35,400 shares of Tropical, at a cost of $1,016,374. All of these buys were made through Glore Forgan. Penphil, which also relied on the advice of Bevan and Hodge, did not purchase any more Tropical shares.

In a letter to Hanley, chairman of the Penn Central's Conflict of Interest Committee, Robert Haslett, the Penphil stockholder who served as Bevan's assistant, attempted to explain these purchases. The letter was dated July 28, 1970. "Our last purchase of stock was on the 15th of October," Haslett wrote. "The following day the company [Tropical] officially filed a registration statement for the sale of 230,000 additional shares of common stock. *This was the first knowledge I had of any proposed financing, and, as a result, no further purchases were made* [emphasis added]."

The question that begs for an answer is: How could Bevan, who sat on Tropical's board and knew of the proposed stock issue, permit the Penn Central, which paid him more than $154,000 a year to manage the railroad's financial affairs, permit the Penn Central to spend another one million dollars in less than one month's time for shares of stock he knew would be diluted in value?

Where was Bevan's responsibility? To Tropical? To Penphil? Or to the Penn Central?

Investigators for Wright Patman's committee asked specifically if Haslett thought Bevan's responsibility to protect the interests of the railroad was greater than his responsibility to Tropical. *"I don't know which one he had a responsibility to first,"* Haslett replied. *"I just can't answer that* [emphasis added]."

Patman's investigators asked Haslett if Bevan knew the Penn Central was buying Tropical stock during this period when Billups, the Penphil stockholder who was also president of Tropical, was desperately fighting to block the Mapco takeover attempt. "Normally, Dave Bevan was aware of Penn Central's Tropical stock purchases, but I'm not sure if he was in this instance," Haslett said. He added that Bevan could not very well have forewarned him not to buy Tropical, asking the investigators rhetorically, "Would that not be inside information?"

Haslett said he continued to buy Tropical for the railroad after Mapco's October 2 offer to acquire Tropical stock through an exchange "because the takeover price made Tropical stock appear cheap." He also said: "I was not aware that Penn Central purchases of Tropical stock were driving the price up."

Significantly, Penphil, which had available to it the same advice that the Penn Central did, avoided buying any more Tropical stock. "It was to Penphil's advantage not to purchase stock during this period because Bevan and Hodge knew the value of all stock would go down," Patman's investigators concluded. "By the same token, it was to Penphil's advantage to let Penn Central take the loss. . . ."

The Arps report on the Tropical–Penphil–Penn Central involvement stated: "Since Mr. Haslett reported to Mr. Bevan in the Penn Central organization, it is difficult to understand why Mr. Haslett would have no information with respect to the proposed issue of common stock in the light of the fact that Mr. Bevan was a member of the board and executive committee of Tropical, and the [Arps] committee has reason to believe that the public offering of Tropical Gas was contemplated as early as August 1, 1968. Further, Mr. Bevan indicated in a statement to Mr. E. J. Hanley that no one would have bought Tropical stock knowing of a proposed issue of additional shares."

The proposed stock issue was subsequently withdrawn, but Mapco lost its fight to take over Tropical. In October 1969, Tropical was merged into U.S. Freight Company. Penphil received 8,900 shares of U.S. Freight for its 10,000 shares of Tropical; the railroad received 79,566 shares of U.S. Freight for its 89,400 Tropical shares.

On October 8, 1970, Penphil deposited $198,339 in its account at Chemical Bank after selling off its U.S. Freight stock. Penphil realized a profit of about $7,000. Because of its substantially higher per-share acquisition costs, Penn Central appeared at that time to have suffered a loss of about $439,000 on its investment in Tropical.

FIRST BANK & TRUST COMPANY, AND
UNIVERSITY NATIONAL BANK

Penphil became heavily involved in Florida banking between September 27, 1966, and February 14, 1969. During that period, it acquired 21,380 shares of First Bank & Trust Company of Boca

Raton at a cost of $332,924, and 4,868 shares of University National Bank, also of Boca Raton, for $94,184.

Penn Central did not invest in either of these banks. But the railroad did own 58 percent of Arvida Corporation, a land development firm with large holdings in Florida, including several valuable parcels of land in the Boca Raton area, home of the two banks in which Penphil had interests.

David Bevan, Charlie Hodge, William R. Gerstnecker (Bevan's assistant), Angus G. Wynne, president of Great Southwest, Brown L. Whatley, president of Arvida, and Joseph W. Davin, vice president of Arvida, controlled the Arvida board of directors. These men were all shareholders in Penphil. Davin acquired 577 Penphil shares on February 19, 1968, and Whatley acquired 1,323 shares the same day.

Thomas F. Fleming, Jr., was chairman of First Bank at this time, and he had large holdings in both First Bank and University National. In August 1968, Fleming became a Penphil shareholder by purchasing 2,285 shares. In a letter to Bevan, dated December 10, 1968, Fleming had this to say about joining Penphil: "This is to advise you that I am thrilled and delighted and want to take all of the stock that is left. Therefore, I am making my plans to pay for 2,300 or 2,400 shares of stock.

"I am so happy to join this exalted group of gentlemen investors about whom I have heard so much. I want to thank you for this opportunity to join your group."[9]

Less than two months after Penphil began buying into First Bank, Arvida money started flowing into that bank.

Among Arvida's holdings was the Boca Raton Hotel and Club, a plush twenty-six story resort. On July 29, 1966, the Arvida board voted to transfer the Boca Raton Hotel and Club operating account from the Boca Raton National Bank, in which Penphil had no interest, to First Bank, into which Penphil was preparing to buy. Arvida's executive committee approved the transfer on October 21, and the account was switched on December 15.

In 1965, gross deposits of the Arvida hotel account with Boca

---

[9] While the transfer of stock to Fleming did not take place until December, the transaction was dated August. Fleming paid $35 a share and realized a paper profit of $11,245 as soon as the stock changed hands.

Raton National came to slightly more than $6 million. There were no gross deposits with First Bank.[10]

In 1966, gross deposits from the Arvida division with Boca Raton National were $6.9 million, with First Bank receiving $97,000. The picture changed dramatically in 1967, after Penphil came on the scene. Arvida hotel account deposits with First Bank jumped to $6.4 million. Boca Raton National received nothing. Hotel account deposits with First Bank were $7.2 million in 1968 and $10.3 million in 1969.

First Bank and University National became part of a registered bank holding company, First Bancshares of Florida, Inc., on October 15, 1970. Penphil's shares in the two banks were exchanged for an equal number of shares in the new company. At that time, Penphil's original $427,000 investment in the banks was worth about $1,244,000, a profit of more than $800,000.

Except for the purchases of Great Southwest stock, the money for Penn Central's investments in the companies listed above came largely from two sources — the Supplemental Pension Plan, with assets of more than $300 million, representing the pension benefits of more than 36,000 railroad employees, and the Contingent Compensation Fund, with holdings of about $11 million, representing deferred payments to some 130 railroad officers and executives.

"Thus, to a large extent, other people's money was being used to finance investments in certain selected companies for the purpose of permitting Penphil and those associated with it to control these same companies," the Patman staff concluded. It also had these questions to ask about the roles of David Bevan and Charlie Hodge:

To whom did David Bevan owe his greatest fiduciary responsibility? A fiduciary responsibility is not supposed to be divisible, i.e., one who

---

10 David Bevan purchased a $46,750 condominium apartment from Arvida's Sabal Point development in Boca Raton on June 23, 1965, with a loan from Chemical Bank. Charlie Hodge bought a condominium in the same development for $47,250 on July 12, 1965. On July 20, 1965, Bevan recommended to the Pennsylvania Railroad executive committee that the railroad acquire control of Arvida.

has a fiduciary responsibility is not supposed to put himself in a position of divided loyalty. It would seem to be impossible for one that was in the position that David Bevan was in to faithfully carry out his duties to all the parties to whom he owed a fiduciary responsibility. Similar questions can be raised for other persons involved with the Penphil–Penn Central–Glore Forgan complex.[11]

Similarly, Charles Hodge and/or his investment banking firm were (1) the principal investment adviser to Penn Central; (2) investment adviser to and broker for the Penn Central Supplemental Pension Plan and the Contingent Compensation Fund; (3) investment banker for Kaneb Pipeline, Tropical Gas and Great Southwest Corp.; (4) a director of Great Southwest Corp., Arvida Corp. and Tropical Gas; and (5) holders of substantial investments in Kaneb Pipeline, Tropical Gas and Great Southwest. How could Charles Hodge give sound objective investment advice to clients of Glore Forgan concerning their investments while being so personally involved in the management and control of these significant corporations?

One significant matter, not dealt with by either Patman or Arps, was the fact that Bevan never saw fit to disclose his interest in Penphil to the Penn Central board of directors or to Stuart Saunders.

After Howard Butcher resigned, the board's Committee on Information, Disclosure and Conflict of Interest prepared several manuals for the guidance of the officers and directors of the railroad and its subsidiaries. With the help of Penn Central's accounting firm, Peat, Marwick, Mitchell & Company, the committee prepared a questionnaire to find out the extent and nature of the outside business activities of the railroad's executives. Among other things, the committee said in its working papers, the questionnaire was to determine "the rank of the individual within the company's organization, the ability of the individual to decide or have a significant influence upon company policies, the ability of the individual to bind the company from a contractual point of view, and the individual's access to sensitive information about the company."

---

[11] In addition to his other duties, Bevan was chairman of the management committee of the Supplemental Pension Plan and was administrator of the Contingent Compensation Fund, giving him control over the investments of both.

In the spring of 1969, this questionnaire was sent to 269 officers and directors of Penn Central and its subsidiaries. Among those who received them were Bevan, Hodge (who was a director of Great Southwest), William Gerstnecker, Robert Haslett, Paul Fox, Cornelius Dorsey and Angus Wynne, president of Great Southwest.

Those who received the questionnaire were asked to provide information about their outside business activities from January 1, 1966, on. One of the key questions asked: "Are you or have you been during the questionnaire period a director, officer, member, consultant, agent, employee, or representative of, or acted in any capacity for, any corporation, partnership, limited partnership, unincorporated association, trust or any entity which at any time during the questionnaire period was not one of the Penn Central companies?"

Bevan's reply, dated April 7, 1969, listed seventeen positions he held outside the railroad, ranging from a directorship with Provident National Bank to various posts he held on committees of his alma mater, Haverford College. He did not mention, however, his association with Penphil, nor did Hodge, Gerstnecker, Haslett, Fox, Dorsey or Wynne.

A second question posed in the questionnaire asked: "Other than your ownership of securities of Penn Central companies, are you or have you been during the questionnaire period (a) the beneficial owner of five percent or more of any class of securities of any corporation or other entity, or (b) the beneficial owner of any amount of such securities as would reasonably be considered material in the context of your own financial position?"

To this question, Bevan replied no, as did the others. When Penphil was organized, Bevan owned more than 5 percent of the total stock. By January 1, 1966, further stock isues had diluted his percentage to 4.7 percent, or three-tenths of a percentage point less than the standard fixed in the questionnaire. The holdings of Hodge, Gerstnecker, Haslett and Wynne were identical to Bevan's, while Fox's percentage was fractionally less. Dorsey never owned as much as 5 percent of Penphil.

Bevan later said he did not report his holdings in Penphil because they amounted to less than 5 percent. The $16,500 he had invested, he said, was not "substantial" and he did not consider it "material" in the context of his own financial position, even though his investment had appreciated by some 600 percent. "There was never any secret about it," Bevan said. "We just regarded it as a highly successful investment club."

After the Penn Central collapsed, the new managers of the railroad did not look upon Penphil as simply a "highly successful investment club." They considered it an "unlawful conspiracy" and, in April 1971, they filed suit in United States District Court for the Eastern District of Pennsylvania against Penphil, Bevan, Hodge, Gerstnecker and F. I. duPont, Glore Forgan, Inc. In the suit, the Penn Central charged:

> Beginning at a time unknown to plaintiffs, prior to 1963, and continuing until June 21, 1970, defendants Bevan, Hodge and Gerstnecker entered into an unlawful combination and conspiracy to exercise their powerful and influential positions in and relationships with Penn Central for their own personal profit, gain and unjust enrichment, and for the personal profit, gain and unjust enrichment of those persons who acted in concert with them, or aided and abetted them, or who were affiliated with them. . . .

> In furtherance of the conspiracy, Bevan, Hodge and Gerstnecker created Penphil, and thereafter covertly utilized and manipulated all of the resources of Penn Central over which they had control not for the best interests of Penn Central and its shareholders, but for their own private, personal profit, gain, aggrandizement and unjust enrichment and that of Penphil and its shareholders and of the companies in which Penphil and duPont had invested or controlled. . . .

The suit alleged that Bevan, Hodge and Gerstnecker had used, for Penphil's profit, the railroad's investment funds, Penn Central's relationships with various banks, the railroad's credit lines and their own special knowledge about the railroad's affairs. The suit also charged that:

> Prior to 1963 Bevan and Hodge, as part of the conspiracy, counselled and advised that Penn Central embark upon a program of nonrailroad diversification. Acceptance of their counsel made substantial assets available for non-railroad related ventures.

> Such availability of large sums for non-railroad related investment created numerous opportunities for personal gain for those in control

of the investment decisions. As part of the conspiracy Bevan and Hodge exploited and utilized for their own personal profit and gain the trust and confidence reposed in them by Penn Central, and they carried out the diversification program and invested Penn Central's funds not for the best interests of Penn Central but in a manner to benefit Penphil and to benefit themselves personally.

In its complaint, the railroad included as part of the conspiracy all of the investments made by Penphil. "Prior to June 21, 1970, and for some time thereafter, Penn Central had no knowledge of the unlawful conspiracy of the defendants, nor of their unlawful conduct and violations alleged in this complaint, nor of any facts which might have led to the discovery thereof. Defendants employed deceptive practices and secrecy to avoid detection, and they fraudulently concealed their conspiracy and violations," the railroad's complaint stated.

Edward C. German and James M. Marsh, attorneys who represented Bevan, in a statement made in response to the suit, said, ". . . it is now obvious that there is a well-defined plan to make Mr. David C. Bevan the scapegoat for the situation, whereas in reality the responsibility rests elsewhere." The lawyers' statement went on to say: "So far as the diversification program was concerned, we do not believe it was susceptible to manipulation. The program itself was heartily endorsed by both management and the board of the Pennsylvania Railroad and a detailed analysis of each company was submitted to and approved by the board before any action was taken to acquire the company involved."

The lawsuit filed by the railroad, said German and Marsh, was "politically inspired." The trustees who took over after the collapse had been unable to stem the Penn Central's losses, they said, and thus they were engaging in "a diversionary action to take the heat off the trustees for the huge losses sustained under their trusteeship." The lawyers said it was "shocking" to have the trustees charge that Penphil contributed to the railroad's failure.

"Mr. Saunders, as chief executive officer, and Mr. Perlman, as chief operating officer, ran the railroad and were responsible for its operations and results," said German and Marsh. "Mr. Bevan had nothing to do with its operation. His primary responsibility was raising money for them to use in operating the railroad as a going business. He did his job; they failed to do theirs."

8

Sidetracked

It was just about midnight on July 1, 1970, when a small group of men arrived at the offices of Executive Jet Aviation, Inc., in downtown Columbus, Ohio. The leader of the group was Bruce G. Sundlun, and he was anxious to get past the locked doors and into the darkened rooms beyond. The man with the keys was Gus Rathgeber, a former Air Force sergeant.

Rathgeber appeared shaken by this late-night foray into the offices of the company that employed him. Nevertheless, he inserted his key into the locked door and swung it open. Sundlun hurried inside. The Great Raid was on.

Sundlun spent the rest of the night sorting and seizing the company's records. He found a bonus when he came across a large stack of color photographs showing Air Force Brigadier General (Ret.) O. F. "Dick" Lassiter, Executive Jet's founder and erstwhile president, in the company of various young women, all of them very pretty and amply endowed.

By the start of business on July 2, Sundlun, a Washington lawyer who had served as general counsel and director of Executive Jet, was in control of the company. Armed Pinkerton guards were stationed at the doors. Lassiter and his aides were barred.

It was an altogether fittingly bizarre end to another misguided Penn Central scheme. An added bit of irony was the role played by Harry Pratt. Pratt was an officer of the Detroit Bank & Trust Company which, since August 1968, had been the trustee for Penn Central's holdings in Executive Jet. On the day of the Great Raid,

Pratt voted Penn Central's stock, which constituted a majority, in favor of a change in management. In effect, Pratt threw out the flamboyant Lassiter and installed Sundlun in his place. He also removed two other retired Air Force generals, W. P. Swancutt and Perry Hoisington, from their positions as officers of EJA.

Three weeks later, Lassiter hired his own squadron of armed guards and tried to physically regain control of the EJA offices. Lassiter's forces, however, were repulsed by Sundlun's Pinkertons.

The railroad's five-and-a-half-year flirtation with Executive Jet grew out of Penn Central's improbable, and illegal, plan to get into the air carrier business. Before the romance was forcibly broken off, Penn Central had lost most of its $21 million investment in the small airline company. It had been hit with the second largest fine in the history of the Civil Aeronautics Board. It had spent many thousands of dollars in legal fees. It had damaged its credit with several major banks. Worst of all, it had lost countless precious man-hours for Penn Central officers who were diverted from the killing problems of the railroad.

The Executive Jet story, like the story of the Penn Central itself, reflects credit on no one. It is a tale marked by deception, mismanagement, questionable business practices and expense account hijinks.

In addition to Lassiter, the major figures in the EJA chronicle are the same men who dominated the Penphil story — David C. Bevan, the Penn Central's chief finance officer, and Charlie Hodge, the investment banker who exerted so much influence on Bevan and, consequently, on railroad financial matters.

Olbert F. Lassiter was a stocky, balding man of medium height when he decided to retire from the Air Force in 1964. Like so many other military men who have risen to high rank while they were still relatively young, Lassiter wanted to embark on a new career before he passed middle age. Unlike so many others, however, Lassiter would not depend on defense contractors to provide him with a sinecure. He had an idea for his own company, an idea so attractive he was able to persuade his Air Force factotum, Gus Rathgeber, to quit the service and go to Columbus with him.

Lassiter incorporated Executive Jet Aviation in Ohio while he was still in the Air Force. His idea was to create a civilian version of the air taxi service he ran for the Air Force. He knew it could work. His special Air Mission Squadron had ferried senior Air Force officers all over the world. It was cheaper and faster to operate the pool rather than have a plane assigned to individual officers, where the plane was sure to be on the ground more than it was in the air.

Lassiter reasoned that the same type of program would be just as successful, and considerably more profitable, if he ran it for civilians. By using a fleet of corporate-sized jets, he could enter into contracts with large firms whose executives did a lot of traveling. The firms would be spared the expense of purchasing and maintaining their own planes, hiring pilots, renting hangar space and the like.

Lassiter discussed his idea with Sundlun, whose law practice had given him wide experience in aviation matters. Sundlun, who was an officer in the Air Force Reserve, found the idea attractive and agreed to become general counsel and serve as a board member. He also agreed to help find financing for the venture.

Others found Lassiter's idea attractive, too. He had no trouble lining up a board of directors that included General Curtis LeMay, the retired Air Force Chief of Staff; movie star James Stewart, who was also a jet pilot; television star Arthur Godfrey, who piloted his own piston plane; James Hopkins Smith, former Assistant Secretary of the Navy; General Hoisington; M. J. Rathbone, former board chairman of Standard Oil of New Jersey, and Fred H. Billups, president of the Tropical Gas Company.[1]

In his search for capital, Sundlun traveled to Manhattan and dropped in on Sam Hartwell, a partner in Glore Forgan, Wm. R. Staats, Inc., Charlie Hodge's firm. Hartwell turned Sundlun's proposal over to Hodge, and thus began the involvement of the Pennsylvania Railroad and, after the merger, of the Penn Central, in the creation of an air carrier. Hodge and Hartwell became members of the EJA board.

The railroad, with one wary eye on the CAB, moved quietly into the air travel business. So quietly, in fact, that many Penn Central directors and officers were unaware of it. "This Executive Jet Air-

---

[1] Billups was also a Penphil stockholder.

craft deal, they sucked $25 million out of Penn Central before anybody knew what was happening," E. Clayton Gengras, president of the Security Insurance Group and a Penn Central director, complained.

The device used to funnel railroad money to EJA was the American Contract Company, a Penn Central subsidiary. David Bevan was the president of American Contract and he served on its board, along with his assistant, William R. Gerstnecker, and three other subordinate Penn Central employees. As a practical matter, Bevan ran American Contract. Because American Contract had its own board of directors, it could spend money without consulting the railroad's board. Bevan, however, maintained that he made a full disclosure of the investment to the railroad's directors. "There was a complete and full disclosure made to the board," he insisted. "The board gave it a unanimous endorsement."

Bevan's claim was not borne out by the statements of some other railroad officials. On February 25, 1970, the day that the board's Conflict of Interest Committee ordered an investigation into Penphil, the same committee directed that an inquiry be made into the railroad's investment in EJA. Basil Cole, Penn Central's vice president, executive department, was placed in charge of the EJA inquiry. His report was turned over to the Penn Central board in May 1970, but the board never acted on it. In the report, Cole makes this statement: "By practice, it appears to have been assumed or implied that the chairman of the finance committee [Bevan] had unlimited authority to make such investments and full discretion as to whether they should be reported to the board."

"They couldn't have picked a man on the railroad who hated me more," Bevan said of Cole. "At one time in the past, I was ready to bypass Stuart Saunders and go direct to the board to ask for Cole's resignation. I've never seen the Cole report, but how can you expect it to be fair?"

Bevan may never have seen the Cole report, but he was fully aware of Cole's investigation into the railroad's investment in EJA, and he resented it. Cole had heard a report that Lassiter had diverted some EJA money to one of his own private enterprises and he had passed this information along to Stuart Saunders. On March 9, 1970, Saunders wrote a carefully worded memo marked "personal" to Bevan. In the memo, Saunders avoided any mention of Lassiter's conduct, but he did quite clearly state for the record that he did not know the railroad's investment in the airline was in danger: "Several days ago you spoke to me about a possible loss in connection with the disposition of our interest in Executive Jet. Within the last day or so Jonathan O'Herron [Bevan's assistant] mentioned something about Executive Jet securing a thirty-day loan extension from the First National City Bank. These were the first indications that I have had that Executive Jet is faced with such financial difficulties."

The internal problems of Penn Central were never more evident than in the circumstances surrounding Cole's investigation. A letter from Cole to Saunders, dated March 13, 1970, showed just how deep-seated these problems were:

Somehow Mr. O'Herron learned that you knew about some funds being diverted from EJA to another enterprise in which Lassiter is interested and immediately passed the information along to Mr. Bevan, who is said to be furious, and by ten o'clock yesterday morning (when I first learned of this) had already accused three people in the financial and legal departments of leaking this to me.

Neither Mr. Bevan nor Mr. O'Herron have asked me about this, but if they do, I will only say that it was a confidence from someone who understood the importance to the company of these and other facts and was indignant because they were being withheld from the chief executive officer, and outraged because the "inquiry" which developed this information was summarily called off after it reached Mr. Bevan, when all of the indications are that this only scratched the surface.

This incident is not in itself important because there is little chance Mr. Bevan will learn how I obtained the information. But the lesson is not lost on anyone who might in the future be tempted to pass anything to you through me. Doors in this building have been slamming ever since the accounting department was returned to Mr. Bevan's jurisdiction. Now, all the cracks are sealed. Also, I am sorry that Mr. Bevan found out about this because it is certain to have an effect in [sic] the answers you get to the questions about EJA's financial condition. I think that his reply would have greater significance if he did not know that you already had access to the true facts.

The first record of railroad money going to EJA that Cole could find was dated November 2, 1964. It was a letter to Gerstnecker from Lassiter and it revealed what the staff of the House Committee on Banking and Currency subsequently described as "an incredibly casual manner" of handling funds. The letter stated:

Dear Bill: Since you had the foresight and interest to advance $275,000 for our project, I thought it important to give you some protection. Enclosed is a note for the proper amount with the interest blank. Thought you'd have a better idea on that subject.

Looking forward to getting this project off the ground with you.

Kind regards,

Dick Lassiter.

The minutes of the meeting of the board of directors of American Contract, held on December 22, 1964, note simply that "the action of the president [David Bevan] in approving and making loans to Executive Jet Aviation, in the total amount of $575,000, evidenced by ninety-day promissory notes" was ratified. The Cole report made this observation: "This established the pattern followed consistently thereafter. The officers of American Contract would purchase stock, make loans, and enter into other financial transactions with Executive Jet, then, at the next meeting of the board — which was usually held only once a year — the directors would 'ratify and confirm' whatever action had been taken in the meantime."

In an attempt to identify how EJA received railroad money, Cole said:

Although it is not possible to trace the original source and flow of all the funds which American Contract invested in EJA, it is clear that most of them came in the form of "advances" from PRR or Pennsylvania Company [the railroad's principal subsidiary]. On June 23, 1965, Mr. Bevan reported to the PRR board — and this is the first such report on EJA that we have been able to find — that the company had advanced funds to American Contract which had made loans in the amount of $4.7 million to Executive Jet and had paid $328,000 for nonvoting stock.

On February 24, 1965, there appeared on the PRR treasurer's report an entry in the loan account indicating an advance of $3,700,000 to American Contract "to restore advance account." And, on twenty occasions during the ensuing thirty-one months, or to September 27, 1967, there were shown on this report advances from PRR to American

Contract for "additional working capital" in amounts ranging from $50,000 to $2,400,000, for a total of about $15.9 million.

The use that American Contract was going to make of these advances was never disclosed on the treasurer's report, and the minutes do not indicate that there was any verbal explanation. The information was there for anyone to question, however, and while there may be room for doubt, this form of report presumably complied with the PRR By-Law.

The staff of the House Committee on Banking and Currency, headed by Congressman Wright Patman, in a special report dated December 21, 1970, gave this breakdown of loans made by the railroad to EJA:

Advances in 1965	$11,182,596.00
Advances in 1966	$ 6,251,518.25
Advances after 1966	$ 4,086,544.00
Interest on certain notes	$ 277,224.56
TOTAL	$21,797,882.81
Less repayments by EJA	$ 5,102,005.50
TOTAL AMERICAN CONTRACT LOANS	$16,695,877.31
Plus loans to EJA by Penn Central through Detroit Bank & Trust Company	$ 4,316,000.00
TOTAL PENN CENTRAL LOANS TO EJA	$21,011,877.31

In addition, the railroad purchased 655,960 shares of EJA non-voting stock for $328,000 in June 1965. This amounted to 58 percent of the company's total equity. Although the stock was nonvoting, it was convertible to voting stock if it were sold to someone else, or if Congress subsequently changed the law forbidding surface carriers, like the Penn Central, to control air carriers. Because the stock was easily convertible under certain circumstances, Harry Pratt, acting as trustee for the railroad's holdings, could later vote the stock to oust Lassiter.

The reason the railroad purchased nonvoting stock was simple. It tended to create the impression that EJA was not illegally controlled by a railroad. The Patman committee investigators found an unsigned memorandum in Penn Central's EJA file, entered in August 1969, that explained the nonvoting stock: "The transac-

tion was handled in this way [nonvoting stock] because of the fact
that rail carriers, under the law, cannot become involved in the
operation of air freight services. The whole project was undertaken, however, in the hope that Executive Jet would expand into
the freight area and at some future date laws might be changed so
that Penn Central would move in."

The most incredible aspect of the railroad's involvement with
EJA is that millions of dollars were being advanced to the airline
even though railroad officials were fully aware of the prohibition
against rail carriers controlling air carriers that is contained in the
1958 Federal Aviation Act. "We knew we couldn't get in directly,
so we tried to get in through an investment," Bevan said. "I talked
to General LeMay and he said with the big planes coming out what
is going to happen to railroad freight business will be beyond belief
by 1975."[2]

On March 31, 1965, the railroad had been told by Hugh Cox,
of the Washington law firm of Covington & Burling, that the
Federal Aviation Act prohibited the acquisition of any "air carrier." The railroad, through David Wilson, its assistant general
counsel, sought another opinion. In doing so, it turned to another
expert in aviation matters: Bruce Sundlun, who happened to be
general counsel for EJA, the firm that was depending on railroad
money to keep it alive. In a letter to Sundlun, Wilson wrote:

As I explained to you, we would like to have an opinion covering
the matters in question in order to permit us to consider the nature and
extent of our relations with EJA in the future. *For reasons of policy,
we would prefer that none of these questions be taken up either formally or informally at this particular time with the agency* [Civil Aeronautics Board] *or any of its staff people if our identity would have to
be disclosed* [emphasis added]. Accordingly, if you conclude that an
approach of that nature would be necessary or desirable, I would
appreciate your advising me about it in advance.

As to the matters on which we desire your opinion, you will recall
that we were at first concerned primarily with the legality of any control relationship between this company and EJA. This is still our main
concern but the question may be broader than we originally contem-

---

[2] Bevan also tried unsuccessfully to dissuade LeMay from running for vice
president on a third-party ticket in 1968 with George C. Wallace.

plated. Instead of our acquiring immediately a majority equity position, we might prefer to begin with a creditor relationship including some convertibility feature, option or other form of stock right, which would permit us to obtain the majority equity position at our discretion in the future.

Sundlun's opinion stated: "We have examined the question as to whether the Pennsylvania Railroad (PRR) can acquire a controlling equity interest in Executive Jet Aviation (EJA) without the approval of the Civil Aeronautics Board. Since it is our opinion that EJA is not an 'air carrier' we have concluded that the economic regulatory provisions (title IV) of the Federal Aviation Act permit PRR both to acquire control of and operate EJA without board sanction."

Sundlun's premise was that, since EJA was at that point engaged only in transporting businessmen under contract, it was not an "air carrier" and hence was exempt under the act. Clearly, the railroad was interested in something far more extensive than jetting businessmen around the country. The business jet concept, so far, was not even proving profitable. EJA, in the year ending August 31, 1966, had lost $1.8 million on revenues of $2.8 million. In August 1966, however, EJA, with the railroad's blessing, took a step that unquestionably placed it in the position of at least wanting to be an "air carrier" as defined by the law. The step was Lassiter's successful negotiation of a deal for EJA to acquire 80 percent of Johnson Flying Service, based in Missoula, Montana, for $1,750,000.

Johnson Flying Service had been awarded a permanent certificate as a supplemental airline by the CAB in May 1966. There was no doubt that if the CAB permitted EJA to buy control of Johnson Flying Service EJA would be an "air carrier" as defined by the law. The only question was whether the CAB would approve the acquisition in light of the railroad's domination of EJA.

Hugh Cox, of Covington & Burling, again warned of the possibility of CAB disapproval in a letter dated August 4, 1966: ". . . if the CAB were to find that EJA was controlled by the Pennsylvania, it would undoubtedly not approve the acquisition of the supplemental air carrier since it would view the transaction as an acquisition by the Pennsylvania and the requirement of the second provision of Section 408 (b) of the Federal Aviation Act could not be met."

The nine other supplemental air carriers predictably opposed EJA's plan to take over Johnson Flying Service. Despite the fact that the CAB scheduled a series of administrative hearings on the proposed acquisition, and despite the strong likelihood that it would be disapproved, EJA — and the railroad — proceeded to advance toward the long-range goal — the establishment of a supplemental worldwide passenger and freight service.

In the fall of 1966, while it was still in the red from its much less ambitious business jet service, EJA ordered four large jets — two 707's and two 727's — from the Boeing Company. The total cost was $26.2 million. The first plane was to be delivered in May and the last in November of 1967. But until the CAB approved EJA's acquisition of Johnson Flying Service, EJA could not legally operate the planes. According to the Patman committee staff, the decision to buy the jets was made by Lassiter, David Bevan and William Gerstnecker. It was only proper that Bevan and Gerstnecker be in on the decision since it was the railroad's money that was keeping EJA alive.

And, with EJA failing to earn a nickel for its stockholders, Lassiter, who did not think small, signed a letter of intent with the Lockheed Aircraft Corporation for the purchase of six L-500's, the civilian version of the giant C5A. If this transaction had ever gone through, it would have cost EJA or, more likely, the railroad, $136.5 million.[3]

The first hole was punched in the EJA balloon on April 11, 1967, when the CAB hearing examiner found that the PRR did indeed control EJA. He recommended that the acquisition of Johnson Flying Service not be approved until an acceptable plan was filed for the railroad's divestiture of its interest in EJA. On June 30, 1967, the CAB adopted the examiner's report and directed that a divestiture plan be filed within six months.

EJA filed its plan on October 27. It provided for the resigna-

---

[3] A lack of CAB authority to operate the four jets, and an inability to lease them out on a steady basis, caused a tremendous drain on EJA's resources. Bevan said the expenses associated with the big jets "ate their heads off."

tions from the EJA board of Charlie Hodge and Sam Hartwell, since the CAB had ruled that Glore Forgan was the railroad's "alter ego" in EJA. It also outlined a plan of financing through an issuance of common stock that would ultimately reduce the railroad's holdings to 39 percent from the 58 percent it then held. On December 22, 1967, the CAB said the plan did not comply with its order and directed that the railroad dispose of its holdings through "a liquidating trust or comparable arrangement."

Despite the unfavorable CAB rulings, the railroad continued to pour money into EJA even after that. It did, moreover, attempt to disguise, or hide, its additional investments. The Cole report made this observation:

The method of supplying funds to EJA changed abruptly after September 27, 1967, and the treasurer's report at the next meeting (October 25) indicates that American Contract repaid PRR $16.2 million. Concurrently, American Contract borrowed $16.3 million from Pennsylvania Company.

Thereafter, the only funds that we have been able to identify originate in Pennsylvania Company. The Pennsylvania Company bylaws do not require reporting of advances to subsidiaries and while EJA's indebtedness to American Contract increased by an estimated $5–$8 million during 1968 and 1969, we were able to find only one advance for $200,000 from Pennsylvania Company to American Contract, this advance being noted in the treasurer's report submitted to the Pennsylvania Company board at its meeting on June 26. It is probable that the money being supplied to American Contract in this period was reflected in the Pennsylvania Company's treasurers' reports as "loans to subsidiaries," since the totals reported in corresponding accounts roughly match. If this is the case, these transactions were recorded in the wrong account (American Contract is not a subsidiary of Pennsylvania Company) and at no time is either the source or the destination of these funds into or out of Pennsylvania Company explained in such a way that the closest scrutiny would reveal that they were ultimately intended for EJA.

The significance of this change in the method of obtaining funds for EJA is that it came shortly after PRR was required to eliminate its economic domination of EJA, a time when those not wise to the ways of finance might have been surprised to learn this investment was steadily increasing [emphasis added].

Bevan disputed this. "The charge that we continued to pour money into EJA with an inference that it was done illegally is untrue," he said. "We actually put money in under the CAB ruling, through a trusteeship. We didn't want them to go under."

If EJA went under, Bevan explained, the railroad could lose its entire investment. If EJA survived, there was still a chance of recovering that investment. Bevan also denied participating in the decision to buy the big jets. "The EJA board made the decision to go ahead and order the four planes, two 707's and two 727's," he said. "The board included General LeMay and Jimmy Stewart. This was their judgment."

Even though EJA had no authority to operate those planes, and even though EJA and the railroad were snarled in the CAB proceedings, the airline and the railroad took another step toward the dream of a worldwide system. This step was to prove the most damaging action that could have been taken.

In February 1968, Carl Hirschmann, a wealthy Swiss financier, bought 90 percent of Transavia, a tiny European airline. Hirschmann was vice chairman of EJA, SA, Executive Jet's European company. Without acquiring CAB approval, EJA leased one of the 707's to Transavia. Transavia could not meet the payments under the lease arrangement, however, adding to EJA's financial woes. Eventually EJA settled for a note from Transavia in the amount of $100,000. The actual debt was more than $1 million. The CAB later found both EJA and the railroad guilty of violating the Federal Aviation Act by leasing the 707 to a foreign carrier without first getting Board approval.

On March 11, 1968, Hirschmann bought 70 percent of International Air Bahamas. International Air Bahamas was not an operating airline at the time, and did not belong to the International Air Transport Association. But it did have landing rights in Nassau and Luxembourg. Once in operation, IAB could sell transatlantic flights below the cost charged by regular airlines since it was not bound by IATA regulations. EJA, as it did with Transavia, leased a 707 to IAB, but this fledgling airline also was unable to meet the payments and soon owed EJA $2.6 million.

Because Hirschmann was EJA's agent, and because both Transavia, which operated out of Holland, and IAB were so heavily in debt to EJA, EJA was found by the CAB to be illegally in control of foreign carriers.

During the summer of 1968, with both airlines deep in the red, Hirschmann disposed of his holdings in Transavia and IAB by transferring them to Ovid Anstalt, a Liechtenstein trust controlled by a German financier named Fidel Goetz. Goetz had played a behind-the-scenes role in the EJA–Penn Central scheme to develop a worldwide air system, helping to arrange for the acquisition of both Transavia and IAB. Goetz also lent EJA $650,000, for which he received a note giving him an option to buy 40,000 shares of EJA stock at $10 per share. EJA repaid Goetz on July 29, 1968.

Although Goetz subsequently sold his interests in the two airlines, he felt that he was entitled to be repaid for the huge sums he had invested in them. The ill-starred affair, he maintained, had cost him $4 million. He did not blame EJA for his loss. He blamed the Penn Central. And he began making plans to recover the $4 million.

Francis and Joseph Rosenbaum were Washington attorneys who had represented Goetz since 1961. In addition, Joseph Rosenbaum had arranged foreign loans for the Penn Central to rehabilitate freight cars. During the summer of 1969, Joseph Rosenbaum was again working on a fee basis for the railroad, which needed $10 million for freight car repairs. He succeeded in putting together a consortium of banks from Germany, headed by the Berliner Bank Aktiengesellschaft, that agreed to advance forty million deutsche marks, about $10 million, to the American Contract Company, the railroad's subsidiary.

Francis Rosenbaum, meanwhile, was in deep trouble at home. He had been indicted by the U.S. Justice Department in the summer of 1968 on a charge of defrauding the U.S. Navy. Rosenbaum was a director of two companies that were prime contractors for navy rocket launchers. At his trial, it was established that Francis Rosenbaum had helped set up dummy companies which ostensibly functioned as subcontractors on the navy projects. These dummy companies billed the navy, through the prime contractors, for supplies that were supposed to have been purchased from European firms. The European firms were also dummies, and the navy ended up paying for materials that were never ordered or delivered. Francis Rosenbaum, upon his conviction, was sentenced to ten years in prison.

Some of the funds obtained in this manner were funneled through Finanz A.G., another firm controlled by Goetz. In the summer of 1969, while his brother was trying to put together the German loan to the Penn Central, Francis Rosenbaum was desperately searching for some evidence that would enable him to beat the charges he faced. He went to see Goetz in Liechtenstein on two occasions, hoping to get an affidavit from Goetz to be used at his trial. During these conversations, Goetz learned of Joseph Rosenbaum's success in putting together the German bank loan, and he started the preparatory work to enable him to recover the $4 million he claimed was owed to him by the railroad.

The bank loan was approved on September 12, 1969. By that time, Goetz had already established still another company in Liechtenstein, where all corporate matters are closely guarded secrets. The new company, which was actually a shell, was called the First Financial Trust of Liechtenstein. Although the date that First Financial Trust became operative is listed in its records as September 15, the railroad had made arrangements three days earlier, the day the loan arrangement was approved, to place the $10 million in the hands of Goetz's shell company. The decision to place the proceeds of the loan in Goetz's company was made by David Bevan. It is usual for loans of this type to be placed in interest-bearing accounts until funds are needed.

On his second trip to Liechtenstein, Francis Rosenbaum, still seeking Goetz's help, agreed to become owner of First Financial Trust and, with his brother, was given full rights to dispose of funds held in the trust. Two Liechtenstein lawyers, Dr. Peter Marxer and Adulf Goop, were retained as sole agents for the trust, giving them the right to act as overseers of First Financial.

At the meeting with Dr. Marxer and Goop, Goetz introduced Francis Rosenbaum as the Penn Central's attorney. Goetz told the two Liechtenstein lawyers that the proceeds of the Penn Central's $10 million loan would soon be deposited in First Financial's account in the Bank of Liechtenstein. When the money was deposited, Goetz said, Dr. Marxer and Goop should transfer 16,-

800,000 deutsche marks, about $4 million, to the account of Vileda Anstalt. Vileda Anstalt was another Goetz company. To support his claim, Goetz produced an accounting of the funds he had lost through his involvement with EJA–Penn Central. Rosenbaum, who had been presented to the Liechtenstein lawyers as a Penn Central attorney, signed the accounting, indicating to Dr. Marxer and Goop that the claim was valid.

The $10 million was deposited with First Financial Trust on September 22, 1969. On the same day, $4 million was transferred to Vileda Anstalt. The loss was not discovered by the Penn Central until after the railroad went broke.

Despite the assistance Francis Rosenbaum gave to Goetz, the German refused to give Rosenbaum the affidavit Rosenbaum believed he needed to escape conviction on the fraud charges. In October 1969, Francis Rosenbaum pleaded guilty to nine of the thirty counts against him and was sent to a federal penitentiary.

During this period, Penn Central was meeting with various firms in an effort to dispose of its EJA holdings. But these negotiations never came to fruition, principally because the railroad insisted on retaining the right to repurchase its interest at some later time. David Bevan told why:

This was a great idea. You couldn't do it with pistons, but you could with jets. You could get anywhere in the United States within two hours from the center of the country. You could use these jets more cheaply than you could maintain your own piston plane. It was the equivalent of Carey Cadillac [a firm that rented cars and uniformed drivers]. Lassiter had run a pool for the Air Force. A lot of jet pilots were leaving the service and he put together the finest pool of pilots anywhere.

LeMay was going to supervise Johnson Flying Service. It would have big planes for freight and passenger charter. Ultimately, it would be an around-the-world non-scheduled operation. You could convert from passenger to freight in an hour and forty-five minutes.

The worldwide ambitions brought into the picture a truly formidable opponent — Pan American Airways. Pan Am had been willing to do business with the New York Central when it built its office building on railroad property in Manhattan, but it was not going to sit back and see the Penn Central compete with it for worldwide air service.

About April 28, 1968, a meeting was held in the New York offices of U.S. Steel to discuss the steel company's acquisition of Penn Central's interest in EJA. Lassiter was there to describe EJA's future prospects. David Bevan and Charlie Hodge were there. So was Roger Blough, the chairman of U.S. Steel, and Robert Tyson, the steel company's finance chairman, and several others. Because Stuart Saunders, the Penn Central chairman, sat on the board of U.S. Steel, he did not attend the meeting. Throughout the whole Penn Central story, Saunders showed a strong aversion to anything that resembled a conflict of interest.

At the U.S. Steel meeting, Lassiter scrawled the names of the foreign airline companies he and Hodge had been in contact with on a blackboard. Then he erased the names.

Lassiter said he did not want to commit anything to writing at that point, to prevent "the competition" from finding out what he had been up to. But there was another reason. The foreign contacts could prove fatal if the CAB found out about them. Without question, this would block the acquisition of Johnson Flying Service, and all hopes of getting a supplemental airline certificate with which to establish worldwide service would be dashed.

The cloak-and-dagger precautions were wasted. Within days, Pan Am's spies learned of the meeting at U.S. Steel. They also found out about the supersecret Blue Book Lassiter had put together with Hodge's help. The Blue Book contained all the basic data about EJA's illegal foreign interests. Somehow, the information in the Blue Book was made available to the CAB.

Burlington Industries was brought into the proposed transfer of Penn Central's interest in EJA to U.S. Steel. On June 3, 1968, the railroad signed an agreement with U.S. Steel and Burlington whereby the two firms would purchase the Penn Central's stock, but with a proviso that guaranteed the railroad the right to repurchase, at $4 a share, up to 659,405 shares, the amount it then owned. But when Burlington learned of the long delay occasioned by the plan to acquire Johnson Flying Service, it withdrew from the agreement and the deal collapsed.

In August of 1968, still trying to comply with the CAB's order to eliminate its control over EJA, Penn Central placed all of its holdings — the loans as well as the 58 percent stock interest — in a voting trust with the Detroit Bank & Trust Company.[4] In November the CAB reopened its hearings to determine what progress, if any, had been made by the Penn Central toward divestiture. Lassiter, Charlie Hodge and William Gerstnecker testified. David Bevan was to be the next witness when the hearings were suddenly recessed until January 1969, to permit the CAB to conduct a search through the files of the parties involved. This search was aimed at corroborating the evidence of illegal foreign contacts made by EJA that was contained in the Blue Book.

When the CAB hearings resumed in January, Bevan was still listed as the next witness. Before he could testify, however, EJA withdrew its application for permission to acquire Johnson Flying Service. The grand plan had collapsed.

The CAB's final ruling was issued on October 14, 1969. It found that the Penn Central and EJA were each guilty of thirteen separate violations of the law. Penn Central was fined $65,000, EJA $5,000. The $70,000 total fine was the second highest in CAB history. In addition, the CAB ordered the voting trust established with the Detroit bank converted to an irrevocable trust and directed the trustees to liquidate the railroad's interest by March 1, 1971. The trustees were more than willing to comply, but they could find no buyer by the deadline. As a last resort, they entered into negotiations with Sundlun and Robert L. Scott, a Philadelphia air-taxi operator, who agreed to purchase, for $1,-250,000, the stock that originally cost the railroad $328,000 and the $21 million in loans that were still outstanding. At best, the railroad could hope to recoup only a fraction of the money it spent on EJA.

In addition to its own funds, Penn Central arranged for at least three different banks to extend money to EJA. One of these was the First National City Bank of New York, a bank on which the railroad relied heavily for its own financing. Altogether, First National City, at Penn Central's urging, lent EJA $14,650,734. In

---

4 The Detroit Bank & Trust Company was chosen trustee because it was one of the few banks in the nation without close ties to Penn Central. Even then, one bank officer had to resign from the board of a railroad subsidiary.

order to swing these loans, the railroad had to agree to subordinate its first claim on EJA aircraft, which had been put up as security for the money advanced by Penn Central. This left the railroad with no collateral for the $21 million it eventually lent EJA.

One 707 was later sold to Caledonian Airways, helping EJA to reduce its debt to First National City to about $2.5 million. The railroad also used its influence to have Philadelphia National Bank lend EJA $2,088,624, and National Newark & Essex Bank advanced the airline $1,076,968 at the Penn Central's request. The outstanding balances on these loans at the end of 1970 were $789,958 and $471,208, respectively.

In addition to its stock purchases and its loans, Penn Central was probably EJA's best customer. From May 1965 to May 1970, the railroad paid EJA charter fees totaling $395,330. Most of these payments were made by Manor Real Estate Company, a railroad subsidiary.

Bevan, and persons who traveled with him, spent by far the most money for EJA flights, a total of $200,033.19. The railroad also paid for Charlie Hodge's trips on EJA, a total of $20,835.94. A considerable number of EJA flights carried Bevan and Hodge between Philadelphia or New York and Boca Raton, where both men owned condominium apartments.

In the midst of EJA's ups and downs, the private little investment club run by Bevan and Hodge, Penphil, was still operating. Lassiter, who also became a Penphil shareholder, knew that Penphil had considered, but abandoned, a plan to try to take over the Fugazy Travel Bureau.

Early in 1968, when railroad executives were presumably devoting all their energies to the Penn Central merger, Bevan was discussing with Lassiter and Hodge the possibility of Penphil acquiring a small travel agency in Tampa. It was owned by Mrs. Irene Bowen and was called Bowen Travel Services, Inc. A friend of Lassiter's, Julian Lifsey, an attorney in Tampa, brought Penphil and Mrs. Bowen together.

Penphil purchased a 51 percent interest in the travel agency, paying $25,000. Mrs. Bowen and Lifsey owned the remaining 49 percent. The agency's name was changed to Holiday International Tours, Inc., and it was moved to Miami.

By the time Penphil purchased its interest in Holiday International Tours, EJA had acquired effective control over International Air Bahamas. To get the airline started, EJA leased one of its 707's to IAB, and EJA supplied the crews to operate the plane, under so-called "wet" leases. It was at this point that the persons involved in the EJA-IAB-HIT-Penphil complex began to resemble a circle of elephants, each bound trunk and tail to the other.

EJA controlled IAB. Three members of the EJA board — Lassiter, Charlie Hodge and Fred Billups — were Penphil shareholders. David Bevan was also a shareholder in Penphil and he represented the Penn Central, which controlled EJA. Penphil controlled HIT. Here the plan began to emerge. Julian Lifsey, in a letter to Charlie Hodge on March 26, 1968, stated:

> Immediately after receiving your approval and authorization to proceed, we met with officials of IAB in Miami and were informed that the company had been capitalized and activated. In these initial meetings we were asked to act as the general tour operator and were requested to organize a tour program on a priority basis and to dedicate our initial first efforts to that program.
>
> After some negotiation we agreed to give top priority to their program for the first three months with the understanding that IAB would pay all of the expenses incident thereto. Subsequently we were asked to consider acting as their general sales agent, and to assist in everything from hiring of reservation personnel to the ordering of ticket stock, flight bags, baggage checks, boarding cards, and so forth, for a fee of three and a half percent of gross sales.

Since there were no gross sales at that time, Lifsey said IAB had agreed to pay the travel agency $5,000 a month for the first three months, to be charged against commissions. This would have covered the entire salary requirements for HIT's staff. John Germany, an attorney representing HIT, put the situation much more succinctly in a letter to Thomas Bevan, David's brother, who was president of Penphil: "As discussed with you on the telephone, the initial concept as outlined by General Lassiter was that Executive Jet Aviation would lease the airplane or airplanes to International Air Bahama[s] who in turn would fly them and Holiday International Tours was set up to be the agent for sales. Under this concept there would be no need for IAB to trouble itself with a sales manager or sales at all."

Lifsey sent a draft of the proposed contract between HIT and IAB to Bruce Sundlun, who was counsel for EJA. On July 10, 1968, Sundlun wrote to Lifsey: "My chief problem with this agreement is that I do not know from which side to approach it, the IAB or HIT side. Actually, I represent EJA, and that company should have an interest in neither IAB nor HIT. On the assumption that sometime in the future EJA may have a desire to acquire an interest in IAB, and on the fact that EJA has currently had close business relationships with IAB, I feel that the proposed agency agreement is excessively favorable to HIT and detrimental to IAB."

Sundlun's letter came at the end of the first three-month period of the agreement between IAB and HIT. The two firms worked together despite the fact that a contract had never been signed. During the first three months, HIT received only $7,000 from IAB, not the $15,000 plus expenses the agency felt it was entitled to. Lifsey complained to Penphil about the shortage of cash it was suffering, and Penphil loaned the agency $40,000, making its total investment in the travel business $65,000.

IAB had other problems to worry about. Although it was operating, it was not making any money. It could not meet the lease obligations, although EJA did not press for the payments early in the relationship. When the debt reached $2.6 million, however, EJA decided to get out. In 1969, IAB was sold to Icelandic Airlines.

With HIT struggling to make a go of it, and EJA's request to acquire Johnson Flying Service entering a crucial stage, Penphil decided to get out of the travel business, at least temporarily, lest the CAB begin inquiring into the relationships between the various companies. On August 28, 1968, Thomas Bevan returned Penphil's HIT stock to Mrs. Bowen. He also sent Mrs. Bowen a note for $25,000 for her signature, $25,000 being the amount Penphil had paid for the stock. The note was interest free.

In September 1969, after IAB had been sold, David Bevan telephoned Mrs. Bowen and demanded that she either pay off the

$25,000 note or return the stock to Penphil. Mrs. Bowen refused to do either. She told Bevan that Penphil owed her at least $25,000. Bevan, and Penphil, decided to drop the matter. The fling into the travel business had cost Penphil $65,000. It was the only unprofitable investment made by the club, although the potential for profit was enormous. The staff of the Patman committee, after reviewing the matter, concluded: "HIT was established and controlled by Penphil primarily if not entirely for the purpose of profiting from the exclusive ticket sales rights on IAB flights. The HIT concept as it was outlined to Penphil relied very heavily on sales of IAB flights between Nassau and Luxembourg. Indeed, had the plan gone according to schedule, HIT would have been in virtual control of IAB through control of ticket sales and reservations. Moreover, it is not beyond the realm of possibility that HIT would have played the same role on a global scale had the Lassiter–David Bevan–Hodge dream of a worldwide air service been realized."

Throughout all this, EJA continued to lose money steadily. By the end of 1969, it was $12.5 million in the red and the company seemed to be disintegrating. A major factor in this situation was the president of the company, Dick Lassiter, and his admitted zest for high living.

While the Penn Central was shoveling huge amounts of cash into EJA's maw, Lassiter seemed to be spending it almost as fast as it came in. Many of his expenditures would later be questioned and would result ultimately in his ouster. In 1968 alone, Lassiter's expense account charges added up to $57,827, nearly equaling his $58,000 salary. The expense accounts for the presidents of Pan American and United Airlines that year were both less than $7,000.

A typical piece of interoffice correspondence from EJA was the following memo from A. W. Estes, EJA treasurer, to Lassiter on November 18, 1967:

This is my periodic memo to you lamenting your personal exposure to the Internal Revenue Service in connection with your travel expenses.

The lack of adequate substantiation of your travel expenses continues to be a source of concern for me, for EJA as a company and for you personally.

In 1967, your travel expenses have averaged between $3,000 and $4,000 a month. For the year, the total will likely come to roughly $40,000. If even half that $40,000 were declared to be personal income to you the additional Federal income tax which you would be called upon to pay could easily be as much as $10,000 in a fifty percent tax bracket.

A recent case in point is an American Express bill for $1,827, nearly all of which was for hotel charges at the Century Plaza in Los Angeles. You indicated that $83.75 of those charges were personal and you paid for them with a personal check. The balance, however, was charged to EJA with no business purpose or other justification for the expense being established, at least in EJA's records.

Lassiter's expense charges to EJA included:

—$2,850 for furniture for his $635 a month apartment in Manhattan.

—$19,300 for use of his apartment on EJA business over a two-and-a-half-year period.

—$2,400 to fly EJA personnel to work on his apartment and on his home in Miami.

—$3,000 to move his furnishings from Columbus to Miami.

Lassiter also spent EJA money to acquire a $116,000 home in Beverly Hills, in which he installed his then-current girl friend (he had been married three times at that point in his life). The money for the house came from $154,000 in EJA funds which Lassiter had advanced to his own firm, Lassiter Aircraft Corporation. He placed on the EJA payroll, at $700 a month, a masseur and physical culture "authority." He equipped EJA headquarters in Columbus with an elaborate gymnasium, complete with sauna baths and handball and squash courts.

At the Indianapolis 500 race on Memorial Day, 1967, Lassiter met a generously proportioned blond named Linda Vaughn. Miss Vaughn was known as "Miss Hurst Golden Shifter," and she toured the auto racing circuit for Hurst Performance Products Company, of Warminster, Pennsylvania, trying to drum up business for the firm. Miss Vaughn became engaged to Lassiter in 1968 and he presented her with a diamond ring which she later estimated was ten carats in weight. During their friendship, Las-

Olbert F. "Dick" Lassiter, the controversial former Air Force general who founded Executive Jet Aviation, with Linda Vaughn, also known as "Miss Hurst Golden Shifter," one of the many pretty girls he squired around. (Courtesy of Executive Jet Aviation)

siter flew her to Europe twice at EJA expense, Miss Vaughn told the Patman investigators. He also provided her with free trips to Georgia, where she visited her parents, and to Nassau, she said.[5]

On March 25, 1968, Frank Conace, EJA vice president, wrote to Lassiter complaining that Lassiter had rehired a girl who had been fired for incompetence and had given her a $75 a month raise and a more responsible position. "The specific points of dismay," Conace noted, were that the girl "is not qualified as a secretary," she "was hired at $75 more than her previous salary, which she presumably didn't earn," and she "made her own payroll change form and 'walked it through,' the only signature on it being yours when it was handed to accounting."

"The credibility of our persistent cost control effort suffers seriously in a situation of this type, and the morale of employees who stick with us while feeling underpaid also suffers," Conace wrote to Lassiter. "As you know, our employee turnover rate is now approaching one hundred percent and no company can possibly sustain this rate very long and survive."

A company study of the turnover rate from 1965 through December 31, 1968, disclosed percentages of 50 percent for the Facilities Department, 107 percent for pilots, 158 percent in the electronics division of the Maintenance Department, and 322 percent in the Marketing Department. The cost to the company in terms of recruiting and training was fixed by the study at $1,-068,000.

"Patman criticized me for not firing Lassiter," Bevan said later. "I couldn't fire Lassiter. I had no authority. If we had said we won't put in any money unless Lassiter was fired, we would have been doing the very thing the CAB accused us of doing — exercising economic domination.

"From an operational standpoint, Lassiter was everything you could want. He won a safety award for EJA. He had letters from hundreds of satisfied customers. He never made any pretense that he was a businessman."

The Patman staff, after reviewing the EJA story, raised what it considered a major point:

---

[5] By 1971, Miss Vaughn wanted nothing more to do with Lassiter. Interviewed by the Philadelphia *Bulletin,* she called him a "baldheaded old buzzard."

The question cries out to be answered why a man of David Bevan's apparent shrewdness, financial acumen, and reputation in the business world would have continued to have PRR make additional heavy investments in EJA after the CAB proceeding made it amply clear that the flow of funds should have been drastically curtailed; and would have continued to the end to resist having Lassiter removed as chief executive officer of EJA despite the repeated advice of reliable management experts and the first hand knowledge possessed by him of corporate waste and the disastrous management problems at EJA. In short, Bevan's actions did not make good business sense.

Under the circumstances, consideration must be given to the possibility that public revelation of certain personal activities that might have been extremely embarrassing to Bevan is inevitably linked to the question of why Bevan acted in the strange way he did throughout the deteriorating EJA catastrophe.

The personal activities the Patman report referred to were raised by Joseph H. Ricciardi, of Miami, who was at one time an EJA employee. Ricciardi met Lassiter in 1964 at a party Ricciardi gave on his houseboat. The houseboat had been used in the James Bond movie *Thunderball*. In June 1967, at Lassiter's urging, Ricciardi agreed to go to work for EJA. Ricciardi had an interesting background; he had at various times operated dance studios, slenderizing salons, charter plane and boat services, and dabbled in show business, real estate and stocks.

Lassiter, Ricciardi and an EJA stewardess flew from Miami to Columbus on July 5, 1967. The three had dinner and stayed overnight in Columbus and Ricciardi was given a tour of EJA headquarters. The next day, the trio flew to New York in an EJA Lear jet to meet with David Bevan and Charlie Hodge.

Ricciardi was dismissed by EJA after working for several months as "a public relations man." He subsequently filed suit against EJA for $42,000 in salary and expenses he claimed was owed him. The suit was settled on February 27, 1969, for $13,000, but no evidence could be found to indicate who paid Ricciardi the $13,000.

The Patman staff believed one possible motive for Bevan's continuing involvement with EJA was contained in depositions given by Ricciardi in connection with his suit against EJA. Excerpts from that deposition, and from a deposition given by Lassiter during legal proceedings over control of EJA, were printed in a Patman committee staff report. Portions of this testimony, with Ricciardi's appearing first, follow:

Ricciardi — That same day [July 6, 1967], I'm trying to follow the sequence, General Lassiter wanted me to meet a gentleman called David Bevan of the Pennsylvania Railroad, who is chairman of the executive committee and executive vice president. We went to his private Pullman car at the Pennsylvania Railroad.

Q: — You mean at the terminal [in New York City]?

A: — Yes. He was trying to show me the type of people I'd be associated with.

Q: — What transpired at that meeting? First who was present?

A: — At first when we arrived there David Bevan was there by himself, and he introduced me.

Q: — You, General Lassiter and Bevan?

A: — Yes. He introduced me as a new employee of Executive Jet and I'd be in New York and he wanted me to get acquainted with him. And about a half hour later Charlie Hodge joined us.

Q: — What was discussed?

A: — Oh, they had a discussion. I just sat down and listened to the last statement of Executive Jet and some of the difficulties they were having trying to get out of the red. And then we discussed having cocktails and dinner all together that evening.

Q: — Where did you have this?

A: — We had dinner at José's.

Q: — Who was present at dinner?

A: — General Lassiter, General Hodge, Dave Bevan, myself and dates.

Q: — Everybody had a date? Do you remember their names?

A: — General Lassiter was with his girl friend at the time, Michelle. I had a young lady, Carol ———, with me; and General Hodge and David Bevan had two young ladies, I don't recall their names.

Q: — What else did you do while you were in New York for EJA?

A: — I could possibly refer to this as public relations. During the first day I was here in New York General Lassiter said I could be of great, great service to him if I would help in the social life of General Hodge and Dave Bevan, since he was under a lot of pressure from them due to the company having financial problems in not getting their supplemental ticket, and to possibly alleviate some of the pressure he was under if I could see to it while they were in New York and they wanted some companionship, that I do what I could to assist.

Q: — Did you do any of this?

A: — Yes.

Q: — What did you do?

A: — On one occasion, General Hodge asked if I knew of any young ladies who would go on a business trip to Europe he was taking with General Lassiter.

Q: — What did you do?

A: — I found a young lady that I — that was agreeable to taking a European trip with an amiable group.

Q: — Do you know her name?

A: — Yes, Helene ———.

Q: — When did this take place?

A: — This took place sometime, I believe, August, early August or late July. I don't recall.

Q: — You say that General Lassiter asked you to do this to take the pressure off him. What pressure was he referring to?

A: — He was under pressure from David Bevan, who represented the Pennsylvania Railroad and that supplied moneys to start Executive Jet, and they didn't seem to be too happy with the monthly statements. There didn't seem to be any improvement in business and that they were having difficulty with the FAA on acquiring a supplemental certificate and I guess they had to keep pouring more money every month into Executive Jet Aviation, and he felt that if they were socially happy it would take some of the pressure off them and off of him and make them very happy.

Q: — Were there any other occasions where you performed these public relations functions?

A: — Yes.

Q: — This is still in New York?

A: — Yes. I would say approximately in August they were acquiring a new Jet Star and they were planning a trip to Las Vegas and Los Angeles, and again General Lassiter asked me if I would find suitable companionship for David Bevan and General Hodge, which I proceeded — I found a couple of young ladies that were willing to take the trip. One was called Beth ———. She was with General Hodge — and a young lady called Corinne ———. And General Lassiter.

Q: — You said General Lassiter and then I —

A: — I said General Lassiter was with the young lady, the same young lady, Michelle. I went by myself.

Q: — Any other occasions where you performed these public relations functions?

A: — During my whole stay in New York I did, on several occasions, have dinner with General Hodge and David Bevan and many times with General Hodge and his date. He seemed to enjoy [the company of] this young lady, Beth ————, very much.

Q: — Any other occasions in New York that you performed these functions?

A: — Yes. I once got a date for David Bevan with a young lady called Norma ————.

Q: — Did you pay for any of the dinners or drinks?

A: — No.

Q: — Did you pay any moneys to these girls?

A: — No.

Q: — To your knowledge, did anyone pay any money to these girls?

A: — I don't know. They all went their own way so I don't know.

Q: — Then it would be fair to say these public relations functions involved fixing up these particular individuals with dates?

A: — As I said, General Lassiter said he was doing this himself but he didn't have the time. He told me he had gotten several dates for them in the past but he just was under such pressure with his own business and doing so much that would I please assist him.

Lassiter was asked about Ricciardi's statements when he gave a deposition in the fall of 1970 in connection with the court fight over control of EJA:

Q: — Did you ask Ricciardi to locate a girl to go to Europe with General Hodge?

A: — I didn't ask him; no.

Q: — Did anyone on behalf of Executive Jet?

A: — Well, you'll have to ask anyone. I don't know.

Q: — Who do you think did it?

A: — Well, I said I don't know. I am not going to make a statement that I am not sure of.

Q: — And do you know who he arranged to go to Europe with General Hodge?

A: — Oh, I remember that there was someone that he arranged, but I don't remember her name. I never saw her again.

Q: — You were along on the trip though, weren't you?

A: — Yes.

Q: — And her name was Helene ————, wasn't it?

A: — I have already answered your question once. I do not know.

Q: — Who did you take on the trip with you?

A: — Miss Michelle ———.

Q: — All right. Did Ricciardi arrange for other girls to accompany Hodge or Bevan?

A: — You'll have to ask them.

Q: — Well, you know whether he arranged it or not, don't you?

A: — No. I don't know for sure what arrangements were made between Hodge and Bevan and Ricciardi. You had better ask them.

Q: — Did you ask Ricciardi to make these arrangements for you?

A: — I can make my own arrangements. I don't have to ask anybody to make my arrangements. To the best of my knowledge, the request was made by whomever wanted something done.

Q: — Did Ricciardi later take the position that Executive Jet owed him substantial sums of money as a result of his making these arrangements purportedly pursuant to instructions from you?

A: — Well, he sued the company, and I'm sure you have a copy of the complaint and the deposition. It was a pure case of blackmail. That's my answer.

Q: — And was he paid anything on account of the suit or in connection with the withdrawal of the suit?

A: — I believe that he was.

Q: — How much were you to pay?

A: — $5,000.

Q: — Who were the others who made payments or were to make payments?

A: — Hodge and Bevan.

Patman's report stated that Hodge denied to staff investigators "all of the Ricciardi allegations regarding Ricciardi's efforts to provide him with female companions."

"Hodge said that he did know Beth ———, but not in the way described by Ricciardi," the report said. "He also said that he was unaware that any settlement of the Ricciardi suit had been made. 'I heard the suit was dropped,' he said."

Edward C. German, Bevan's attorney, also denied all of Ricciardi's allegations. German issued this statement, attributable to Bevan:

Without qualification, I deny all charges of personal misconduct. The staff report of the Patman committee incorporates statements by a disgruntled former employee several years ago in a suit later withdrawn.

As far as I am personally concerned, these statements are untrue and unfounded.

With respect to Executive Jet Aviation, this was an investment, not a subsidiary, and was managed independently by its own board of directors.

Our investment in this company was made with the approval of the chief executive officer and by the board of directors of the railroad and periodic reports were filed with the board from time to time with respect to EJA. The allegations and conclusions reached in the report as to why we continued to advance funds to EJA are false. All advances were made purely from a business standpoint and seemed justified at the time.

Bevan later said that he doubted he had seen Ricciardi more than four or five times in his life. He called him "Ricciardo."

9

Highballing to Nowhere

The union of the Pennsylvania and New York Central railroads on February 1, 1968, the most ambitious business merger in American history, created a truly awesome monument to the free enterprise system. Smaller companies fought to be associated with the Penn Central. Coldhearted bankers showed it the same solicitude and tolerance that they would show for the town's wealthiest dowager. "Banks considered it an honor to do business with the railroad," Nochem S. Winnet told us. Winnet, a former Philadelphia judge, was counsel to the First National City Bank of New York, one of the largest of Penn Central's 100,000 creditors.

Consider the dimensions. Penn Central, on Merger Day, had assets of from $6.5 to $7 billion. The railroad alone was valued at more than $4.5 billion, and it owned or controlled 186 companies. It was the biggest transportation company in the nation, the largest real estate dealer. It had pipelines, trucks, barges, water companies, coal mines, factories, hotels, amusement parks, warehouses.

But underneath all the gilt and glitter, the railroad was not really the wealthiest dowager in town. It was, rather, like a proud but aging widow secretly selling off her jewelry and silver to keep up appearances, to keep the suitors knocking at her door. The house was big and impressive, but there was very little money to heat it and the pantry was nearly bare.

On the day of the merger, despite all its huge holdings the Penn Central had only $13.3 million in cash, and $7.8 million of that came from the smaller New York Central. This would be roughly equivalent to the man who owned a $45,000 house, drove a $5,000 car, but had less than a dollar in his bank account.[1]

When the railroad went broke, 871 days later, the cash on hand was $7.3 million. The fact that the railroad had $6 million less in cash on June 21, 1970, than it did on opening day was not, of course, the reason the Penn Central failed.

During its brief existence as a totally private corporation, more than $4 billion in cash and on paper passed through the railroad's hands. "Passed through" is the correct terminology, for the Penn Central was able to hold onto almost none of it.

Perhaps each bankrupt company goes broke in its own fashion. Certainly, the incredibly complex scope of the Penn Central's dealings and its mind-boggling bookkeeping and accounting practices did set it apart. But in one respect, the railroad was just like any other business failure. It spent far more than it took in and, eventually, the money had to run out.

The Penn Central corporate structure essentially consisted of three tiers. At the top was the Penn Central Company, a holding company, whose only asset, until early 1970, was the railroad.[2]

The heart of the merged company was the Penn Central Transportation Company, the railroad. The railroad was the second tier. It was the railroad that owned or controlled the 186 companies. It was the railroad, and its holdings, that generated about $2 billion

---

[1] The railroad, obviously, had a constant flow of cash coming in so that the balance varied widely from day to day. But the cash balance on Merger Day was far too low. David Bevan, the company's chief finance officer, told us that the rock-bottom minimum cash balance the railroad *should have had* on hand was $40 million.

[2] The holding company was voted into existence on October 1, 1969, by the railroad's 118,000 stockholders. The vote permitted the newly formed Penn Central Co. to acquire all of the 24,111,881 shares of railroad stock outstanding at that time and, in exchange, the holding company issued, on a one-for-one basis, 24,111,881 shares of its own stock. While the stockholders thereafter had shares in the holding company, their real stake was in the railroad, upon which they depended for dividends and appreciation. The management said the creation of the holding company would provide greater "flexibility" for its diversification program. Early in 1970, the holding company acquired two small oil companies, Southwestern Oil & Refining Co. and Royal Petroleum Corp., through an exchange of stock. In February 1971, at the insistence of the managements of the oil companies, this acquisition was rescinded.

in revenues annually. And it was the railroad that spent almost all the money.

The Pennsylvania Company, which was wholly owned by the railroad, represented the third tier. Pennco, as it was known, owned most of the nonrail assets, including the real estate and the pipelines.

The first and third tiers of the Penn Central empire were not forced into bankruptcy on June 21, 1970. It was only the Penn Central Transportation Company, the railroad, that went under. Although it owned all of the outstanding stock of the railroad, the holding company did not really figure in the bankruptcy. For the most part, while there were grand plans for it, Penn Central Company was little more than a shell, totally dependent on the railroad.

The Pennsylvania Company, because it used the railroad's money and was, in turn, used by the railroad, did figure in the collapse, but it was not the decisive factor. Once the railroad failed, Pennco preferred stockholders and bondholders filed suits charging that the railroad had milked the investment company. Congressional leaders and the Interstate Commerce Commission maintained that Pennco was responsible for draining cash *away* from the railroad.

There is evidence to support both positions. In the final analysis, however, it was the railroad that failed and it is to the railroad and the nature of its operations that one must turn for the answers.

When the U.S. Supreme Court, on January 15, 1968, removed the final legal obstacles to the merger, the two railroads did not view their impending marriage as a device to permit them to return to the days of the robber barons, to plunder the nation. To the railroads, the merger was purely and simply a matter of survival.

Back during the days of World War II, long before the St. Lawrence Seaway and before the jet plane, business boomed and the railroads earned big money carrying troops and cargo for the government. But these profits were to prove costly in the future. Because of the war effort, both the PRR and the Central were operating around the clock. Their plants, already aging, were seriously depleted. Except for absolutely essential maintenance, very little money was spent on equipment, roadbed and trackage. At the end of the war, the two railroads found themselves with virtually worn out equipment. The result was that, in the immediate postwar years, both lines had to more than double their capital expenditures just to stay even.[3]

In the fifties, the PRR and the Central started on a decline which was never really reversed. On June 29, 1956, President Dwight Eisenhower added to their troubles by signing into law legislation to construct and improve 41,000 miles of interstate highways. The concrete that went into this program, Eisenhower boasted, would form "six sidewalks to the moon." We have already described how the trucking industry, thus subsidized by the government, began making serious inroads on the railroads and the railroads fought back with a disastrous undercover propaganda campaign.

In the twelve years that ended in 1963, the PRR and the Central realized an average annual return on their investment of 1.28 percent and 1.84 percent, respectively. This was far less than an investor could receive from government savings bonds or ordinary bank savings accounts, and far, far less than the 6 to 9 percent other utilities were earning.

From 1963 through 1967, results were similar except for the year 1966. Then the Central system earned $50 million, or about 2.7 percent, and Perlman thought he had a "depression-proof" railroad. In no other year did the two railroads return as much as 2 percent.

The last year before the merger took effect, 1967, was operationally unprofitable. On a combined basis, the two railroads had revenues from transportation operations of $1,506,834,000. Transportation expenses, however, amounted to $1,592,581,000, meaning the railroads had lost $85,747,000. Nonrail income of more

---

[3] Capital expenditures by the PRR and Central in the seven years following World War II:

	PRR	*Central*
1946	$ 33,720,000	$ 41,200,000
1947	$ 52,675,000	$ 48,368,000
1948	$106,337,000	$ 90,170,000
1949	$105,770,000	$100,549,000
1950	$ 87,798,000	$ 70,560,000
1951	$215,593,000	$125,659,000
1952	$123,321,000	$148,398,000

than $94 million enabled the two companies, on a combined basis, to show a modest net of some $9 million for the year.[4]

In order to survive, the two companies had to reduce the crushing costs of operating the railroads. That was the reason for the creation of the Penn Central. With merger, it was believed that economies could be achieved that would at last place the railroad on a solid foundation. Without the realization of these economies there could be very little hope because, dollar for dollar, the Penn Central was the most expensive privately owned railroad in the world to operate.

A railroad functions best when it can assemble unit trains (where all cars are bound for the same destination) for long-haul trips. Under these conditions, operating costs are lower, and there are fewer delays and fewer misrouted shipments. If, at the final destination, there are loop tracks leading to the terminal, so much the better. Loop tracks enable the train to leave the main line and approach a terminal to unload cars, then reenter the main line. This eliminates the costly and time-consuming process of stopping the train, uncoupling the car or cars to be unloaded, then switching them onto the spur leading to the terminal or dock. This kind of an operation provides high utilization of equipment and manpower, matters of efficiency that all railroads strive for.

The Penn Central, when it opened for business, did not have this type of operation. It was a "yard heavy" railroad, burdened with an overabundance of terminals.

While there were many long-haul and unit shipments among its 1,720 daily freight trains, the Penn Central, proportionately, operated far more trains made up of individual carloads than any other railroad. This type of train is the most expensive to assemble. It requires the efforts of dozens of yard crews to bring the cars to be shipped to various connecting points. These crews use yard equipment to do the job, equipment that demands heavy power, which is

---

[4] The PRR and the Central filed a joint annual report for 1967. The report showed that railroad operations lost a total of some $265 million for the year. This was a bookkeeping item, since $275 million had been charged off as merger-connected expenses. While the loss was taken in 1967, the $275 million was not actually spent that year. As merger expenses cropped up, they were charged to the 1967 account.

also expensive. Moving the cars is a slow process, and classifying the cars at the connecting points for shipment to the final destination is just as slow.

Once at the destination, the same costly, time-consuming process must be reversed. The train must be broken down, the individual cars assigned to yard crews, who then transport them to the owners' docks or terminals.[5]

The inefficiency connected with this type of an operation was something the Penn Central never overcame. The railroad spent more than fifteen cents out of every freight revenue dollar it received for yard transportation expenses. On other railroads, the average yard transportation expense was less than ten cents on a dollar. This difference cost the Penn Central about $80 million a year.

In addition, the Penn Central was beset with the problems attached to operating in the urbanized and industrialized East. Much of its trackage ran through highly taxed urban areas. Its freights moved slower, and were more susceptible to vandalism. Congestion in the Penn Central yards caused unbelievably long delays for shippers.

The average Penn Central freight car traveled only thirty-seven miles in a day. It covered those thirty-seven miles at an average speed of seventeen miles per hour, only slightly faster than a man running a four-minute mile. A major reason for the slow average speed was the poor condition of much of the Penn Central rails. More than 10 percent of the total trackage, 2,103 miles, was in such poor shape that "slow orders" were imposed on it. Slow orders were the bane of shippers who depended on fast delivery. They required the freights to reduce their speeds to a tortoiselike five to ten miles an hour, depending on the condition of the track. As a result, the average Penn Central freight car earned revenue for less than three hours a day, and fully 20 percent of its cars failed to generate $100 in revenue on any given day.

---

[5] A comparison of the yard crew operations of the Penn Central and the Southern Railroad, which is half the size, was made by the PC trustees in late 1970. The PC had 2,636 yard crews at 381 locations, with seventy-nine of the locations having ten or more crews. The Southern had only 511 crews, at seventy-seven locations, with fifteen locations having ten or more crews.

It was a difficult situation, but Alfred Perlman, the new president, had never been a fainthearted man. Perlman had demanded, and received, the tools he thought were necessary to do the job. These tools gave him control over budget administration, accounting, taxes and insurance, which had previously been in David Bevan's domain.

The one thing Perlman did not ask for control of was raising money; this continued to be Bevan's responsibility. The friction caused by this unfortunate division of duties generated sparks continuously over the next eighteen months. It was an unhealthy situation: The man who raised the money had little control over how it was spent; the man who spent the money had no responsibility for raising it.

Perlman's spending habits and Bevan's objections kept the railroad in turmoil throughout 1968. The massive task of integrating the two systems was still ahead of them, but Penn Central executives used precious hours engaging in office intrigues. The result was that many matters simply weren't attended to. The incompatible computers were still misdirecting trains at the end of 1968, just as they were on Merger Day.

Bevan, recalling the first days of the merger, said he was stunned when Perlman presented the board with an "estimate" of what the operating expenses of the railroad would be for 1968. Perlman was proposing to spend more than $1.5 billion to run the railroad during the year. But he had no formal budget, no precise figures to show where the money would come from, or how it would be spent. "I wanted an incomes budget, where we would know what was coming in and what was going out," Bevan said. "He said, 'You can't run a railroad on an incomes budget.'"

Perlman revised his "estimates" several times during that first year. But the revisions, according to Bevan, were always proved to be wrong. To get an accurate picture of what was happening, it was necessary to wait for the quarterly reports, which came out only after the fact.

Perlman did prepare a capital budget, however. For 1968, he projected expenditures for equipment and road of about $300 million. This budget was lacking in two respects. It contained no provision for financing — that is, how the money would be raised

— and it underestimated expenses by some $34 million. In addition to everything else, Perlman neglected to inform Bevan, the man responsible for raising the money and the purported finance chief of the railroad, that he had prepared the capital budget.

From that point on, a steady flow of memos emanated from Bevan's offices on the seventeenth floor of the Transportation Building in Philadelphia. Most of them were directed to the offices of Stuart Saunders, the chairman, one floor above. Virtually all of them dealt with the need to cut spending. On August 30, 1968, Bevan wrote to Saunders a memo forecasting a cash shortage for the year of $125 to $150 million. Bevan went on to say: "In my judgment, we are faced with the most serious problem, from a financial viewpoint, that I have encountered since I have been with the railroad. I see no alternative but to stop all capital expenditures which represent a cash drain until such time as we can establish a positive cash flow."

The Alfred E. Perlman Freight Classification Yard near Selkirk, New York, which opened on September 25, 1968, was costing far more than construction estimates, Bevan noted later. In 1969, the railroad told its stockholders the Perlman Yard had cost $29 million; Bevan maintained the actual cost was $36 million, $11 million over budget. Even excluding the heavy costs of starting up the merger, the Penn Central found that one railroad is not necessarily cheaper to operate than two. The railroad, in 1968, was *losing $400,000 a day.* Losses on passenger service alone were costing more than $250,000 a day.

Revenue was down. Despite a freight rate increase granted by the ICC in 1967 that should have produced additional revenue of at least $28 million in 1968, railroad operating revenues increased by only $7 million.

The federal government continued its policy of diverting mail away from the rails to trucks and planes. In 1968, Penn Central's mail revenue fell to $59.5 million from $74.9 million the year before. In 1969 it fell again, to $50 million.[6] This diversion of mail saddled the Penn Central with an excess of 1,000 mail han-

---

[6] In 1960, the combined mail revenue for the two railroads was $91.2 million.

dlers, employees who were left with nothing to do. The railroad was faced with paying these employees off — about sixteen months' salary for each, more than $14 million — or finding other jobs for them. It tried to fit them into other posts within the system, but there was nothing the Penn Central could do about the millions of dollars worth of mail-handling equipment that was forced to sit idle because of the loss of mail business.

Money seemed to be leaking out everywhere. The railroad's operating ratio was 83.62 in 1968, meaning that, for every dollar taken in, 83.62 cents was spent just on operations. In 1969, the operating ratio climbed to 85.60. This was a good ten cents more on each revenue dollar than either the Chesapeake & Ohio–Baltimore & Ohio system or the Norfolk & Western, the Penn Central's principal competitors, were spending.

Railroads customarily use freight cars belonging to other railroads. When they do, the borrower is charged a per diem fee by the lender for the use of the freight car.

Because of a chronic shortage of cars, the Penn Central borrowed more cars than any other railroad and it ran up enormous debit balances in the per diem category. In 1967, the combined PRR-Central debit balance for the hiring of freight cars was $138 million. In 1968, the debit balance jumped to $160 million, and it increased in 1969 to $168 million.

Despite the fact that freight traffic was growing in the area served by Penn Central, the railroad actually reduced the number of freight cars it owned by 35,000 during the five years immediately preceding the collapse. This was a reduction of some 20 percent and was a major factor in the railroad's relatively low revenue level. It simply did not have the equipment needed to provide first-rate service for shippers.

(The railroad's control over its own equipment was so bad that, during the last half of 1970 and the first quarter of 1971, at least 305 good boxcars, worth more than $1 million, were removed from the Penn Central's lines wtihout anyone noticing. In a suit filed on April 8, 1971, to recover the missing boxcars, the Penn Central gave this account of how the equipment had vanished: The railroad, through three separate agreements, had under lease from the Equitable Life Assurance Society of the United States 3,500 boxcars, each forty feet long. On January 20, 1970, the railroad notified Equitable that it was terminating agreements covering 466 boxcars because they "were in such disrepair as to preclude their possible use in the shipment of freight."

On May 6, 1970, Equitable informed the Penn Central that the 466 faulty boxcars had been sold to Diversified Properties, Inc., of Essex Fells, New Jersey, and asked the railroad to ship them to the LaSalle and Bureau County Railroad Company, Inc., a tiny line with fifteen miles of track in northern Illinois. The Penn Central started shipping the cars on June 2, 1970, and completed delivery in March 1971. During that period of time, however, the 305 usable boxcars found their way onto the LaSalle tracks.

According to the Penn Central, the 305 good boxcars were repainted "to reflect markings and numbers of the LaSalle and Bureau County Railroad." Some of the worthless boxcars, the railroad said, had been altered to resemble the good boxcars, which the Penn Central still had under lease from Equitable. In effect, the railroad said Diversified Properties was buying worthless boxcars and trying to switch them for good boxcars. After disguising the good boxcars as LaSalle and Bureau County Railroad property, the Penn Central said, Diversified Properties fed them back into the systems of the Penn Central and other railroads and charged rental fees for their use. Presumably, the Penn Central was paying money to use its own boxcars. The suit was settled on June 15, 1971. Under the settlement, the railroad was to recover 352 boxcars plus a cash payment of $150,000. The Penn Central did not explain how the number of missing boxcars, originally estimated as 277, had risen to 305 and finally to 352.)

Besides the shortage of equipment, the Penn Central also suffered from poorly maintained equipment. At any given time, 9 percent of its freight cars were out of service awaiting repairs. This large volume of "bad trip" cars, compared to the industry-wide average of 4 percent, further reduced revenue. "Bad trip" cars do not earn money.

James Beggs, undersecretary of the U.S. Department of Transportation, said that the state of the railroad's equipment was directly related to the loss of business, especially high-quality business, the Penn Central experienced after the merger. "It had over

10,000 bad trip cars in the shops, 13,000, and they weren't repairing them," Beggs said. "Plus they had a car shortage. So it would get worse. They had to hire cars, and they had to pay per diem charges, which further worsened the picture. They were short of locomotives, and shippers were complaining. They were still losing whole trains between Harrisburg and other points. Maybe they weren't losing whole trains, but they did lose manufacturers' shipments of eight, nine and ten cars. They would be sitting on a siding somewhere and nobody knew where they were. I had one shipper that had a valuable cargo in one car and it couldn't be found. He was so mad that he went out and walked the lines until he found his car."

After the collapse, Perlman was able to give wide circulation to his contention that Saunders and Bevan had interfered with him, preventing him from running the railroad. One story that originated with Perlman had it that Bevan, with Saunders' approval, refused to release $25 million for the repair of 12,000 freight cars in 1969.

Saunders was outraged by these stories, and he privately denounced Perlman in bitter terms. But, in an interview with us, he refused to put himself on the record as a critic of Perlman, although he did take steps to counter what he believed was a propaganda effort by Perlman. One of the first things Saunders did was to prepare a list of the freight cars that Perlman said he had been prevented from repairing. The list showed that the cars, contrary to what Perlman said, had been repaired, and it contained the serial numbers of the cars and the dates they had been in the shop.

In private, and in material he prepared for Sen. Vance Hartke, the Indiana Democrat who was chairman of the Senate Commerce Committee's Subcommittee on Surface Transportation, Saunders maintained that Perlman had complete responsibility for running the railroad. This material purported to prove that Perlman, until he was eased out of his job, never once complained to Saunders or the board that he was being hamstrung by former Pennsylvania Railroad officers. Saunders privately insisted there was not a word of truth in Perlman's later complaints. The board of directors, the material compiled by Saunders showed, never turned down any of Perlman's requests.

Saunders was also infuriated by stories that indicated Perlman had voted against the quarterly dividend approved by the board in June 1969. He accumulated copies of company records to prove that Perlman had not opposed the dividend. These records indicated that Perlman attended the finance committee meeting and the board meeting at which the dividend was approved. There was no dissent.

Even if Perlman did have sufficient equipment in good working order, which he did not, the Penn Central would still have had serious problems. Good equipment could not change the rigid rate structure imposed on the Penn Central and on all railroads.

Nowhere was the damage inflicted by this rate structure more evident than in the below-cost rates in hundreds of categories the Penn Central was forced to live with because these rates were considered to be in the public interest. In effect, the below-cost rates compelled the railroad to transport goods for prices that did not even cover the cost of providing the service. For the most part, the rates were fixed by the ICC, but in some cases the rates were set by regulatory authorities in the sixteen states served by the railroad.

The Penn Central carried chemicals to keep municipal water supplies uncontaminated, and it transported coal to provide power for utilities and heat for schools. In some of these cases, and in various others where local regulatory agencies wanted to protect favored industries that dealt intrastate, rates were kept artificially low. Some categories were historically low, while others were kept that way as a result of pressure from lobbyists.

The molasseslike response of the ICC to requests for rate increases contributed to the railroad's problems. Each year the railroad was faced with higher labor costs, as it was in 1968, as a result of contracts negotiated the previous year with union leaders. In 1969, after new contracts were agreed upon, wage raises were made retroactive to January 1.

Although the railroads themselves caused many of their own problems in seeking rate hikes, the ICC routinely delayed for months before approving such increases. The ICC decisions, when they finally came, came late in the year.

The Penn Central, at the start of 1968, saw its labor costs go up by 9 percent, or some $90 million annually. It was not until June

24 that the ICC granted an interim 3 percent rate rise. Its final verdict authorized a total increase amounting to 5 percent for the year, effective November 28.

The 5 percent, had it been granted early in the year, would have meant $65 million on an annual basis to the Penn Central, not enough to cover the full $90 million in higher labor costs but enough to cushion the blow. Because of the long-delayed decision by the ICC, the railroad realized only about $20 million during the year.

In January 1969, the ICC modified slightly the rate increase granted the previous November, but the newer tariffs remained basically the same. Labor agreements negotiated that year amounted to about a 7 percent increase in wages, or a total of $75 million for the year. Again, it was not until November that the ICC approved a 6 percent rate increase. On an annual basis, the 6 percent increase would have brought an additional $80 million to the railroad. Because it was so late in coming, the Penn Central realized only $7.6 million.

Rate increases, unlike pay raises, cannot be made retroactive. "This time lag alone costs Penn Central hundreds of millions of dollars," Stuart Saunders told us.

In 1970, the year the railroad went broke, the same situation developed, although on this occasion the railroads themselves were as much at fault as the ICC. "The railroads are the only industry in this country that can get together and fix prices because they have immunity under the antitrust laws," Saunders said. "But they can't ever agree. Their competitive interests are so different. Even now [late 1970] they've got this 15 percent proposal before the ICC. The Southern Railroad won't go along with it. They're going along with 6 percent. Last year we went for 6 percent — I wanted to go for 12 percent, and I thought we should have that. And a number of Western railroads agreed. But the Southern Railroad said no. It took months to get them to go for anything [in 1970] and they finally went along with six. And the Commission gave us five."

The railroads asked for a 6 percent increase in March 1970. In June, when the Penn Central was on its last legs, the ICC approved an interim 5 percent rise. For the last half of the year, this meant an additional $36 million for the Penn Central, but the cost of the new labor agreement was $62 million, retroactive to January 1, 1970.

The cost of labor was by far the railroad's biggest expense. It had an annual payroll of more than $1 billion. Sixty-six cents out of every dollar it took in went to meet the payroll. Again, the Penn Central lagged behind its competitors, who only spent fifty-eight cents out of each dollar to pay employees.

Eight months after the Penn Central filed for reorganization under Section 77 of the Federal Bankruptcy Act, the four trustees appointed to oversee the reorganization concluded that the railroad could not continue to function indefinitely unless labor costs were drastically reduced. By that time, there were some 94,000 persons working for the railroad. At the time of the merger, there were more than 102,000.

"Of this 94,000 total," the trustees said, in a report filed with the U.S. District Court for Eastern Pennsylvania in February 1971, "approximately 10,000 were retained solely because of (1) the retention in three states (Indiana, Ohio, and New York, in which Penn Central has large operations) of full crew laws — which all other states except Arkansas have repealed because they do not make sense under present circumstances; or (2) various work rules which have been repeatedly considered by various Presidential Boards or Commissions and have uniformly been found to be unjustified; or (3) other work rules which in the light of modern conditions can no longer be justified by management."

Stated simply, the trustees were saying that variations of the rail unions' famous and controversial reliance on featherbedding were still being used to keep unneeded employees on the payroll. The annual cost to the Penn Central for these employees was $120 million in 1970.

Al Lupini, president of Local 4889, United Steelworkers of America, believed he had personal knowledge of the railroad's use of unneeded employees. Lupini represented steelworkers employed by United States Steel Corporation's Fairless Hills plant, located outside Philadelphia.

The Fairless works had 105 miles of railroad track running

across its 3,000 acres. It had twenty-three locomotives, and a railroad department of 200 employees, all Local 4889 members. According to Lupini, who obviously was hoping to expand his membership, Penn Central employees worked from sixteen to eighteen hours a day on U.S. Steel property, checking switches and transporting cars. This work, said Lupini, could have and should have been done by U.S. Steel employees. Lupini estimated that this "extra" work cost the Penn Central about $120,000 yearly.

U.S. Steel, whose board of directors included Stuart Saunders, was one of the railroad's major shippers. Despite Lupini's complaints, Penn Central quite naturally wanted to keep U.S. Steel happy, and $120,000, considering the immensity of the railroad's operations, appeared to be small enough. The underlying question, though, was how many other shippers were receiving similar favors from the railroad?

Much of the railroad's heavy labor costs were directly traceable to the merger itself. After the merger agreement was signed, in 1962, the twenty-three labor unions that represented the railroad's employees announced their opposition to the proposed consolidation.

Saunders was fully aware of the power of the unions. As head of the Norfolk & Western in 1959, he incurred the wrath of the unions when he was attempting to bring about the merger of the N&W and the Virginian. Under the Interstate Commerce Act, any rail merger must provide protection for employees of the merged system for at least four years. The details of the protection arrangement are left up to the railroads and the unions.

On May 20, 1964, Saunders and Perlman, in anticipation of the merger, signed an agreement with the labor leaders. While it followed along the lines of the arrangement worked out in the N&W-Virginian case and in other mergers, it gave the unions more concessions than any other previous agreement. Where the earlier agreements provided job protection for four years, the Penn Central pact offered lifetime protection. Any person on the payroll at the time the merger agreement was signed could not be dismissed except for cause. If any employee was laid off, he had to be given a year's severance pay. Anyone who lost his job between the time the agreement was signed and the effective date of the merger had the right to be rehired.[7]

In exchange for this, the unions agreed to drop their opposition to the merger. This was the most important factor to Saunders. The concessions that labor offered seemed small when compared to what the railroad had given up. Under the agreement, the railroad could reduce its work force by 5 percent a year, but only through attrition. This was the normal rate of attrition anyway. It did very little to help the railroad operate more efficiently. Attrition did not afford management the opportunity to choose which jobs could be eliminated. The choice was thrust upon the railroad. If a key post became vacant because its occupant had died, retired or resigned, the railroad would still have to fill it. If employees the railroad considered superfluous chose not to resign, Penn Central either had to keep them on the payroll or pay them severance. The railroad did receive the right to transfer workers, a provision earlier agreements lacked. But in doing so, it had to pay all moving expenses. If the employee refused to move, the railroad was again faced with the same choice — keep him on the payroll or pay him severance.

At the time of the pact, the railroad calculated that the Merger Protective Agreement would cost it $78.2 million over an eight-year period. For an unexplained reason, railroad negotiators based their estimates on 1961 wage scales, even though the negotiating was done in 1964, when wages were higher, and even though the agreement would have to be lived up to in future years when, presumably, wages would have climbed still higher.

In 1968 and 1969, the cost to the railroad of the agreement was $64.7 million. In 1970, the agreement cost Penn Central another $28 million. In just three years, the cost estimate had been exceeded by $14 million. The internal costs generated by an inability to furlough ineffective or unnecessary employees cannot be calculated.

Saunders, after the collapse, remained highly sensitive to crit-

---

[7] About 5,000 employees who had been furloughed between the date of the Merger Protective Agreement and February 1, 1968, were eligible for reinstatement because of the pact. About 2,400 asked to be reinstated and they were rehired.

icism about the Merger Protective Agreement. He insisted the agreement "saved us a great deal of money."

"Now, you might ask, how do you get that?" Saunders said. "You see this merger agreement protects these people for life whereas this other is four years from the date of the merger or the date affected. But the reason you can take that is attrition. Your attrition is sufficient to take care of all the jobs that you can vacate anyway. In other words, on the Penn Central at the time of the merger we had roughly 105,000 employees. Well, your attrition rate is at least 5 to 6 percent a year. So you've got 6,000 jobs a year coming vacant. By death, resignations and so forth. And with your right to transfer the work and the jobs, that's — in four years you've got 25,000 jobs. That's more jobs than you need."[8]

Not everybody agreed with Saunders. E. Clayton Gengras, the Hartford insurance executive who joined the Penn Central's board in December 1969, thought the labor agreement was cause enough to call off the merger. "The death came with the merger," Gengras said. "It should never have been permitted. The day Stuart Saunders signed the deal with the unions he gave the farm away. It was all downhill after that. It was impractical and impossible."

Saunders' elimination of 6,000 jobs a year never came to pass. By March 15, 1970, more than two years after the merger, employment had been cut by only 8,410. Reviewing this reduction, Undersecretary of Transportation James Beggs had this to say: "This is a cut that is substantial, but it is not near what was projected at the time of the merger as being the manpower savings possibilities of the merged road. I think this reflects somewhat a lack of aggressive action on the part of the management, and it also reflects the fact that the labor agreements have been hard to

---

[8] When the *Wall Street Journal* printed an article critical of the agreement on August 25, 1970, Saunders had Guy W. Knight, former Penn Central vice president for labor relations, write a long letter to the newspaper defending the pact. "The fact is that, without the Merger Protective Agreement, the labor unions would never have withdrawn their opposition," Knight wrote. "You refer to the labor protection agreement as 'the Saunders Agreement.' Actually all of the negotiations were conducted jointly in 1964 by Messrs. Perlman and Saunders. The agreement was signed by both Messrs. Perlman and Saunders."

administer, and that labor has been difficult in responding when the various cutbacks were proposed."

Despite the foul-ups and the $400,000 daily loss on rail operations, Saunders, and Perlman, told the stockholders, in a letter attached to the 1967 annual report, that everything was going beautifully. The letter, which was dated March 15, 1968, and was mailed April 1, said:

Although we are just getting started, the transition and progress of our merger has been smoother and more rapid than we had anticipated. Sound and comprehensive planning while we awaited consummation enabled us to evolve a close working relationship between the two companies.

A remarkable spirit of cooperation and enthusiasm is manifest throughout our new organization [emphasis added]. We are confident that we have a talented, experienced and well-qualified management team for the years ahead, and we consider this a very important asset.

The letter also said that earnings for 1968 "should show substantial improvement over 1967." The optimistic tone of the letter was to become characteristic of Saunders' attitude. In the face of adversity, he was always hopeful. Until almost the very end, he preached faith and ignored the barrels of red ink the railroad was using up in its accounting department. This optimism was to be partially responsible for his ultimate undoing.

Saunders' optimistic outlook was not a recent development. On November 21, 1966, David Bevan wrote the chairman a note warning of the implications of such optimism: "The policy may be instituted of maximizing earnings to the greatest extent possible within the limits of good accounting practices," Bevan wrote. "In the last several years this has been done in accordance with your expressed desires. It does mean, however, that we tend to create a wider and wider difference between reported income and cash flow."

A year later, this attitude had changed not at all. William S. Cook, vice president and comptroller, wrote a note to Bevan marked "personal and confidential" on October 5, 1967. In the note, Cook requested that the salary of Charles S. Hill, manager of general accounting, be raised from $25,500 to $27,500. As justification, Cook said: "His imaginative accounting is adding millions of dollars annually to our reported income."

Saunders' optimism prevailed after the merger, and the Penn Central continued to maximize its earnings. Thomas J. Russo, an auditor in the ICC's bureau of accounts, inquired into the railroad's accounting practices after the collapse and came to this conclusion: "In general, the management of the merged Penn Central adopted the former Pennsylvania Railroad's policy of maximizing income. The result was an increase in income without a corresponding increase in cash flow, thus obscuring the carrier's true financial condition."

On the same day that Saunders and Perlman mailed their optimistic letter, April 1, 1968, David Bevan had a decidedly different opinion. He told a stockholders' meeting the railroad's income was "alarmingly low in relation to our investment in transportation facilities." Bevan was in a position to know, since he had to raise the money. In May 1968 he received the board's permission to begin selling commercial paper. Commercial paper is little more than an IOU. In the late 1960's, it became a convenient, if potentially dangerous, way for established corporations to borrow money. Its popularity grew, in large part, because of the tight money situation in the country at that time and the unavailability of credit at the banks. During the first part of 1970, the commercial paper outstanding exceeded $40 billion. This figure was reduced after the Penn Central collapsed.

Issuers of commercial paper (in effect, borrowers) need not register with the Securities and Exchange Commission. They simply sell a written promise to pay back to the buyer the amount the paper was sold for, plus interest. There is no collateral. The seller's word is his bond. The transaction is short-term, usually ninety days and rarely more than six or nine months. The danger is that the money must be repaid quickly or the paper must be "rolled," that is, resold at the same, or higher, interest rates. In a situation where cash is tight, this can bring on a crisis of the first magnitude.

Bevan, and the Penn Central, had no choice. The railroad was spending money in huge quantities and cash had to be acquired. In August 1968, Bevan sold $35 million in commercial paper. It was the first time any railroad had ventured into this market. The application of the commercial paper, however, was as effective as applying a Band-Aid to a severed jugular vein. The money continued to gush out.

By the fall of 1968, Bevan was back before the ICC, asking permission to increase the amount of commercial paper the railroad could sell. On December 17, the ICC gave the Penn Central authority to issue up to $100 million in commercial paper. The railroad was to return again and again to this well, until it ran dry.

Another Bevan proposal was approved by the board at its June 1968 meeting, but it was of a different nature. This was a proposal that the railroad buy a $10 million insurance policy from Lloyd's of London to protect the company's officers and directors against personal liability in the event that claims were filed charging any of the officers or directors with wrongdoing. The policy, for a three-year period, cost $305,000 and was paid for by the railroad.

Policies of this type are not unusual in industry. But there were some curious circumstances surrounding the Penn Central policy. Pennsylvania law, until November 30, 1967, prohibited corporations from paying the full premium on officers' liability policies. Then the law was changed.

Evan Williams, a Republican member of the Pennsylvania State House of Representatives, sponsored legislation to permit corporations to buy such policies. Williams, who later became a judge, told the Associated Press that the legislation had been written by John J. Brennan, a Philadelphia lawyer whose firm (among others) represented the railroad. Brennan said his interest in the bill came about because his principal client, the Pennsylvania Bankers Association, wanted the legislation passed. Brennan said he sent ten copies of the bill to the railroad's legal department. On February 28, 1968, Bevan reported to the board that the bill had been signed into law by Governor Raymond P. Shafer.

On September 7, 1968, three months after the Penn Central bought the policy, a railroad shareholder from New York, Simon Kaminsky, accused railroad director Howard Butcher III of taking advantage of "inside" information to sell off stock he owned in the Penn Central. Butcher was a Philadelphia stockbroker who had long been an enthusiastic purchaser of railroad stock. He was elected a director of the Pennsylvania Railroad in 1962 and continued on the board after the merger. On September 24, three weeks after Kaminsky made his charges, Butcher resigned from the Penn Central board.

Trading on inside information, i.e., using information not available to the public but available to an officer or director, is a federal offense. After the railroad collapsed, a blizzard of lawsuits descended on the Penn Central and many of its officers.

Bevan was a prime target in these suits, because of his own sales of Penn Central stock and because of his involvement with Penphil and Executive Jet.

Lloyd's of London, along with other insurers participating in the policy, began court action in February 1971 to rescind the policy. Lloyd's claimed the policy was invalid because Bevan had failed to disclose his connection with Penphil and his handling of the Executive Jet matter. By failing to disclose this information, Lloyd's said, Bevan had deliberately misled the insurance company.

The first year of the merger was not a happy one for the railroad, despite Stuart Saunders' optimistic forecasts. The divisions in the executive suites, rather than diminishing, had deepened. The tremendous problems — how to get the computers to work, how to consolidate duplicate facilities in thirty-five cities, how to appease the shippers, what type of marketing system would be used — remained unresolved.

Worst of all, the railroad suffered staggering losses. An unsophisticated stockholder reading the 1968 annual report would conclude the railroad lost $5,155,000, a not inconsiderable sum. The actual net operating loss of the rail system was an astounding $142,367,000.

In 1968, the railroad had total operating revenues of $1,514,-071,000. Railroad expenses were $1,656,438,000, or more than $142 million over and above railroad income.

The Penn Central was able to reduce this loss to $5,155,000 because it included in the transportation company's statement of earnings $137,212,000 in other, nonrailroad, income. This brought total income to $1,651,283,000.

The validity of this "other" income was later brought into question. Was it cash or was it just paper? Did it really help the railroad or did it simply prop up a dismal earnings picture? At least one director, John Seabrook, was dubious. He described this "other" income as "Chinese money."

But, considering the disastrous performance of the railroad, which was spending real dollars, the consolidated earnings statement of the Penn Central, reflecting the total income of the corporation, did not look too bad, even if it did contain some Chinese money. Consolidated income was listed as $2,108,634,000, while consolidated expenses totaled $2,020,845,000. This enabled the company to report net earnings for the year of $87,789,000.

The stockholders, unaware of the huge flow of cash away from the railroad, were presumably happy. In July of 1968, Penn Central shares sold for $86.50, which would be the highest in the merged company's history. The board of directors voted to pay out $55.4 million in dividends for the year. This was a hefty dividend, 63 percent of reported earnings, and at least some of those earnings were John Seabrook's Chinese money. The dividends, however, were paid in cash. In the six years prior to merger, the average PRR dividend payout was 36.14 percent of earnings, while the Central's average payout was 43.79 percent. In any event, the Penn Central kept alive the PRR's record of never letting a year go by without paying the stockholders a dividend. The record began in 1848, and the railroad had the longest string of dividend-years on the New York Stock Exchange.

Saunders and Perlman, in their annual letter to stockholders were again the optimists: "We finished the year ahead of our schedule for transforming two formerly competitive railroads into a single entity compatible in philosophy, practices and objectives," they wrote. "The outlook for 1969 is brighter than it was for the past year, especially with regard to our railroad system. . . . We are projecting a gain of at least $65 million in gross revenues from the higher level of freight rates, and we anticipate a substantial increase in traffic volume."

Saunders got his $65 million increase in gross revenues and, thanks partially to the New Haven Railroad's inclusion in the system, even a little more. In 1969, railroad revenues increased by almost $138 million over 1968. But railroad expenses went up by $188 million.

Among the items that cost the railroad more in 1969 was interest on debt. This jumped from $68.7 million in 1968 to $96.7 million. The interest was the natural consequence of borrowing, and the railroad had to borrow to stay alive.

David Bevan, at the start of the year, was midway through the $950 million borrowing program. It was a program that was modified as the need arose during 1968 and 1969.[9] There were no true fixed goals behind this borrowing; it was almost entirely improvised. When the railroad needed money, Bevan looked around for some asset that was not already pledged as collateral for a previous loan and went out and mortgaged it.

Surveying the wreckage after the collapse, Robert Bennett, assistant secretary for congressional relations of the Department of Transportation, told the authors: "Apparently, whenever they had a money crisis, they'd scurry around to find something that wasn't mortgaged and mortgage it. There was no plan. It was a helter-skelter kind of thing. Relations with their subsidiary companies were terribly fouled up and there was a bizarre relationship between the president and the chairman and the financial officer. This was hip-pocket management of a corporation with $7 billion in assets. All the nonrail assets are mortgaged. They might be able to find a typewriter here and a coffee table there [that weren't mortgaged] but it's that kind of operation."

The railroad began 1969 with a working capital deficiency (the excess of current liabilities and debt due within one year over current assets) of $171 million. This was a situation which clearly pointed to a possibly fatal cash shortage at some moment of crisis.

The railroad's capital position was further worsened by the inclusion, as of January 1, of the bankrupt New Haven Railroad in the Penn Central system. The ICC had ordered the New Haven included as a condition of the merger. This was one question on

---

[9] Bevan borrowed these funds in what he described as "the tightest, most difficult money market of the century." The $950 million was spent in this way: $560 million for capital expenditures, including $379 million for equipment and $181 million for road purposes; $245 million to meet debt maturities, and $145 million to help finance the railroad's operating deficit.

which Bevan and Perlman were united. Both men correctly predicted that the New Haven would do great harm to the Penn Central.

The New Haven, even while in trusteeship, under which most debts and taxes are suspended, had lost $22 million in 1968. It carried this deficit into the already overburdened Penn Central. In addition, the Penn Central was forced to spend another $22 million to refurbish the New Haven's equipment.

Before long, the railroad found itself squeezed even more between the pressures of inflation *and* recession. While other businesses were damaged by these economic conditions, the Penn Central was damaged far more than most. Unlike other private firms, the railroad was largely inflexible. It could not scale its prices to meet the laws of supply and demand. It did not operate in a market economy. It was a highly regulated company, and the ICC, never quick to respond, is not easily moved by economic vicissitudes. The railroad, thanks to the Merger Protective Agreement, could not cut back on its work force. It was approaching a cash bind and it could not afford to lay off any employees when it meant paying those employees about $12,000 each.

Suddenly the railroad found that it was losing *more than $500,000 a day*. The memos from Bevan's office to Saunders' office increased. Again and again, Bevan warned that expenses had to be cut, that Perlman was spending far too much money. Bevan urged that Saunders retain outside experts to study the railroad's operations. During the first half of the year, all Bevan got from Saunders was silence.

Bevan was the one who had to deal with the banks. Despite the strong standing of the railroad in the financial community, some banker, sooner or later, was going to notice the torrent of cash streaming away from the railroad. So far, nobody had. But Bevan was being forced to rely more and more on the "other" earnings of the railroad to induce the bankers to come across with loans. If the "other" earnings were diluted with Chinese money, the bankers didn't know it in 1969.

On April 1, 1969, Bevan pulled off a coup rivaling that of his 1965 performance when he sold the worthless Long Island Rail Road, which hadn't earned any money in more than a generation, to the state of New York for $65 million. When he first went to the PRR, Bevan set up a $50 million revolving credit plan. First National City Bank of New York was the lead bank in the deal. Now, with the Penn Central in a most difficult cash position, Bevan was able to increase the amount of the revolving credit to $300 million. First National City was again the lead bank in a consortium that eventually numbered more than fifty.

As collateral, Bevan pledged all the common stock of the Pennsylvania Company, the third tier in the Penn Central complex. Since Pennco, at that time, was worth an estimated $900 million, the collateral was on a $3 for $1 basis. All $300 million was used by the railroad, which eventually defaulted on the loan. First National City was stuck for $35 million. Irving Trust Company and Morgan Guaranty Trust Company were owed $25 million each. Manufacturers Hanover Trust was out $20 million, and four other banks were owed $15 million each. They were Bankers Trust, of New York, Chemical Bank New York Trust, First National Bank of Chicago and Continental Illinois Bank & Trust Company.[10] The last bank, Continental Illinois, figured prominently in later developments. Before he left to become Secretary of the Treasury in the Nixon Administration, David Kennedy was head of Continental Illinois. Kennedy was one of the first men Stuart Saunders approached when he was seeking government help for the railroad in 1970.

Bevan later said in an interview that the banks had received all the information they had requested concerning the financial position of the railroad. But, inside the railroad, Bevan was not receiving the information *he* wanted. Perlman, again, had prepared no formal budget for 1969 operations. Bevan, again, pressed for an incomes budget, but got none. Saunders seemed to ignore his complaints. The board routinely approved the management's decisions.

Publicly, there was no hint of the difficulties the railroad was

---

[10] The Penn Central in May 1971 began negotiating with 53 banks for the sale of Pennsylvania Co. to satisfy the $300 million debt. Upon completion of the agreement, the railroad was to receive a line of credit from the banks, but it appeared unlikely that it would realize any cash from the deal.

experiencing. At a stockholders' meeting on May 13, in Philadelphia's Civic Center, Saunders said the Penn Central's "prime objectives are to improve service and put our railroad in the black at the earliest possible date." Speaking at the same meeting, Perlman said that the merger had enabled Penn Central to shave twelve to forty-eight hours off the shipping time on some of the railroad's busiest routes. This time-saving, he said, was made possible through more direct routing as a result of the railroad's consolidation of twenty-three freight terminals.

By the end of 1969, terminals in thirty-five cities had been consolidated, at a cost to the railroad of $121 million. There was no evidence, however, that shippers were overjoyed at the Penn Central's performance. The file of complaints about Penn Central service at the ICC never stopped growing. It was by far the largest such file for any railroad.

Bevan also appeared at the May 13 stockholders' meeting. He disclosed that he had successfully sought ICC permission to increase the amount of commercial paper the railroad could sell to $150 million. By the end of the year, commercial paper authorization was increased to $200 million. In another successful effort to raise money, Bevan told the stockholders he had, for the first time, borrowed $50 million in Eurodollars. (At the risk of oversimplification, Eurodollars are American dollars deposited in Europe.)

Nobody mentioned that the railroad was already spending more than $260,000 a day on interest payments. Or that passenger losses were amounting to $275,000 a day. Or that the railroad was losing more than $500,000 a day. If the stockholders were fooled, they weren't the only ones. Some Wall Street analysts also thought the railroad's prospects were bright. One of the most bullish of these analysts was Murray Harding, who wrote a report published in January 1969 by Equity Research Associates, a Manhattan investment research firm. In the report, which ran to twenty-one pages, Harding predicted "a considerable turnaround by the railroad." He advised readers to buy Penn Central stock.

David Bevan did not take Harding's advice. While other investors were reading Harding's report predicting good things for the railroad, Bevan was unloading a large proportion of his stock.

The *Wall Street Journal,* which investigated insider selling by

Penn Central officials, reported that Bevan sold 15,000 shares of railroad stock between January 6 and June 25, 1969. The sales brought him a total of some $840,000. According to information on file with the Securities and Exchange Commission, Bevan bought 20,000 shares of railroad stock under an option plan in November 1964 at a total cost of $420,000, or half what he received when he resold 75 percent of them five years later. Bevan subsequently said he sold off his stock because he had to reduce a bank loan.

Altogether, the *Journal* reported, fifteen Penn Central officials sold stock they owned in the railroad between January 1969 and early 1970. Among them were five members of Penphil, the investment club organized by Bevan. In addition to Bevan, the Penphil members who sold were William R. Gerstnecker, former treasurer and vice president of the railroad, who sold 5,000 shares for an undisclosed amount between January and May 26, 1969; Theodore K. Warner, Jr., vice president for accounting and taxes, who sold 4,000 shares in September 1969, for $164,000; Robert Haslett, vice president for investments, who sold 3,000 shares on July 15, 1969, for $130,000, and Paul D. Fox, vice president for administration, who sold an undisclosed number of shares. One officer who did not sell was Stuart Saunders, the chairman of the railroad. Saunders held onto the 45,341 shares that he owned at the time, and suffered a tremendous loss. Asked if he knew that some of his officers were selling off their Penn Central stock, Saunders said: "No."

"I wrote a letter in April of 1965 to all the officers of the Penn Central and cautioned them about insider trading," Saunders told us. "I said it shouldn't be done without the approval — they shouldn't do it — I couldn't tell them not to, but before doing it they should clear it with the general counsel's office. And then in 1968, along about April, Mr. Bevan and Mr. Prizer [vice president and general counsel John B. Prizer] wrote a letter to all of the officers of Penn Central to the same effect. No officer ever consulted me but one exception. And I told him then I wasn't going to advise you about this. If I was you, I wouldn't do it. But I said you talk to general counsel about that; that's his responsibility.

"A lot of these sales I think were perfectly legitimate. I know Bayard Roberts.[11] His wife was in the hospital; he was in the hospital for a long time. I imagine he had to sell because he needed the money. And then I know about one other case. An officer had a loan and I'm sure this is probably true of others. They had loans that the banks were calling and that made them sell their stock. But even under that — I wouldn't — I haven't sold a share of mine. And I've lost millions of dollars in the process."

Asked why he didn't sell, Saunders replied: "Because I didn't think I should, first. Secondly, I had confidence in the company. But I didn't think it was right. And I would never trade in any securities — I've never traded in any securities of subsidiaries or anything else. And nobody can ever find a thing that I've done wrong in that regard. Or anywhere else. I said I'm never going to sell any stock as long as anybody can accuse me of any inside information. And I purposely do not receive any reports now about the company. All I know is what I read in the newspapers. Another reason why I moved out of the office building. I've never been in it since the first of August [1970]. I'll get along. But I lost over $5 million."

Actually, if Saunders had sold out during the same period Bevan was selling, he would have gotten more than $2.5 million, or a profit of about $1.6 million. Based on the price of Penn Central stock in March 1971, he would have suffered a loss of some $720,000.

Even while Bevan was selling, he was desperately trying to find money to keep the railroad alive. After increasing ICC authorization for Penn Central's commercial paper, and after arranging for the $300 million revolving credit, he decided to take on what he

---

11 Bayard Roberts was secretary of Penn Central and was identified by the *Wall Street Journal* as one of those who sold his stock. The others named by the *Journal* were Guy W. Knight, vice president for labor relations; John G. Patten, vice president for freight sales; David E. Smucker, executive vice president; Henry W. Large, executive vice president; Robert W. Minor, senior vice president for legal and public affairs; Jonathan O'Herron, vice president for finance; Malcolm P. Richards, vice president for purchases and materials; William A. Lashley, vice president for public relations, and John E. Chubb, vice president–Baltimore. Lashley was the only executive to consult with Saunders before selling his stock.

considered the biggest of Penn Central's many liabilities — Alfred E. Perlman, the president of the company.

By June 1969, the sheen had been rubbed off Perlman's reputation. For some months, Saunders had been quietly trying to find a replacement for the railroad's president. There was never any doubt about Bevan's low opinion of Perlman. Saunders noticed that even some board members who had previously supported Perlman were changing their minds.

Saunders, understandably, was becoming apprehensive. The rail losses were gigantic, and it was only a matter of time before some alert stockholders realized what troubles the railroad was having. When that happened, it could be the end of them all, Saunders and Bevan as well as Perlman. But Saunders had so far been unable to find a man to replace Perlman. Perlman was unaware of Saunders' secret efforts to oust him and, in mid-1969, he believed his position was secure. Bevan recalled that Perlman, at the June 1969 board meeting, predicted the railroad *would earn $50 million in 1969.*

It was at this point that Bevan made his move. He wrote a long, emotional letter of resignation to Saunders. While he said he was electing early retirement as of March 1, 1970, or earlier, Bevan was in fact quitting over Perlman's method of running the railroad. Although he mentioned nobody by name, his target was clearly Perlman. There had been no improvement in the railroad's operations, Bevan wrote. In fact, things had become worse. He was not interested so much in the mechanical operation of the railroad, but in the financial end of it. Penn Central could not continue to pour huge sums into the railroad without a rational basis for doing so and without some indication that there would be a return on the money that Bevan was borrowing at 8, 9 and 10 percent. The $300 million revolving credit agreement should see the railroad through 1970, Bevan said. But after March 1, the Penn Central would have to find somebody else to raise the money.

In effect, Bevan told Saunders, "You've got to choose between me and Perlman." Bevan's timing was perfect. As recounted earlier, Saunders had decided late in 1968 or early in 1969 that Perlman had to go but, until he received Bevan's letter in June 1969, he had been unable to implement his decision. He had no love for Bevan, and in fact considered both Bevan and Perlman his two biggest problems. But if he had to choose between the man who raised the money and the man who spent the money, there was really no choice at all. Perlman had to go. Costs had to be cut.

After several weeks of negotiation, Bevan accepted the deal offered by Saunders: Perlman would be removed as president and kicked upstairs into the meaningless position of vice chairman. Bevan would regain control of the budget. A Bevan protégé, Jonathan O'Herron, then executive vice president of Buckeye Pipeline Company, a railroad subsidiary owned by the Pennsylvania Company, would become Bevan's vice president for finance. And Bevan would be invited to sit once again on the board of directors.

Saunders quietly obtained the approval of key board members to purge Perlman, who had a contract that ran until November 30, 1970.[12] When the contract expired, Perlman would be three years past the retirement age of sixty-five. Saunders believed the railroad could not afford Perlman's leadership for that length of time. It would be cheaper to forcibly retire him, even though it meant that Perlman, under his contract, would receive about $800,000 from the Penn Central by the middle of 1981.

One of the things that bothered Saunders, and several board members, was that Perlman was almost sixty-six years old when the merger became effective. Yet there was no one whom he was grooming to succeed him. It seemed, in fact, as if he intended to run the railroad forever.

Even after he had been informed that he was being kicked upstairs, but before his successor took over, Perlman found himself being criticized for his spending. On September 12, 1969, Saunders, in a tactfully worded note, again sought to pressure Perlman to cut expenses. "I know that you and your people are already making an intensive effort to control the outflow of cash and in view of our current situation, I ask that you re-double your efforts along this line. It is absolutely vital that this be done," Saunders wrote.

---

[12] Unlike Perlman, Saunders never had a contract and never asked for one. See James Symes letter in Chapter Three.

More than anything else, it was the money. Saunders felt that Perlman was spending far too much. This was, after all, stockholders' money, and they were entitled to a decent return. Saunders and Bevan did not believe that the way to make money out of the railroad was to invest more money in equipment and roadbed improvements. Perlman did. He was constantly finding new ways to invest in the railroad's plant, promising that the investment would yield returns of from 30 to 300 percent. In December 1969, when Perlman became vice chairman, E. Clayton Gengras joined the Penn Central's board. Gengras had mixed feelings about Perlman. "From what I'm told, Perlman would never stay within the figures they gave him for operations," Gengras said. "He was a guy who spent a lot of dough. There was tremendous conflict among the management and over operating philosophies. Perlman was far superior as an operations man, but when he tried to operate, they kept forcing the Pennsy people in there. He couldn't do anything. He didn't have the people."

Saunders did not believe that Perlman was a superior operating executive. Privately, he was saying that Perlman never earned a dime on railroad operations either on the Penn Central or on the New York Central. So he set out to find a replacement, someone who knew something about cost controls.

Saunders' approach to Louis Menk, the highly regarded president of the Burlington Northern Railroad, had failed when Menk said no in March 1969. Saunders next turned to a high executive of General Motors. The executive was interested in the job until he heard the salary — $175,000 plus deferred compensation, a total of about $250,000 a year. This was less than the executive was making at General Motors and he, too, refused the presidency.

Finally, Paul A. Gorman's name came up. Gorman had recently retired as head of Western Electric. One director said that Charlie Hodge, of Glore Forgan, recommended Gorman. Another said Gorman's name was supplied by railroad director John Dorrance, who served with Gorman on the board of the Campbell Soup Company. Gorman was sixty-two and was widely known as a blunt, unsophisticated man of unquestioned honesty. His cost control programs at Western Electric had been highly successful. And he was interested in the job. After some negotiation with Saunders,

Paul A. Gorman answers newsmen's questions on June 9, 1970, the day after Stuart Saunders, Alfred Perlman and David Bevan had been fired. Gorman was named chairman and chief executive officer in addition to his post as president of the Penn Central as a result of the shakeup. (Philadelphia *Bulletin* photo)

where Gorman let it be known that he would continue to live in
Summit, New Jersey, Gorman agreed to become president of the
Penn Central. Although Gorman was much admired in the business world, he was totally without experience in railroading. Asked
why he had chosen a nonrailroad man to run the railroad, Saunders told us:

Well, for two reasons. In the first place, I couldn't find any railroad
men that I thought could do the job. Or that would take it. In the
second place, I thought — and I still think — you've got plenty of
expertise to run the railroad but what we needed most of all at this
particular juncture was cost control, budgeting and better management
of our financial affairs. And I thought that Gorman — and he was —
an excellently qualified man to do this job. If he'd been given an opportunity I think he would have. But we didn't have the cost control. And
we needed more — and we still need more — of industrial management
practices in the railroad industry. I thought that a man of his stature,
capabilities and experience, having charge of accounting personnel in
a large industrial company — and not being able to find a railroad man
who would fit the bill or we could get — that it was a good thing
to do."[13]

After he was ousted, Perlman was again able to persuade a good
many people in government, the news media and the industry that
it was *his* decision to give up the presidency, because he could no
longer function under the restrictions imposed on him by Bevan
and Saunders.

Saunders resented this. He did not state so publicly, but he let
his associates know that he engineered Perlman's removal and had
encountered great resistance from Perlman. Perlman had no intention of quitting, Saunders said, and had threatened to contest his
ouster in a showdown before the board.

On August 26, the day before a scheduled board meeting,
Saunders called Perlman into his office and broke the news to him.
He was being effectively retired a year early, on November 30,
1969. On December 1, he would have to surrender his presidency
to Gorman. Perlman argued angrily with Saunders and made his
threat to take the matter to the board. But it became clear to him

---

[13] Perlman refused to discuss with us charges that his spending practices
got the railroad into difficulty.

that Saunders would not have struck unless he was sure the board would support him.

Perlman reminded Saunders that he had a valid contract. If the Penn Central failed to pay him what the contract specified, he would bring in his lawyers. He demanded, and received, assurances that he would have secretarial help, the use of a company car after he became vice chairman, and would retain his office in New York. He would not give up the perquisites of the presidency.

At the August 27 meeting of the board, David Bevan was elected a director. Saunders told the board that Perlman was giving up his duties as president as of November 30. On December 1, Perlman would be booted upstairs to the office of vice chairman. On September 24, the board elected Gorman the new president of the Penn Central.

Gorman obviously did not know how serious the situation was. Shortly before his election, he called Bevan and told him he had some personal affairs to clean up before moving to Penn Central. Because of this, he said, he couldn't possibly take over until December 1. Since it was so late in the year, he told Bevan, why didn't they just wait until January 1, 1970, to have him take over.

"You'd better get here as early as possible," Bevan told Gorman.

"It's that bad?" Gorman asked.

"It's worse," said Bevan. "I'll buy you all the time I can but you're going to have to cut the hell out of expenses."

Gorman took office on December 1.

Before Gorman moved in, however, the full dimensions of the railroad's disastrous position were finally being perceived by the management and the board. Persistent rumors along Wall Street had it that the railroad was going to omit its usual fourth-quarter dividend. Responding to these rumors, Penn Central stock hit its 1969 low on November 12, $28.75, down from a high that year of $71.75.

The stock rallied somewhat after that, based in part on large purchases made through the Philadelphia brokerage firm of Butcher & Sherrerd, headed by Howard Butcher III, the former Penn Central director who had been accused of "insider" selling and who was one of the largest individual shareholders in the railroad. On November 26, the stock closed at $31.25. But on November 26, the board confirmed the Wall Street rumors by voting to omit the last quarter dividend. Saunders placed the blame for the omitted dividend on "general business conditions."

Even then Saunders remained optimistic. On the day the dividend was omitted, he said he noticed several "encouraging developments." Among these he listed the promise of lower per diem costs in 1970, a 6 percent freight rate increase approved by the ICC on November 18, and the possibility of congressional action to reduce the crushing passenger losses.

And still the search for cash to feed the railroad went on. In July 1969, Bevan had arranged for the Pennsylvania Company to sell $35 million of 8¼ percent collateral trust bonds. Pennco then used the $35 million to buy securities from the railroad. It was purely and simply a device, using Pennco's assets, to get cash to the railroad. By December, the $35 million was gone, and Pennco was tapped again to raise cash for the Penn Central. This time it was $50 million, through an issuance of 9 percent sinking fund debentures. As soon as it had the cash, Pennco loaned it to the railroad.

Even this was not enough. The railroad was being eaten alive by inefficiency and the insidious combination of rising prices and slumping business. Late in December, Bevan went to Europe and returned with a commitment for $59 million in Swiss francs. The interest was 10.1 percent.

By the end of 1969, costs directly related to the merger — severance pay, consolidation of terminals and the like — amounted to $193 million. Ironically, the railroad's operating loss for 1969 was just about the same figure, $193,215,000.

Because of its complicated relationships with its subsidiaries, and the method of preparing its earnings statements, the railroad was able to reduce this loss to $56,328,000. And, in the end, was able to show earnings for the consolidated company on ordinary operations of $4,388,000.

In 1969, total railway operating revenues were $1,651,978,000. Railroad expenses were $1,845,193,000, meaning that the railroad spent $193,215,000 more than it took in. Added to railroad revenues, however, was $136,887,000 in "other" income. Subtracting this "other" income from the railroad's deficit reduced the loss to slightly more than $56 million.

The railroad selected 1969 as the year it would write down to salvage value its investment on long-haul passenger service facilities west of Harrisburg and Albany. The reason it took this action, the railroad said, was that "prior operating losses make any possibility of recovery of such investment through future operations clearly remote."

The write-down on long-haul facilities was fixed by the railroad at $126 million and it was recorded as an "extraordinary" (not chargeable against ordinary earnings) loss for the year. This "extraordinary" loss, added to the loss on railroad operations shown on the earnings statement, reflected an *admitted* loss on rail operations for 1969 of $182,328,000. Added to the *actual* rail loss of more than $193 million, the extraordinary loss brought the 1969 rail deficit to $319,215,000.

The consolidated earnings statement showed ordinary earnings for the year of slightly more than $4 million. The ordinary earnings statement tended to indicate that Penn Central, from its vast holdings beyond the railroad, was at least making some money, no matter how little. These ordinary earnings, however, were made possible *only by writing off the $126 million in long-haul facilities.* The write-off was considered "extraordinary" (which it actually was) so it could not be charged against ordinary earnings. While the write-off did produce an overall loss of $121,612,000 (the $4,388,000 in ordinary earnings less $126,000,000), it nevertheless left ordinary earnings intact. The stockholder, reading the annual report, would notice ordinary earnings, the true measure of a company's performance, and would disregard the write-off because it was a one-shot event.

If the long-haul facilities had not been written off, the consolidated earnings statement for ordinary operations would have been forced to show a loss for 1969.

The long-haul facilities, had they not been written off, would have cost the Penn Central depreciation expenses of $4,500,000 during 1969. *Depreciation is chargeable against ordinary earnings.* This would have reduced the consolidated ordinary earnings of

$4,388,000 by $4,500,000. And this reduction would have meant a loss on ordinary operations for 1969 of $112,000.

The gloomy figures seemed to affect even Stuart Saunders. In his annual report for 1969, Saunders was not quite as optimistic as he had been in the past. "The year 1969 was a very difficult one for Penn Central," Saunders told the stockholders, in a letter. "Our problems were principally centered in the transportation company, and some of them were beyond our control."

The "most troublesome" problems, said Saunders, were inflation, which he claimed cost the railroad $100 million; delays in getting rate increases; a business slowdown; the passenger deficit; merger start-up costs; abnormal weather conditions; and strikes and threats of strikes. But Saunders did find one ray of sunshine: the diversification program. "Income of $137 million — derived from real estate operations, investments and tax payments from subsidiaries — was used to support our railroad operations during the past year," Saunders wrote.[14] "We have not taken a penny from the railroad to pursue diversification. On the contrary, the railroad benefits greatly from the earnings of these enterprises."

The question of diversification was a touchy one inside the railroad's offices. Perlman opposed it, because he believed the railroad's funds would be more wisely spent improving the railroad. Saunders and Bevan viewed diversification as the company's salvation. They believed that, since the railroad was obviously not making any money, the company should make investments with a view toward getting some return.

Bevan, testifying before the Senate Commerce Committee on August 6, 1970, said the railroad could not have continued operations if it weren't for the diversification program. "All in all, from the Pennsylvania Railroad side, we invested a total of approximately $144 million of cash in this diversification program, of which only about three-quarters of a million in total came from the

---

[14] Companies acquired by Penn Central were given refuge in the railroad's huge tax shelter. The railroad had not paid any federal income taxes since 1954 and it had an annual tax-loss carry forward adequate to insure that its subsidiaries could avoid income taxes. In lieu of federal income taxes, the subsidiaries were assessed a comparable amount by the railroad. The railroad did pay about $64 million in local taxes each year.

transportation company," Bevan said. "The system realized a return of $146 million from these investments from the date of acquisition through 1969, aproximately five years in all. Those dividends and income from other non-railroad properties have served to blunt the losses from passenger service and have provided the margin necessary for continued operation of the railroad."

Both the Pennsylvania and the Central, before the merger was contemplated, had considerable nonrail holdings. These were scattered through an amazing assortment of companies the railroads had acquired over the years. There was no plan or order discernible in this empire. It was just a vast agglomeration of assets, some valuable, some less so.

With the merger approved by both companies, Bevan began an aggressive program to acquire substantial nonrail companies in 1964. This time, there was a plan. The Pennsylvania Company, the third tier in the Penn Central complex, would be developed into a holding company as well as an investment company. All future significant acquisitions would be made by Pennco.

The Central brought some choice Manhattan holdings into the merger. Its Despatch Shops, Inc. owned Realty Hotels, Inc. Realty owned five major New York hotels — the Waldorf-Astoria, the Barclay, the Biltmore, the Roosevelt and the Commodore. The Waldorf was leased out, but the Penn Central, through its subsidiary, operated the other four and advertised these four on Metroliner ticket jackets.

The Penn Central also owned twenty-nine acres of valuable land in mid-Manhattan, running from 42nd Street north to 52nd Street and from Madison Avenue east to Lexington Avenue. The major office buildings that rose from this land included Grand Central Terminal; the Pan Am Building; Graybar Building; Vanderbilt Building; Yale Club; Vanderbilt Concourse Building; New York General Building; Union Carbide Building; Chemical Bank New York Trust Building; Bankers Trust Building; International Telephone and Telegraph Building; Manufacturers Hanover Trust Building; 466 Lexington Ave.; 383–85 Madison Ave.; 250 Park Ave.; 245 Park Ave., and 299 Park Ave. Farther south, the railroad owned Pennsylvania Station, 24 percent of Madison Square

Garden and 24 percent of the New York Knickerbockers basketball team and the New York Rangers hockey team. The New York real estate, in 1969, produced more than $20 million for Penn Central.[15]

In the long run, however, Pennco was to be what Bevan described as the railroad's "jewel." Pennco had been around since 1870, but it was not until 1963 that it really shone.

Pennco acquired control of Buckeye Pipeline Company in 1963 through cash purchases of its stock totaling $28,170,000 and an exchange of its preferred stock for Buckeye stock. It acquired 100 percent ownership of the pipeline over the next two years by paying another $2,211,000 for stock. Total cash expended for Buckeye stock: $30,381,000.

Buckeye was the eighth-largest processor of crude oil in the United States. Every day, 42 million gallons of crude and refined products were fed through its 7,600–mile network of pipes. It supplied 3 million gallons of jet fuel to New York's Kennedy International Airport every day, and it was a major fuel supplier to Miami International Airport, Greater Pittsburgh Airport and various Air Force bases.

From the time it acquired Buckeye through 1970, Pennco paid dividends on its preferred stock. For Buckeye, which had received Pennco stock as part of the acquisition price, these dividends amounted to $19,488,000. This raised the total cash expenditure by Pennco for Buckeye to $49,869,000.

In return, Buckeye paid dividends to Pennco. Through 1970, Buckeye dividends to the railroad's subsidiary totaled $37,331,-000, meaning that, through the period of the collapse, Buckeye had drained off from Pennco, in cash, $12,538,000. Buckeye was probably the soundest acquisition Pennco made.

What interested the railroad's management, and with considerable justification, was Buckeye's earnings picture and what it could

---

[15] The Penn Central, in June 1971, placed all of its mid-Manhattan real estate except Grand Central Terminal on the market. Although this real estate had been one of the railroad's few consistent sources of earnings, it was offered for sale both in an attempt to generate capital and to appease Congressional critics who wanted the Penn Central out of everything but the railroad business.

contribute to the parent company's earnings statement. In 1968 and 1969, the two critical years in the merger, Buckeye had net earnings of $26,034,000. This total amount was carried on the Penn Central's books as part of its earnings. However, the actual cash the railroad received was only $12,600,000. The railroad was thus, legitimately, reporting more than $26 million in income, but it had the use of less than half that. Nevertheless, Buckeye appeared to be a sound investment.

Great Southwest Corporation and Macco Corporation were something else again. Pennco began acquiring Great Southwest in 1965 and Macco in 1966. By 1969, it controlled 90 percent of the stock and merged the two companies into one survivor — Great Southwest. The total cash investment by Pennco (meaning the railroad) was $87,365,000. By the end of 1970, Great Southwest had returned to Pennco $4,256,000 in dividends. The cash drained away from the railroad: $83,109,000.

Here again, the railroad was interested in something besides dividends. What could Great Southwest contribute to a bleak earnings picture that was threatening the parent company? It could contribute quite a bit, if one didn't look too closely.

In 1968 and 1969, Great Southwest reported net earnings of $61.7 million. The railroad's share of this, since it owned 90 percent of the company, came to about $55.6 million. This helped bolster the Penn Central's poor earnings statement, even though the railroad had the use of only a little more than $4 million of it. But the potential for fancy bookkeeping, in the Great Southwest case, was far greater, because it was Great Southwest that dealt in John Seabrook's "Chinese money."

Great Southwest was a Texas land development firm with large holdings in the western part of the nation and Hawaii. It also owned, at one time, two amusement parks — Six Flags Over Texas and Six Flags Over Georgia. Because it was involved in land sales, many of Great Southwest's deals were long-term arrangements. That is, if a substantial sale were made, the buyer would be permitted to pay for his purchase over a period of years. Despite this, Great Southwest routinely credited its income account with the full purchase price for the year in which the sale was made, even though only a fraction of the money had been collected and the full balance might never be paid. Pennco, in a prospectus for a debenture sale, acknowledged this: "Great Southwest records sales of lands and buildings in the year of sale and generally takes the full sales price into income *even though in many instances a substantial portion of the sales price is payable over an extended period of time and may not include personal liability of the purchaser so that collection of the total purchase price may be dependent upon successful development of the property.*"[16]

Abraham J. Briloff, professor of accountancy at the Baruch College of the City University of New York, made an extensive study of one Great Southwest transaction, and published the study in *Barron's Weekly*. Professor Briloff found that Great Southwest, in 1969, sold its Texas amusement park for $40 million.

Great Southwest received a cash down payment of $1.5 million and a note for the $38.5 million balance. Annual payments on the note were fixed at $2,315,685, principal and interest. The debt would have been paid off in the year 2005. But the note contained this caveat: "The sole recourse of such holder for the collection of the Amusement Park Note shall be against the property covered by the Amusement Park Mortgage. The Amusement Park Note will provide that neither Fund [the purchaser] nor any general or limited partner of Fund shall be liable personally for the payment of the Amusement Park Note or for the payment of any deficiency upon foreclosure under and sale of the property covered by the Amusement Park Mortgage."

Great Southwest, then, received $1.5 million in cash, a greatly hedged promise to pay off the note, and very little else. Yet, it recorded from that sale $17.5 million in after-tax income, *or more than half its total net income for 1969.* And 90 percent of this Chinese money found its way onto the Penn Central's books.

Great Southwest's sales increased by a little less than $16 million in 1969, over 1968. Yet, its accounts receivable shot up by more than $70 million. Clearly, these paper transactions were of no help to the railroad, except insofar as they brightened the sagging earnings picture.

In 1965 and 1966, Pennco paid $22,047,000 in cash to acquire

---

[16] Emphasis added. Taken from a prospectus for a $100 million debenture issue proposed by Pennco in May 1970.

58 percent of Arvida Corporation, a Florida land development firm. Arvida, through mid-1971, never paid out a dividend. Cash flow away from the railroad: more than $22 million. Arvida's total net earnings for 1968 and 1969 amounted to $3,749,000, of which the railroad's share was about $2.1 million, not enough to greatly affect Penn Central's earnings picture but far more than Arvida actually contributed.

The Executive Jet story has already been told. In 1970, the railroad wrote off as a loss the $21 million investment it made in EJA.

In 1969, the railroad, through Pennco, increased its holdings in Madison Square Garden by buying $2 million more in stock. The railroad also advanced an additional $2,802,000 to Madison Square Garden. Total flow of cash away: $4,802,000. Cash returned: none.

In 1966, the Central acquired the Strick Holding Company for $15 million cash. Before selling Strick for $15 million in December 1968, the Penn Central had made loans to the trailer company amounting to $9,437,000. Net cash drained from the railroad: $9,437,000.

The diversification program, then, resulted in at least $153,021,-000 in cash flowing away from the Penn Central. The ICC, in a special study of nonrail investments dated November 18, 1970, concluded the cash drain was actually $209,000,000.[17] It arrived

---

[17] The railroad's diversification program, which began on January 1, 1963, and ended when the railroad collapsed seven and a half years later, contributed significantly to the company's poor cash position. The table below, prepared from figures compiled by the Interstate Commerce Commission, illustrates the negative cash impact of the program:

CASH SPENT BY PENN CENTRAL	
— For stock purchases	$157,138,000
— For dividends to subsidiaries	19,488,000
— For loans and advances	32,982,000
TOTAL CASH SPENT	$209,608,000
CASH RECEIVED BY PENN CENTRAL	
— In dividends	$ 41,587,000
— From sale of assets	15,000,000
TOTAL CASH RECEIVED	$ 56,587,000
NET CASH DRAINED AWAY BY DIVERSIFICATION	$153,021,000
ESTIMATED INTEREST CHARGES	$ 56,394,000
TOTAL NEGATIVE CASH IMPACT ON PENN CENTRAL	$209,415,000

at this figure by adding $56,394,000 to the amount that was readily identifiable as having been paid out for stock acquisitions, dividends and loans. The additional $56 million, the ICC said, was what it cost the railroad in interest charges over the seven and a half years of the diversification program to borrow an amount equivalent to what it invested in nonrail ventures. The Penn Central could have saved this $56 million, the ICC stated, simply by reducing its borrowing by the amount it invested in cash for the diversification program.

The railroad did realize some benefits from this program, however. For a time, its interest in Great Southwest appeared to be worth perhaps $900 million. When Pennco borrowed to help the railroad, its limits were extended because Great Southwest stock had, for a time, appreciated. But when Pennco's stock holdings depreciated, as they did in 1970, the railroad was brought up short.

In a briefer study restricted to the railroad's investment in four companies — Great Southwest, Buckeye, Arvida and Macco — Rep. Wright Patman and the staff of the House Committee on Banking and Currency concluded that the diversification program had drained off "at least" $175 million from the Penn Central. "Investigators for the committee have determined that ill-advised investments by Penn Central resulted in a heavy drain of cash so critically needed to operate the railroad," Patman said, on November 2, 1970. "This is in direct contradiction to the claims put forward by David C. Bevan, the former chief financial officer of the Penn Central, that the diversification program had provided great benefits and income for the operation of the railroad."

While diversification did siphon cash away from the railroad, it also provided an opportunity for the Penn Central to bolster a dismal earnings statement. The evidence appears strong that the railroad, above all else, was interested in showing a good earnings picture to its stockholders and to its directors. "There was a completely unrealistic approach to the real estate holdings," railroad director E. Clayton Gengras said: "Unfortunately, they were allowed to do it and it wasn't illegal. In retrospect, I really don't think it was proper. For example, they had this property, worth about $10 million, and they syndicated it. They registered it and it was all legal. I don't want to mention the name of the property. They syndicated it and, instead of spreading the proceeds over a number of years, they reported a profit on it of $20 million that year. They didn't even have the money yet. It was just a flock of paper, but it looked good on the balance sheet and to the stockholders. It was really a valley of frenzied finance. These were forced earnings.[18]

"They had a highly profitable leasing company, involved with piggy-back trailers. They needed cash, so they took $10 to $15 million out of it, in cash. They broke the company."

Gengras said the railroad management really believed diversification was a great boon to the Penn Central. "If anyone had looked at this long enough and hard enough they would have realized it was just a house of cards," he said. "I can't see anywhere where there was a definite, underhanded, dishonest or planned approach of screwing anyone. It was more pressure to make things look good, more forcing of earnings that was, actually, depletion, more drive to keep the thing afloat."

The Penn Central trustees, in a statement to the Senate Commerce Committee on November 23, 1970, concluded that the diversification policy was not in the best interests of the railroad.

"The 'diversification' policy which was in effect at PCTC [Penn Central Transportation Company] was in our judgment, given the advantage of hindsight, a mistake," the trustees said. "It conceivably postponed the showdown at Penn Central. Some of the investments soured. Some, particularly in real estate development projects (especially Great Southwest Corporation), involved a need for additional cash just at a time — 1969 and 1970 — when credit opportunities tightened up severely. Under different economic conditions, the policy might have worked. But as things

---

18 In August 1970, *Fortune* magazine said the railroad, in 1969, "showed a $14.5 million dividend from its wholly owned truck line, New York Central Transport Co., which had a 1969 profit of only $4.2 million. To get the dividend, Penn Central virtually cleaned out all the Transport's shareholders' equity." *Fortune* also said the railroad collected a $2 million dividend from Manor Real Estate Co., another subsidiary, which lost $714,000 in 1969, and received a $4.7 million dividend from another trucking affiliate, Merchants Despatch Transportation Corp., which earned only $2.8 million in 1969.

turned out, the diversification policy often meant (i) the unavailability of cash to support the railroad operation, and (ii) *opportunities for bookkeeping and reporting practices which had the effect — whatever their purpose — of postponing a day of reckoning at Penn Central which would have been less bleak if it had dawned earlier* [emphasis added]."

Penn Central, the trustees said, should be taken out of "every business not significantly connected with running the railroad."

"In a significant and meaningful sense, we would, if this were possible, simply put For Sale signs on the non-railroad properties held or controlled through subsidiaries by Penn Central," the trustees said, anticipating the action they were to take in the spring of 1971. "This would include the Pennsylvania Company itself, its three principal subsidiaries — Buckeye Pipe Line, Great Southwest Corporation, Arvida Corporation, the New York City hotels, and the 24 percent interest in Madison Square Garden Corporation."

The trustees also commented on the Penn Central's 1969 financial reports, which were prepared by Peat, Marwick, Mitchell & Company, the railroad's $600,000-a-year accounting firm.

"Without questioning the consistency of the 1969 report with generally accepted accounting practices, it appears to have reflected a corporate policy at that time of putting the best conceivable face on the facts — *to the point that these facts were dubious allies of the truth* [emphasis added]," the trustees stated.[19]

The unanswered question is, just how much valuable time was spent by railroad officials on the diversification program that could have been better spent on Penn Central's problems? By the end of 1969, it was obvious that the railroad was still committed to the program. The annual report noted: "Earnings from Pennsylvania company's diversified holdings continued to contribute significantly to Penn Central's results."

Perhaps buoyed by the illusion that the Chinese money was real, the Penn Central continued to pay dividends until the last quarter of 1969, although these dividends were clearly not being earned.

---

[19] On December 7, 1970, the Penn Central retained the firm of Haskins & Sells to assist in handling its accounts. By June 1971 Haskins & Sells had become the railroad's accountants and Peat, Marwick, Mitchell & Company was dropped.

Even with the suspended final quarter dividend, the total payout to stockholders during the year was $43,396,000.

This was not as advantageous to the stockholder as one might think. If someone had bought a share of railroad stock early in the year, he would have paid about $70 for it. By the end of the year, the stock was down to around $30, or a loss in value of $40. He had received three quarterly sixty-cent dividends, for a total of $1.80, hardly enough to cover the loss in value. And, on top of that, the $1.80 was subject to ordinary income taxes.

Another ominous sign was that, in 1969, Penn Central's working capital deficit had again increased, this time by $35 million. The deficit at the start of 1970 was $206 million.

But a new year was beginning and, as always, the railroad was optimistic. Even David Bevan was hopeful. The finance chairman knew the railroad was in a bad way. But Perlman, for all practical purposes, was gone, and there was a new president, Paul Gorman. At last Bevan could institute his incomes budget, because Gorman also believed in living within one's means.

10

End of the Line

Nineteen sixty-nine had a white Christmas. The snow began to fall early in the day. The fluffy white flakes swirled down from the skies like bits of cotton candy, silently and steadily, coating the twinkling Christmas lights with a frosty icing. By dusk the next day almost six inches of snow were on the ground in Manhattan, Philadelphia, Baltimore and Washington. Twice as much and more covered parts of upstate New York, western Pennsylvania and the Midwest. Penn Central's locomotives and boxcars, its freight yards and its 20,000 miles of track in sixteen states, were buried under a thick white mantle of snow.

It was a good time for Christmas sleds and skis and ice skates. It was not a good time for the railroad. Snow cost money. Ice on electrical lines meant power failures, which translated into delays and missed connections for holiday travelers. Freight operations, which brought in almost 82 percent of the Penn Central's revenue, were affected even more.

David Bevan was not too concerned about the first snowfall of the winter of 1969–1970. In fact, for the first time in two years he felt almost confident. The railroad's appetite for cash remained enormous, but he believed he had found means of satisfying it, at least for the immediate future. Bevan had arranged for the railroad to receive, on the last day of 1969, $59 million in Swiss francs. The interest on this loan, which was backed up by Penn Central International, a shell company established in Curaçao for the sole purpose of making the loan possible, was 10.1 percent for a one-year period. Earlier, on October 29, 1969, the ICC had agreed to permit the railroad to sell up to $200 million in commercial paper. But in granting its permission, the ICC made what turned out to be a prophetic statement: "Although we are sympathetic to applicant's [the Penn Central] problem, short-term financing has traditionally been relied upon to finance short-term needs and is not normally regarded as a proper source for long-term financing of capital expenditures or for refinancing of maturing long-term debt. . . . The exhaustion of short-term credit to refinance maturing long-term debt or to finance long-term capital expenditures could expose a carrier to a serious crisis in the event of an economic squeeze, at which time a carrier may require short-term financing for traditional use."

In the next paragraph of its decision, however, the ICC said, "On the whole, applicant is in a strong financial condition. . . ."

Bevan also had managed to get commitments for equipment trust certificates to finance the purchase of 147 new locomotives and 1,838 new freight cars, to be delivered in 1970. He needed an additional $100 million to see the railroad through 1970. Raising $100 million had proved no problem to Bevan in the past, and he foresaw no difficulty in doing so again. Besides, he was starting the new year with a new president, Paul A. Gorman, whose business-like approach impressed Bevan.

"Gorman came in and worked like hell," Bevan said. "We adopted an incomes budget for the first time and I was encouraged. He said come hell or high water we're going to live up to the incomes budget. We had got all the equipment financing for 1970 done. We just needed this last $100 million to carry us through 1970."

Bevan's budget forecast a net loss on rail operations, after the inclusion of "other" income, of $55 million for 1970. In the first quarter of the year, always the worst quarter for Eastern railroads, a loss of $49 million was anticipated. This was the same loss the railroad had experienced during the first three months of 1969, and Bevan did not expect any change in it, even though prices and interest charges were rising and labor costs would go up, effective January 1, as soon as new contracts were signed with the unions. Bevan was relying on the railroad's subsidiaries to shrink the rail losses to manageable proportions.

The Christmas snow was still on the ground when 1970 began.

The start of the year was not promising. A mass of frigid air blanketed the Penn Central region, in which 100 million people lived, and new snow started piling up. On January 6 and 7, the major cities were hit with six more inches, while the northern and western regions again received a foot or more. In only one of the thirty-one days in January did the temperature stay above freezing in the eastern cities. For much of January and February, the mercury was below ten degrees, and on many of those days it fell to zero or below.

The effect of the weather on the railroad was devastating. Power lines snapped and switches froze. Sections of steel rail split like dry timber under an ax. Trains of 100 cars or more, crammed with freight, were stranded outside clogged yards. The railroad's most expensive computer classification facility, the $36 million Perlman Yard, at Selkirk, New York, was paralyzed. Cars broke down but the bitter weather made it impossible to repair them out of doors, where repairs were usually made. Shippers screamed their objections as schedules were jettisoned, but the railroad could not conquer the winter weather. The inability to move cargo already on hand prevented the Penn Central from taking on new cargo, and revenues declined. Per diem charges shot up.

When Stuart Saunders appeared before the Senate Commerce Committee on July 22, 1970, he placed much of the blame for the railroad's collapse on the severe winter. "It was worse than any strike we ever had," Saunders said. "For three weeks or over three weeks the Penn Central was paralyzed over a great portion of its railroad. We couldn't get a car through Selkirk yard for days. As I say, it was worse than a strike. You have to expect bad weather every year but the unprecedented bad weather we had in the first quarter of this year cost Penn Central at least $20 million."

Gorman, unfamiliar with the railroad's operations, soon found himself hip-deep in red ink. During his first weeks as president, he searched frantically for some way to save money, for some kind of tourniquet to squeeze off the huge amounts of cash that were spurting out. But he could not do it.[1]

---

[1] Testifying before the Senate Commerce Committee on July 23, 1970, Gorman said: "I had the responsibility for the operation of the railroad. And believe you me, that is a tremendous job."

Snow and ice removal alone cost the railroad $8.5 million in January and February. Losses on passenger service mounted to more than $375,000 a day. A postal strike and continued diversion of mail away from the rails reduced mail revenues for the first quarter by another 25 percent. Interest charges for the first three months went up $9 million. Operating expenses increased by almost $49 million over the same period in 1969, while revenue decreased.

The Penn Central's 1970 first quarter was probably the most disastrous in American railroad history. Receipts from rail operations totaled about $5 million a day. But the railroad was admittedly spending more than $6 million a day. Even for the Penn Central, this was an intolerable situation. How long could any business continue to lose more than $1 million a day?

The management was not yet fully aware of the magnitude of the losses. The reports would not be in until April. Bevan, in the meantime, was looking ahead. In 1970, the railroad was faced with debt maturities of $106 million and Bevan's job was to find the money to meet these maturities.

The solution, inevitably, was more borrowing. While the railroad was digging out of the winter storms, while hundreds of day laborers were lining up outside Penn Central offices to earn some money shoveling snow, Bevan was putting the finishing touches to a proposal that would raise the funds the railroad needed.

Bevan presented his preliminary plan to the ICC on March 25. It was built around a bond issue to be floated by the Pennsylvania Company, the railroad's wholly owned subsidiary. Pennco was to issue $100 million worth of debentures, with a life of twenty-five years, at an interest rate of 10.5 percent. The proceeds were to be used by Pennco to buy three companies from the railroad. The railroad would then use the cash to meet its debt maturities. Although all of Pennco's stock was pledged to secure the $300 million revolving credit, on a $3 for $1 basis, the market value of the investment company's holdings appeared at that point to be substantially more than $1 billion, giving it sufficient leeway to manage the bond issue.

Three investment banking houses — First Boston Corporation, Glore Forgan, and Salomon Brothers & Hutzler — had agreed to head up the list of underwriters for the issue. Despite the fact that the railroad was losing money at an enormous rate, it was obvious that the faith of Wall Street and the banks in Penn Central's soundness remained unshaken.[2]

The railroad was by this time surviving on credit. In addition to the $106 million coming due in 1970, it had long-term debt amounting to $1,585,000,000. It owed the consortium of banks $300 million for the revolving credit it had used. Other bank loans due in 1970 added up to $30 million. By the end of the year $193.4 million in commercial paper was due. Interest charges for the year would reach $132 million.

Nevertheless, the financial community believed in the Penn Central. Nothing could happen to The Railroad. Its dividend record was above reproach, 122 uninterrupted years. In the two years since the merger, the railroad had paid out almost $100 million in dividends, and that was an impressive performance. So impressive, in fact, that everyone tended to overlook a very basic circumstance — during those two years, despite the addition of "other" income to the earnings statement, the railroad was in a negative cash flow position.

Because of the railroad's sterling reputation in the financial world, Bevan was confident he could pull it off, could raise the necessary $100 million. The interest rate on the Pennco bonds would be extraordinarily high, but money was tight and the price had to be paid. The rating services, at that time, still classified Pennco bonds as suitable for institutional investors.

So, while the gloomy first quarter figures were being compiled, the details of the proposed $100 million offering were sent to the printer. Before the prospectus rolled off the presses, the bad news

---

[2] An example of this faith can be found in an internal memo of the First National City Bank of New York, dated March 6, 1970. The memo concerned a long overdue debt of Executive Jet Aviation, and the possibility of selling off an EJA jet put up as collateral to satisfy the debt. The memo said, "In consideration of the future Penn Central relationship and certain assurances from the railroad's financial officers, FNCB has agreed to postpone liquidation of collateral for a period of time in order to permit the railroad to locate a credit worthy purchaser for EJA. Hence, it is our recent decision to be cooperative with the railroad's financial officers, given their present efforts to work out this situation." The memo was turned up by investigators for the House Committee on Banking and Currency.

came in. On April 22, the railroad reported that it had lost $62 million in the three months ending March 31. The actual rail losses, however, amounted to almost $102 million over the first quarter. These losses were reduced by some $23 million in "other" income and by the sale of a coal company to Pennco for $16.9 million.

The figures had reached Bevan a few days earlier, at the beginning of a budget meeting. In the first quarter, operating revenues were $402,972,000, down $4 million from the previous year. Expenses were $504,572,000. The loss, before other income, was $101,600,000. "When the figures came in I was stunned," Bevan recalled. "Saunders took one look at my face and said, 'Is this going to affect the Pennsylvania Company offering?' I said, 'I don't know. I'll have to study it.'"

Gorman was also shaken by the first quarter report. He had never seen such an earnings statement at Western Electric. But Gorman was game, and at the budget meeting he vowed to make up $15 million of the overrun in the second quarter. It was a promise he would be unable to keep.

The stock market had been soft for some months. In April, it suddenly worsened. On April 27, the Dow Jones Industrial Average plunged to its lowest point since the assassination of John F. Kennedy on November 22, 1963. The market's most recent peak had been on December 3, 1968. Over the next sixteen months, culminating with the April 27 plunge, investors suffered paper losses of almost $200 billion.

The Pennsylvania Company was among those that suffered significantly. Its most attractive holding was Great Southwest Corporation, the real estate firm. At its zenith, the Great Southwest stock owned by Pennco was worth, on paper, about $980,000,000. Because of the slump in the market, and because of its own internal problems, the value of the Great Southwest stock had fallen to some $230,000,000. By the end of 1970, Great Southwest had written down its value to a mere $50 million.

Two days later, on April 29, a first draft of the prospectus for Pennco's $100 million issue came back from the printers. It was not an auspicious event. The market decline which caused the value of Pennco's holdings to shrink substantially raised doubts about the ability of the railroad's investment company to support the $300 million in revolving credit as well as the bond issue. The reduction in the market value of its stock meant that the collateral value of these holdings was also reduced. Without sufficient collateral, the bond issue could not be floated. Another damaging circumstance was the fact that the railroad had lost almost $102 million in the first quarter.

Even though the outlook for the bond issue appeared bleak, the prospectus was sent back to the printer to incorporate later financial data into an amended version. The amended version of the prospectus was to be ready on May 12. In the meantime, the pace of events began to pick up.

Stuart Saunders was not the railroad's financial expert. He was the "outside" man, the chief executive officer who was paid to deal with the ICC and Congress and the White House. Although he was not a financial expert, a loss of $102 million meant as much to him as it did to Bevan or Gorman. Shortly after the budget meeting, Saunders telephoned John Volpe in Washington. Volpe, a former Republican governor of Massachusetts, was secretary of the Department of Transportation in the Nixon Administration.

Volpe agreed to meet with Saunders and the railroad's vice president for finance, Jonathan O'Herron, on April 30, in his Washington office. This was the latest in a series of meetings between railroad and government officials. On February 24, Saunders, O'Herron and Gorman had met with the ICC to lobby for freight rate increases and to point up the problems Penn Central was having. Over the next two weeks, Saunders had met three times with Volpe to discuss the rate increase, passenger losses and the general condition of the railroad. Saunders also had arranged a fourth meeting, on March 13, between him, Gorman and O'Herron and Volpe, Undersecretary of Transportation James Beggs and Assistant Secretary Charles Baker. It was at this meeting that Saunders had complained that the snowstorms were costing the railroad millions of dollars. Volpe asked for precise figures, but Saunders could not supply them. Volpe told Saunders to come back when the figures were available.

On April 30, the figures were available, and the same group of men sat down in Volpe's office. Bevan was not present. "Bevan didn't come," Beggs remembered. "We never saw Bevan. Bevan never came down here." Saunders told Volpe the situation was "critical" and urged the nationalization of passenger service. O'Herron provided the details of the Penn Central's financial condition. At the end of the meeting, Volpe said he would meet with other members of the government to discuss possible solutions and he promised to put Saunders in touch with Secretary of the Treasury David Kennedy. But before Saunders met with Kennedy, he was faced with the first in a series of crises to hit Penn Central during the spring of 1970.

The board of directors, so long somnolent, was at last waking up. At least, part of the board was. Six directors, all members of the finance committee, had received telephone calls from bankers who were concerned, finally, about the railroad's performance. The most persistent of the callers was Walter Wriston, head of the First National City Bank of New York. First National City had put together the consortium that established Penn Central's $300 million revolving credit. The railroad was into Wriston's bank for $35 million under the revolving credit plan. The total railroad indebtedness to First National City was more than $300 million.

The finance committee members, at this point, did not need much encouragement from the bankers. They were already alarmed by the earnings statement, and they decided to take some tentative action. The six directors were:

— E. Clayton Gengras, sixty-one, board chairman of the Security–Connecticut Insurance Group. Gengras' firm owned 220,-900 shares of Penn Central. Gengras lived in West Hartford and had run unsuccessfully as a Republican for governor of Connecticut in 1966. While he lost that race, he did become friendly with another New England Republican — John Volpe. Gengras joined the Penn Central board in December 1969.

— Edward J. Hanley, sixty-seven, chairman of Allegheny Ludlum Steel Corporation. Hanley was from Pittsburgh and he was a close associate of Richard King Mellon, who then had only a month to live.

— Seymour H. Knox, seventy-one, from Buffalo. Knox was chairman of Marine Midland Banks, Inc., a Penn Central creditor.

— Franklin J. Lunding, sixty-four, a lawyer from Melrose Park,

Illinois. Lunding was Finance Chairman of Jewel Companies, Inc.

— Thomas Lee Perkins, sixty-four, from Rye, New York. Perkins was a lawyer, a director of Morgan Guaranty Trust Company, another railroad creditor, and chairman of the trustees of the Duke Endowment.

— John M. Seabrook, fifty-three, from Salem, New Jersey. Seabrook was a scion of the Seabrook Farms family, and chairman and chief executive officer of International Utilities, Inc. International Utilities owned 500,000 shares of Penn Central stock, making it the largest investor in the railroad.

Although these men were not close personally, adversity brought them together. Acting on their own, they scheduled a secret meeting of the finance committee. To this meeting, they summoned Saunders, Bevan and Gorman. The conference was held in the railroad's New York offices, where Alfred Perlman spent his time. Perlman, however, was not invited to the meeting, even though his future would be discussed.

The meeting got underway, as planned, on May 5. Seabrook, tall and urbanely handsome, acted as spokesman for the six outside (i.e., not part of management) directors. Seabrook began slowly. The $100 million debenture issue, Seabrook said, appeared to be in danger. The banks were unhappy, he said. Very unhappy. Seabrook said that Walter Wriston was demanding that changes be made in the railroad's management.

"Wriston was furious at his loan officers for getting his bank so deeply involved without knowing what a hole the Penn Central was in," one of the six directors told us. "He was mad at them, so he took it out on Bevan. He wanted Bevan removed. Wriston wasn't the only banker that was mad. They were all mad. Nobody believed the railroad's figures and they blamed Bevan. Bevan had lost his credibility with the banks, and so had the railroad."

Seabrook, as gently as he could, told Saunders, Bevan and Gorman that the management of Penn Central had to be "reorganized." Seabrook was an engineer, a graduate of Princeton (Phi Beta Kappa), and belonged to clubs in New York, London and Philadelphia. He had the easy grace of an aristocrat and took great pride in his skill as a coachman. He did not deliver the finance committee's verdict with triphammer blows; he sketched the outlines of the reorganization broadly, almost vaguely.

First, Seabrook said, Saunders' policy of calculated optimism had to be abandoned. Emphasizing nonrail earnings and minimizing rail losses hadn't worked. A deliberate policy of pessimism had to be adopted. "We want the railroad's losses emphasized," Seabrook said. "We want the government to know how desperate we are financially."

"We believed that although the reports of the losses would scare some investors and might dry up private sources of credit, it would hasten government help," one finance committee member told us. "We wanted to alert the government so that it would step in and help us and maybe even take over the railroad, or at least the unprofitable parts of it."

This was a bitter pill for Saunders to swallow. Just five months earlier, he had rejected similar advice from another railroad director, William L. Day, chairman of the First Pennsylvania Banking & Trust Company. On December 1, 1969, Day had written Saunders:

> The other evening I sat beside Harold Geneen of ITT and had an interesting talk with him about the outlook for conglomerates and his general philosophy regarding the course of American business. He said he thought that Penn Central was making a great mistake in not "exposing the railroad in all its nakedness to the public" so that the public and, in particular, legislators would realize what a poor performance, under present rate-making practices, the railroads are experiencing. It seems to me there is a great deal of merit in this suggestion. I realize that we must present the consolidated picture to Penn Central stockholders but we have been tending to cover up the poor results from the railroad rather than exposing them.
>
> The second broad suggestion I have is that some regular schedule be established for reviewing operations of our subsidiaries in detail. Major changes in relationships have occurred and are occurring at the level of the subsidiaries which I don't think the directors know of or comprehend. For instance, I have before me a release of October 27, 1969, which says that Richardson Homes Corp. has been acquired by a Great Southwest subsidiary, Macco Corporation, for $20 million. This is a major transaction and directors should have some knowledge

as to how this was financed and what our long term plans and commitments are in this new venture.

A week later, on December 8, Saunders replied to Day:

I recognize that there is merit in "exposing the railroad in all its nakedness to the public." On the other hand, if we go much further than other railroads go in this regard, our figures are not comparable. Moreover, I think our picture is bleak enough to achieve most of the results that we need from the point of view of legislation and regulatory agencies. If we go too far in this regard, we also get ourselves in greater trouble so far as our financing is concerned. I am, however, in complete accord with you that the board should have all the facts.

Seabrook's suggestion clearly would require Saunders to make a major adjustment in his business philosophy. But Saunders raised no objections. At the end of the meeting, the finance committee believed it had gotten across to Saunders, Bevan and Gorman what it wanted done: Saunders was to be relieved of his duties as chief executive officer and kicked upstairs. He would retain the title of chairman, but his role would be limited largely to presiding over board meetings. Bevan was to be retired. Perlman was to be retired. Gorman would become chief executive officer and would try to recruit a railroad man to run the railroad.

Gengras told us the finance committee had made its intentions perfectly clear at the May 5 meeting. He also said that Gorman expressed unhappiness at the situation he found himself in. "He had begun to realize what the story was and he wanted to be on the record that he didn't approve of the way things were going," Gengras said. "When they brought him in, Gorman was under the impression that his pension was fully funded and there was no question about it. He found out later this was a mistake. He was angry with Saunders. Seabrook did a lot of talking. It was properly expressed that Bevan had served his purpose. Saunders had had it."

Another director told us Perlman was discussed only briefly. "It had been so long since Perlman had done anything that we just didn't think about him much," he said.

It soon became obvious that Bevan and Saunders had not gotten the message the finance committee believed it had delivered. As soon as the meeting ended, the two men went right back to work trying to bail out the railroad.

For Bevan, it was an unsettling experience to encounter difficulty in his dealings with the banks. He was to spend much of the next month in New York, trying to tap the money markets, but the first quarter loss had cast him in the unfamiliar role of supplicant. It did not occur to Bevan to stop trying, because he did not believe the finance committee had indicated any desire to have him retire. His only recollection of the meeting, he said later, was that the committee let it be known that Saunders had to be removed.

Saunders, who divided the next month between New York and Washington, could not remember any discussion of his future at the May 5 meeting. As far as he was concerned, the committee's chief interest seemed to be the firing of Bevan. Perlman had not been invited to the meeting and nobody bothered to tell him about it afterward. The finance committee took no further direct action to implement its decision, and so Bevan and Saunders simply continued working.

The revised circular announcing Pennco's $100 million bond issue came out on May 12. Even though this, too, was a preliminary circular, the new information it contained doomed the offering. On top of the $102 million first-quarter rail loss and the stock market decline, the Penn Central was forced to admit publicly that it was caught in a run on its commercial paper. The run was not unlike a run on a bank where depositors clamor for their money, and the cause was the same: Lack of confidence. The bankers and the brokers no longer believed in the railroad. This damning information was contained in a single paragraph on page four of the fifty-three-page circular. "Between April 21, 1970 (the day preceding the announcement of the operating results of Railroad for the three months ended March 31, 1970) and May 8, 1970, maturities and payments of commercial paper exceeded sales of commercial paper by $41.3 million," the circular stated. There could be no doubt that investors who had money in the Penn Central wanted out. The loss of confidence was pushing the railroad to the brink.

An essential part of Bevan's plan to keep the railroad alive was to "roll" the $193.4 million that Penn Central had outstanding in 1970. That is, he had hoped to avoid redeeming the paper as it came due by reselling it to the original purchasers or to new lenders at the same, or higher, interest rates. This could have permitted the railroad to continue to pay interest charges instead of paying off the principal amount. The loss of confidence in the Penn Central made it clear that this plan would not work. Redemptions of the paper in just three weeks had cost the railroad more than $40 million in cash it could not spare. This left $152.1 million still to be paid off in 1970. By June 30, $75 million of this was coming due, and Bevan knew the purchasers would demand that the principal amounts be paid off. The Penn Central could no longer "roll" its commercial paper. A good part of the $59 million Swiss loan the railroad had obtained went to redeem the commercial paper that came due by May 8.

In the past, the banks had always been there when the railroad needed them, which was often. This was not surprising, for the Penn Central was one of the best bank customers in the world. The Penn Central was also able to maintain cordial relations with the banks for another very important reason. Bankers had always been well represented on the railroad's board, and the railroad's inside directors sat on the boards of some of these same banks. It was a cozy arrangement while it lasted, and it lasted for a very long time. The railroad had easy access to bank money, and the banks earned millions from the Penn Central in interest charges and fees.

"Preliminary investigation reveals heavy involvement by banking institutions in nearly every one of Penn Central's operations," the staff of the House Committee on Banking and Currency stated in a report dated June 27, 1970. "Every aspect of the issues involved in the collapse of the corporation appears to lead back to some banking institution."

Sixteen of the railroad's twenty-three directors sat on the boards of fourteen commercial banks. In all, these sixteen directors held a total of twenty-four directorships in the fourteen banks. As of December 31, 1969, the railroad was indebted to at least eight of the fourteen banks. The total amount of this indebtedness was

$262,920,063. In addition, seven banks, including two that were represented on the Penn Central's board, held 12.9 percent of the outstanding stock of the railroad through various nominees. The railroad debt held by these seven banks amounted, at the end of 1969, to $534,660,867.

Reviewing what it described as the "massive interlocks between the board of directors of the corporation and major commercial banks," the House Committee on Banking and Currency staff raised these questions: "Which interests were directors of Penn Central representing in negotiating such loan agreements when they were also connected with the banking institutions lending money to the railroad? Was it ever possible for these men to act objectively without violating their fiduciary responsibility to at least one of the several parties they were supposed to be representing?"

On May 12, 1970, these were the interlocks between railroad directors and major banks, including the railroad's indebtedness to some of these banks:

Stuart Saunders, chairman of the board
— Chase Manhattan Bank & Trust Co. ($7,832,500)
— First Pennsylvania Banking & Trust Co. ($18,004,766)
— First National Exchange Bank of Virginia
— Philadelphia Saving Fund Society
David Bevan, finance chairman
— Provident National Bank ($57,074,895)
Paul Gorman, president
— Bankers Trust Co. ($26,063,106)
John T. Dorrance, Jr., chairman of Campbell Soup Co.
— Morgan Guaranty Trust Co. ($90,972,957)
Thomas L. Perkins, counsel, Perkins, Daniels & McCormack
— Morgan Guaranty Trust Co.
Alfred E. Perlman, Penn Central vice chairman
— Marine Midland Grace Trust Co. ($1,083,651)
Louis W. Cabot, chairman, Cabot Corp.
— New England Merchants National Bank
— Suffolk Franklin Savings Bank
Otto N. Frenzel, chairman, Merchants National Bank & Trust
— Merchants National Bank & Trust Co., Indianapolis

Walter A. Marting, president, Hanna Mining Co.
— Bankers Trust Co.
— National City Bank of Cleveland
R. Stewart Rauch, Jr., president, Phila. Saving Fund Society
— Philadelphia Saving Fund Society
— Girard Trust Bank ($49,408,188)
John M. Seabrook, chairman, International Utilities Corp.
— Provident National Bank
William L. Day, chairman, First Pennsylvania Banking & Trust Co.
— First Pennsylvania Banking & Trust Co.
— Philadelphia Saving Fund Society
R. George Rincliffe, chairman, Philadelphia Electric Co.
— Philadelphia National Bank ($12,480,000)
— Philadelphia Saving Fund Society
Gaylord P. Harnwell, president, University of Pennsylvania
— First Pennsylvania Banking & Trust Co.
Seymour H. Knox, chairman, Marine Midland Grace Trust Co.
— Marine Midland Grace Trust Co.
Robert S. Odell, president, Allied Properties
— Wells Fargo Bank

The directors who did not sit on the board of any financial institution were E. Clayton Gengras, chairman of the Security Insurance Group; Edward J. Hanley, chairman of Allegheny Ludlum Steel Corp.; Franklin J. Lunding, finance chairman of Jewel Companies, Inc.; R. Walter Graham, Jr., a manager of personal investments from Baltimore; Carlos J. Routh, vice chairman of the Pittston Co.; Daniel E. Taylor, a West Palm Beach investment counselor, and Fred M. Kirby, chairman of the Alleghany Corp.

Despite the close ties between the railroad and the banks, Bevan could make almost no progress in raising new money in May 1970. It was not that the banks did not want to help the Penn Central; they did, after all, have hundreds of millions of dollars tied up in the railroad. The last thing they wanted was for the railroad to go under, dragging with it their considerable investment. But the railroad's financial condition had reached such a perilous state that to advance it even more money would have been reckless. The banks made it clear to Bevan that the only way the railroad would receive more money from them was if the banks were given some sort of ironclad guarantee that the money would be repaid.

Providing this guarantee was largely the project of Stuart Saunders. On May 9, Saunders went to the annual meeting of the Business Council in Hot Springs. John Volpe was there. So was David Kennedy, Secretary of the Treasury. Volpe set up a meeting between Saunders and Kennedy, and Saunders, for the first time, asked Kennedy for some form of emergency government assistance. The nature of this assistance was not fully developed at the Hot Springs meeting, but Kennedy was put on notice that unless some kind of minor miracle occurred to rescue the railroad, Saunders would be back. Saunders subsequently had a few brief meetings with Volpe and Kennedy, but the two Cabinet members turned over the task of helping out the Penn Central to their chief assistants, Undersecretary of Transportation James Beggs and Undersecretary of the Treasury Paul A. Volcker. Kennedy, it should be noted, was president of Continental Illinois Bank & Trust Company before joining the Cabinet. The Penn Central, at this time, owed Continental Illinois $15 million.

"Sometime in the middle of May Saunders asked for another meeting," Beggs recalled. "This was after he had met with Kennedy. This was after he had gone out and gotten into trouble with the debenture issue, but before it was withdrawn. He brought his new financial man, O'Herron, with him.

"They presented a projection for the year that looked pretty dismal. There would be a negative cash position. We looked at it and Volpe turned to Saunders and said, 'Get together with Beggs and see what can be done.'

"Saunders said the only possibility was a government loan guarantee. He said he had no confidence that he could get the money out of the private sector, he had no confidence in the debenture issue. I asked him how much they needed and he threw out a figure of $50 million. He thought that would get them through."

Beggs said he and Charles Baker, Assistant Secretary of Transportation, started going through the railroad's financial records. "Baker and I dug into it and it was pretty obvious we were not talking about $50 million but about maybe $200 million," he said.

"We insisted that O'Herron supply us with better figures. We told O'Herron we wanted a projection at least through 1971, solid, and a five-year projection. He told us they didn't even have one for 1971. 'The railroad doesn't make its projections until November,' he said.

"It was obvious that the numbers for 1970 were no good. I said, 'Jim Beggs ain't gonna help you until you get me those figures. You're talking $200 million now, more in 1971, and it could go on for years.' I smelled a mouse and I was getting concerned. The railroad lawyer was there and he told O'Herron what I was asking for was reasonable. O'Herron reluctantly agreed to get the figures, but he got no assurances from us. He admitted that we were talking more like $200 million."

While the negotiations were going on, the railroad continued to lose hundreds of thousands of dollars a day. Based on the railroad's figures, the loss for the second quarter, after the inclusion of "other" income, would amount to $41 million. By the end of 1970, Penn Central had lost an incredible $431 million, the most disastrous year in American railroad history.

The bills did not stop coming in just because the Penn Central was having difficulty. But the railroad could no longer guarantee that it would pay its bills. On an average day, the railroad consumed an enormous amount of power — power charges per day from only three companies[3] totaled $50,000 — but Penn Central, in May, was unable to pay its electric bill.

The railroad was always cash poor. Considering its serious cash position, Beggs found the Penn Central amazingly lenient in its handling of accounts receivable. "The ICC requires that all railroad invoices be paid by shippers within seven working days," Beggs said. "We went over their books and found they had twenty-eight days of receivables, four times what they should have. Based on a year's revenues, this amounts to $150 million in cash owed to them that they were letting sit idle at one time. They weren't billing

---

[3] Consolidated Edison of New York and the Philadelphia Electric Company billed the railroad about $20,000 each for an average day. The Pennsylvania Power and Light Company's average daily bill was about $10,000.

properly. They weren't settling shippers' claims, so the shippers just weren't paying their bills."

The average investor and the general public were still unaware of the Penn Central's dangerous position. But the men who dealt on Wall Street were beginning to suspect what Beggs was learning first hand: The railroad was on the edge of disaster. Their suspicions were confirmed when the revised prospectus for the $100 million bond issue, which clearly showed the $102 million first quarter loss and the run on the commercial paper, came back from the printer on May 12.

Howard Butcher III, the sixty-eight-year-old senior partner in the Philadelphia stock brokerage firm of Butcher & Sherrerd, had had a lifelong romance with the railroad. Butcher's great-grandfather, Washington Butcher, had been one of the first directors of the Pennsylvania Railroad. For many years, Howard Butcher had been the largest individual holder of railroad stock. Except on rare occasions, his advice to his clients and friends was consistent: Buy Penn Central. And he took his own advice. He and his family owned, at one time, about 200,000 shares. International Utilities Corporation, which Butcher served as board chairman, owned 500,000 shares. International Utilities held onto these shares after Butcher was succeeded as chairman by John Seabrook, who was also a railroad director.

One of Butcher's clients, whom he served as a labor of love, was the University of Pennsylvania. Butcher was a Penn trustee and was chairman of the university's investment committee. His firm also acted as one of Penn's investment brokers. Under Butcher's guidance, Penn had acquired 94,714 shares of railroad stock, which made it the second largest holding in the university's portfolio.[4]

Butcher was a railroad director for six years, until he resigned on September 24, 1968, after a Penn Central stockholder filed suit alleging that Butcher had acted on "inside information" in selling

---

[4] During much of this time, Penn's president was Gaylord Harnwell, who also sat on the railroad's board. After the collapse, Harnwell became chairman of Penn Central Company, the holding company, for a short period of time.

some of his railroad holdings. At the time, the broker said he was resigning because his continued presence on the board "could be misconstrued." Butcher and his associates later resigned from the boards of all other publicly held companies on which they served in order to avoid, Butcher explained, "potential conflict of interest which might be embarrassing to any broker." Nevertheless, he retained his affection for the railroad and, in the early part of 1970, was still trumpeting the virtues of Penn Central stock.

In mid-May 1970, Butcher's long affair with the railroad came to an abrupt, and costly, end. Butcher later told the Philadelphia *Bulletin*'s economic columnist, J. A. Livingston, that the romance began to die when he picked up the revised prospectus on Friday, May 15, and took it home with him to study over the weekend. By Monday morning, he told Livingston, he had decided to get out.

There is some evidence that Butcher's ardor actually cooled a few days earlier. On May 13, a report prepared by Butcher's research department advised selling Penn Central. But, in any event, he was in the vanguard of the wildest selling spree in the history of the railroad. From March 30 through April 3, Butcher & Sherrerd sold only 21,100 shares of Penn Central. During the week of May 11 through May 15, the firm's sales shot up to 175,000 shares, and the following week, the total sold reached 202,900.

Before the month of May ended, Butcher & Sherrerd had sold off a grand total of 484,566 shares of Penn Central. Of these, 86,000 were owned by Butcher and his family and his firm. Butcher & Sherrerd clients owned 303,852. The single largest owner was Penn, with 94,714 shares sold. Butcher and his wife, Elizabeth, and the Butcher & Sherrerd firm, received an average of $16.57 per share sold. Penn received an average of $14.10 a share, or $2.47 less per share than Butcher sold for. Butcher determined his loss, and the firm's, to be $883,313. Penn's loss amounted to $3,029,807.

Butcher did not have the Penn Central market to himself. Before long, railroad stockholders were clamoring to sell. Turnover in Penn Central stock increased by an amazing 300 percent. From April 1 to June 26, stockholders sold off 6,727,000 shares, more than 27 percent of all outstanding Penn Central stock. Many of those shares went for less than $10, a far cry from the $86.50 a share price that prevailed less than two years earlier. The following table illustrates the selling pattern of some brokers:[5]

Date	Butcher & Sherrerd	Salomon Bros.	Goldman Sachs	Shields & Co.
Mar. 30–Apr. 3	21,100	none	none	200
May 11–15	175,000	63,900	4,900	200
May 18–22	202,900	12,600	62,100	5,200
May 25–29	6,500	1,600	153,600	169,900

As the selling neared tidal-wave proportions, the Penn Central was struck by another blow. In mid-May, Standard and Poor's, a leading financial rating service, decided that Pennco bonds should be moved down a notch in grade. This downgrading removed Pennco bonds from the category described as acceptable for institutional investors and put them in the category defined as speculative. Even if the bonds could be sold, interest payments as a result of the downgrading would be forced upward by as much as $10 million over the twenty-five-year life of the issue. The practical effect of the rating change was to kill all hopes for the bond issue.

David Bevan met with representatives of First National City Bank and Chemical Bank in New York on May 21 to convey this information to them. He told them the bond issue was dead. It was after Bevan's meeting with executives from the banks that an additional wave of selling of Penn Central stock swept Wall Street. This time the sellers were the trust departments of several large banks, including Chase Manhattan, which numbered Stuart Saunders among its directors. The coincidence in timing led Rep. Wright Patman to charge, in March 1971, that the banks had benefited from "inside" information not available to the public.

The railroad's finance committee met in Philadelphia on May 27 to formally bury the proposed bond issue. The full board later that day approved the committee's recommendation that the issue be withdrawn. Bevan described in detail the impact of the run on Penn Central's commercial paper and informed the board that the final $50 million available under the $300 million revolving credit

---

[5] Source: Special Subcommittee on Investigations of the House Committee on Interstate and Foreign Commerce.

plan had been drawn down and was being used to pay off the paper. The amount outstanding had been reduced to $110 million. Before the board meeting ended, the directors agreed that government guaranteed loans were now the Penn Central's only hope. The board granted Bevan authority to enter into such loan arrangements, if the government agreed to provide the guarantees.

On the following day, May 28, the railroad announced its decision to withdraw the bond issue. The announcement triggered the final widespread sale of stock by the public, for the withdrawal signaled to even an unsophisticated investor that the Penn Central was in deep, perhaps fatal, trouble. A rush of trading on the last two days of the week boosted the total sales for that week to 751,700 shares, and the price of the stock tumbled down close to $10.

Another event that occurred that same day was not publicized by the railroad. This was the resignation of one of its directors, Louis W. Cabot, chairman of the Cabot Corporation. Penn Central did issue a news release later in June that Cabot had resigned, but it never disclosed Cabot's reasons. In a letter to Saunders dated May 28, Cabot assigned one reason: "Another conflict of interest is my position as chairman of a major shipper of Carbon black and other products on the nation's railroads, *where it is my obligation to negotiate for lower, not higher, freight rates* [emphasis added]."

Cabot had only been on the board since 1969, but his letter raised an interesting point. Could a shipper fulfill his obligations as a railroad director when the shipper's primary responsibility was at times in conflict with the railroad's best interests, as in the case of higher versus lower freight rates? It was a question that should have been answered long before, but wasn't. The Penn Central board contained several important shippers, but apparently the question of conflict-of-interest had never been explored. Besides Cabot, other shippers who served as railroad directors were John Dorrance, chairman of Campbell Soup Company; Edward J. Hanley, chairman of Allegheny Ludlum Steel Company; Franklin J. Lunding, chairman of the executive committee of Jewel Companies, Inc.; Walter Marting, president of Hanna Mining Company, and R. G. Rincliffe, chairman of the Philadelphia Electric

Company. Eventually, all of them resigned. But, so far as is known, none cited a potential conflict arising out of their roles as shippers.

The trains went on a holiday schedule over the Memorial Day weekend, and many railroad employees were given time off to relax with their families. For the men at the top of the Penn Central, especially Saunders and Bevan, the weekend was agony. On Monday morning, June 1, the desperate race had to be resumed. Bevan had to talk to the bankers. Saunders had to persuade the government.

One of Bevan's toughest tasks was to restore the Penn Central's usually good relations with First National City Bank of New York, the railroad's largest creditor. The deterioration in this relationship was particularly distressing to Bevan. He had been friendly with J. Stillman Rockefeller when Rockefeller was president and then chairman of First National City. When George Moore succeeded Rockefeller, he and Bevan became warm friends. But Bevan was not friendly with Walter Wriston, who was president of First National City in June 1970.

"I made a date with First National City and took O'Herron and Hill [Penn Central vice president and comptroller Charles Hill] with me," Bevan recalled. "I assumed they would have top representation there. They always did. I reviewed the budget with them for almost an entire day, but the vice president for transportation didn't come. He was too busy. I arranged a second meeting and the same lowly guy was there. The vice president for transportation didn't show up. These were not the guys I was used to dealing with. I dealt with George Moore and Stillman Rockefeller."

While Bevan was having difficulty getting in to see the top officers of Walter Wriston's bank, Walter Wriston was in touch with other members of the railroad. On Tuesday, June 2, Wriston contacted Paul Gorman and told the railroad president he wanted to see him and Stuart Saunders in First National City's offices. A meeting was arranged for 10 A.M. Friday, June 5. Bevan was not invited.

Bevan succeeded in seeing Wriston on Wednesday, June 3. He was accompanied by Randolph Guthrie, President Nixon's former law partner. The railroad had quietly retained Guthrie to help it through its difficulties. Bevan remembered having a "cordial conversation" with the banker. At Bevan's request, Wriston arranged for some ninety bank officers from most of the banks involved in the $300 million revolving fund to meet with Bevan on June 4. Bevan outlined the railroad's position to this group, explaining that Penn Central was hoping to receive government assistance and doing his best to calm the bankers' fears of losing the money they had advanced to the railroad.

While Bevan was talking with Wriston, some of the most powerful men in Washington were gathering in the White House to discuss the Penn Central. They included Attorney General John Mitchell, Federal Reserve Board chairman Arthur Burns, Secretary of the Treasury David Kennedy, Secretary of Commerce Maurice Stans, chairman of the Counsel of Economic Advisers Paul McCracken and Budget Bureau director Robert P. Mayo. Most of those present were concerned about the possible effect on the rest of the economy if the Penn Central failed. At that point, most felt that the government should provide assistance if it became necessary, but no definite plan of action was decided upon.

By Friday June 5, the situation at the railroad was rapidly building toward a climax. Just how rapidly, and the exact nature of the climax, were still unknown to Saunders and Bevan. Perlman had long ago been removed from all activity and was no longer considered a real part of the Penn Central operation.

For the first time since they had joined the railroad, Saunders and Bevan found themselves almost totally at the mercy of strong outside forces. These external forces were influencing the railroad's policies and Saunders and Bevan were powerless to do anything about it. Indeed, they were not always sure just who these external forces were. They did not know which directors were being contacted behind their backs. They did not know to whom the government was talking, nor what it was saying.

One of those external forces was Walter Wriston, and he had reached the end of his patience with the railroad. Wriston was one of those to whom the government had been talking, and both the government and Wriston had reached the same conclusion: There had to be a change in management.

When Saunders and Gorman walked into his office, Wriston was prepared. He told the two men point blank that Bevan had to go before his bank would consider making further loans to the railroad, even *with* government guarantees. Wriston said the Department of Transportation was in agreement with this position.

"We decided that it was absolutely necessary that there be a change in management," Undersecretary of Transportation James Beggs remarked. "We had talked to the money people in New York, mostly to the First National City Bank, the lead bank, and they insisted that management had to be changed. A number of people were after Bevan. They felt Bevan was the biggest problem in management. We thought Bevan had to go."

June 5 was not a good day for Bevan. He was again in New York, working on the bankers, trying to line up support for $200 million in loans backed by government guarantees. What really disturbed him, however, was that his good friend Richard King Mellon was being buried that day. Mellon had been known as "Mr. Railroad," and with good reason. He became a director of the Pennsylvania Railroad in 1934, at the age of thirty-six. The vacant seat he filled had been, for the previous eight years, the seat of his father, Richard B. Mellon. Mellons had sat on the Pennsylvania board since 1856, and Richard King Mellon, who was richer than Rockefeller, carried on that tradition until he retired thirty-five years after becoming a railroad director.

Mellon had liked Bevan. Saunders and Perlman did not receive invitations to Mellon's 18,000-acre estate in Ligonier, outside Pittsburgh; but Bevan did. Mellon liked Bevan so much that he had once asked him to take over as head of the Mellon Bank. Bevan refused, but when he later reviewed what happened to the Penn Central, he said ruefully: "Maybe I should have taken it."

Now Mellon was dead; the long career of "Mr. Railroad" was ended. But none of his friends on the railroad, including his special friend, David Bevan, could make it to the East Liberty Presbyterian Church, outside Pittsburgh, for the funeral. They were too busy trying to prevent the funeral of the Penn Central from taking place.

After the meeting with Wriston, Gorman and Saunders separated. Saunders had decided to call a special meeting of the board on Monday, June 8, to do what must be done — fire Bevan. Gorman bumped into Bevan after both men had had lunch, although they had not dined together. Gorman engaged Bevan in a brief conversation, but he failed to mention the meeting with Wriston. Bevan was becoming suspicious.

Later that day Saunders and Bevan had what was for Bevan a cryptic conversation on the telephone. Saunders was the one who placed the call.

"Saunders called me and said he wanted to set up a board meeting for Monday," Bevan recalled. "I said, 'What for? There are no new developments.' He said he just felt we ought to have a board meeting."

Saunders confirmed that the primary purpose of the meeting with Wriston was Wriston's desire to have Bevan ousted. Later that evening, Saunders made a second call to Bevan. "Walter Wriston was very critical of you," Saunders told Bevan. "I want to warn you about this. I won't go any further."

At that time, Saunders was unaware that the same strong external forces were still at work, and they were working against him.

After Saunders and Gorman met with Wriston, Saunders thought that was the end of it. It was not. Walter Wriston, and other bankers, could also use the telephone. One of them picked his up and called Gorman. Not only must Bevan go, this banker told Gorman, Saunders had to go, too. There had to be a complete housecleaning. And the Department of Transportation also had agreed to this. Saunders did not know who called Gorman. Bevan had no doubt that the call was made by Wriston.

"Saunders just didn't know what was going on," said the Transportation Department's Beggs. "He was the company's outside man and he had a way of delegating authority that worked to his disadvantage. He relied on others. Saunders had to go for appearance's sake.

"We felt there had to be a complete turnover in management. It had to be shaken up from top to bottom. They had to go out and hire a guy to run the railroad. There was a meeting in New York and the bankers let them have it straight. The management had to be changed. We talked to [E. Clayton] Gengras and [William L.] Day [railroad directors], but mostly we dealt through the banks."

While Saunders and Gorman were meeting with Wriston on June 5, Sen. Hugh Scott was concluding his address to the graduating class of Jefferson Medical College in Philadelphia. Scott was the Republican leader in the Senate and one of the most powerful men in Pennsylvania. He had known Richard King Mellon as a friend and as a premier contributor to the Republican Party. Scott would not miss Mellon's funeral.

At Philadelphia's International Airport, Scott was met by Thomas Bayard McCabe, the seventy-seven-year-old chairman of the Scott Paper Company, and Thomas Sovereign Gates, Jr., chairman of the executive committee of Morgan Guaranty Trust Company. McCabe had served for three years as chairman of the Federal Reserve Board, from 1948 to 1951. He had been appointed by Harry S Truman even though he was a prominent Republican and was to become Pennsylvania's Republican National Committeeman, Gates had been Secretary of the Navy and Secretary of Defense in the Eisenhower Administrations.

The three men went directly to McCabe's private hangar to board an eight-seat jet, owned by Scott Paper, for the trip to Pittsburgh and Mellon's funeral. At the hangar, Scott found a message waiting for him. Secretary of Transportation John Volpe was trying to reach him. The matter was "urgent."

Volpe was in a White House jet flying from San Francisco to Seattle when Scott's call was patched to him by the U.S. Signal Corps through the White House communications system. Volpe's flat, Yankee voice boomed over the ground-to-air connection as he told Scott the reason for his call. The Penn Central, he told Scott, was on the verge of a collapse. The company was having trouble paying its bills. The railroad could be saved, Volpe said, but he needed Scott's help. He wanted Scott to set up a meeting for him with leaders from both parties in Congress. Volpe wanted the meeting held on June 9, the day after the special Penn Central board meeting at which changes in management were to be proposed. Volpe was not going to put himself in the position of asking Congress to bail out the railroad until he was certain the railroad was willing to change its management.

Scott agreed to arrange the meeting. He walked out to board McCabe's plane with a troubled look on his face. He was running for reelection and the Penn Central was a major industry in his state. Not only were there thousands of railroad workers, and their families, to worry about; there were thousands more whose jobs depended on the railroad, dockworkers, warehousemen, factory hands. As the little jet taxied toward the runway, Scott began repeating his conversation with Volpe to McCabe and Gates.

The three men talked almost exclusively of the Penn Central and its troubles on the trip to Pittsburgh. The plane made one stop, at Harrisburg, to pick up Lieutenant Governor Ray Broderick. Broderick was the Republican candidate for governor of Pennsylvania, running against Democrat Milton Shapp, and he had been assigned to fill in for Governor Raymond P. Shafer at Mellon's funeral. Broderick was not familiar with the railroad's situation and he took almost no part in the conversation.

By the time McCabe's jet touched down at Pittsburgh, the three men found themselves in agreement: The railroad had been mismanaged. Stuart Saunders was the chief culprit. McCabe had no direct connection with the railroad, but he was friendly with several Penn Central directors and served on other boards with some of them. Gates was by far the most critical of Saunders and the railroad's management. Six feet two inches tall, handsome, and with the unflappable confidence born of old wealth and an impeccable Philadelphia family background, Gates knew all about the Penn Central.

Just the day before, a representative from Gates' Morgan Guaranty Trust Company had attended the meeting where David Bevan had outlined the financial condition of the railroad for the banks participating in the $300 million revolving credit plan. Morgan Guaranty had advanced the Penn Central $25 million through the plan. Thomas Lee Perkins, a railroad director, was also a director of Morgan Guaranty. Gates was not on the Penn Central board, but he was kept up to date on the railroad. He was also familiar with the operations of the railroad. His father, Thomas Sovereign Gates, Sr., who had been president of the University of Pennsylvania and a partner in J. P. Morgan, Morgan Guaranty's predecessor, served as a director of the Pennsylvania Railroad from 1930 to 1948.

The services for Mellon lasted less than thirty minutes. When Scott joined the other mourners filing out of East Liberty Presbyterian Church behind the body, he was accompanied by David Kennedy, Secretary of the Treasury. Scott, who was returning to Washington, accepted Kennedy's offer of a lift on a White House JetStar and canceled a seat he had held on a United Airlines flight.

On the trip to Washington, the conversation again dealt with the Penn Central. Kennedy, like Gates, was bitterly critical of Penn Central's management, particularly Saunders. There was another similarity between the positions of Gates and Kennedy. Kennedy's former bank, Continental Illinois Bank & Trust Company, was also a participant in the $300 million revolving fund. The railroad owed Continental Illinois $15 million.

Saunders knew he was being criticized in some circles, but he did not know that his criticism had reached into the highest councils of the government.

Since his friend Lyndon B. Johnson was no longer president, perhaps Saunders should have been prepared to encounter hostility from the government; but he was not. On June 5, he was concerned primarily with the meeting he was calling for Monday, June 8, the meeting at which Bevan would be fired. As it turned out, Saunders was not prepared for what happened at this meeting either.

It was June 8, 1970. The directors began arriving in midmorning. A short, somber Negro, clad in the dark cotton suiting favored for employees by the railroad hierarchy, acted as butler. He greeted the directors as they stepped off the elevator on the eighteenth floor of the Transportation Building in Philadelphia's Penn Center Plaza. The butler steered the directors to the hushed board room at the end of the hall, where the armchairs, each with a brass plate affixed to it bearing the name of the director who sat in it, were ranged around the huge polished table. The butler was unnecessary; it was a nice touch of gentility, but the directors knew where the board room was. What they did not know was precisely what they were going to do.

By 11 A.M., fourteen directors were in their seats. They were David Bevan, William L. Day, John Dorrance, Otto Frenzel, E. Clayton Gengras, Paul Gorman, R. Walter Graham, Edward J. Hanley, Seymour Knox, Franklin J. Lunding, Alfred Perlman, R. George Rincliffe, John M. Seabrook and Stuart Saunders.

Five men were absent. They were Gaylord P. Harnwell, Walter A. Marting, Thomas L. Perkins, R. Stewart Rauch and Daniel E. Taylor. Resignations had left six vacancies on the board.

Saunders opened the meeting with a general statement about the condition of the railroad and briefly referred to the efforts being made to raise money to keep the company afloat. He then asked Gorman to deliver a report on these efforts.

Gorman told the directors that the government appeared willing to provide loan guarantees of up to $200 million to cover the railroad's cash needs for the next four to six months. The Department of Transportation, Gorman said, also was supporting legislation to provide $750 million in long-term loans to assist railroads in financial trouble. About $300 million of this would be available to the Penn Central. The minutes of this meeting, transcribed by company secretary Bayard Roberts, describe what happened next:

The president [Gorman] stated further that interested banks have expressed a willingness to consider making loans or advances on the basis described [with government guarantees], but have made it clear that they will insist upon three conditions among others:

(*1*) A reorganization of top management acceptable to the banks must first be accomplished.

(*2*) All cash provided through new loans must be restricted to the essential needs of this company and not be channelled into subsidiary companies.

(*3*) The banks insist on the right to dispose of part or all of the collateral in case of a default in any payment due under the loan agreement.

Perlman suddenly became alert. If he hadn't known what was planned, the reference to a "reorganization of top management" must have tipped him off that the skids were being greased for somebody. He did not like the whole business.

Bevan spoke briefly, advising the board that the papers necessary for new loans were prepared and the last dollar of the $300 million in revolving credit had been drawn down. Then Saunders invited into the room Randolph H. Guthrie, of the New York law firm of Mudge, Rose, Guthrie & Alexander.

After he lost the election for governor of California in 1962, Richard M. Nixon moved to New York and began practicing law. The firm he joined was Mudge, Rose, Guthrie & Alexander. In his book, *The Resurrection of Richard M. Nixon,* Jules Witcover describes Randolph Guthrie as the man Richard Nixon felt closest to when he first joined the firm. Another partner in Mudge, Rose, Guthrie & Alexander was John N. Mitchell, who would become Attorney General of the United States after Richard Nixon was elected president in 1968.

Guthrie's firm, like literally hundreds of others, had represented the railroad on various matters over the years. But Guthrie had never before been invited into the board room. On June 8, Saunders escorted Guthrie across the threshold and introduced him to the board as "a member of the Nixon firm." Guthrie, Saunders told his fellow directors, was "close to the White House." He had been retained to represent the Penn Central "on legal aspects of its proposed financing" through government-guaranteed loans. According to the minutes of the meeting, this was the extent of Guthrie's participation on June 8: "Mr. Guthrie reviewed very briefly the financial program which had been described by the president [Gorman]; expressed the view that a number of government officials were astonished to learn how serious is the condition of the railroad industry as a whole, and this company in particular; and stated that the government appears to be anxious to attempt a solution of the problem of such an important segment of industry."

Guthrie's relationship with the railroad ended several weeks later. John Volpe was particularly distressed when he learned the railroad had retained Nixon's old friend to represent it in negotiating terms of the government-guaranteed loans. It looked to him like a blatant political power play that would backfire on both him and President Nixon, and he demanded that the Penn Central sever its ties to Guthrie.

"Guthrie was wholly in the background," Saunders said later. "So far as I know, he's never been paid for anything. We never made any agreement to pay him anything. I never did. Never even discussed any figure."

When Guthrie had finished his presentation, Saunders told the board that he, Bevan, Gorman and Perlman would leave the room to permit the directors to freely discuss the "reorganization of top management." This was another move that Perlman did not like. The minutes noted: "Before leaving, the chairman of the board and chairman of the finance committee both offered their complete cooperation in any decision which the board might take affecting their relationship to the company."

Perlman's contract had almost five months to go, but he did not approve of the direction in which this meeting was moving. He did not know what was going to happen, and he would not pledge his cooperation in advance. Gorman did not need to make such a pledge; he knew his position was safe.

The four men left the room, followed by Bayard Roberts, the secretary. It was up to the ten outside directors. Franklin J. Lunding was elected by the board to preside over the meeting.

Lunding waited until the door had closed behind the management. Then, he went around the table soliciting the views of the directors.

John Seabrook, smoothly and confidently, outlined the plan he believed he had developed at the secret meeting that was held on May 5. Under this plan, Bevan and Perlman would be fired, Saunders would retain the title of chairman but would be stripped of all executive duties, which would go to Gorman, who would remain as president and try to recruit a railroad man to run the railroad.

When Seabrook mentioned that Saunders would have to lose all of his powers, one director told us, there was a clearly audible, "Oh, dear, oh dear," from William L. Day, chairman of the First Pennsylvania Banking & Trust Company, Philadelphia's largest bank. Saunders was a director of First Pennsylvania. "Mr. Day spent a lot of time wringing his hands," one director recalled.

Nevertheless, Seabrook pressed on. This appeared to be the best plan, he said. He was confident Walter Wriston, and the banks, would accept it.

There was some disagreement over the plan. Various directors tried to put in good words for either Saunders or Bevan. These men were friends. They moved in the same circles, belonged to the same clubs, visited each other's homes. Nobody mentioned Perlman. He did not move in the same circles, did not belong to the same clubs. Finally, when it appeared that opposition to the plan had been overcome, E. Clayton Gengras spoke up.

Gengras, the New England insurance man, had attended the May 5 meeting and had approved of the plan outlined by Seabrook. Since that time, he had been asking questions and meeting with important people like his fellow New Englander, John Volpe, and other officials of the Department of Transportation.

Gengras was not tall like Seabrook, or aloof like some of the other directors. He was an aggressive, short, sandy-haired man who chain-smoked cigarettes and drank black coffee. He was a self-made millionaire who had built an auto agency in Hartford into an empire, and ended up with hospital wings named after him. "Saunders has to go," Gengras told the startled members of the board. There was immediate resistance to this pronouncement. Why make a messy situation even messier? Saunders would be kicked upstairs under the Seabrook plan, out of everybody's way. There was no need to fire him outright.

Gengras refused to budge. He maintained that Saunders was a liability to the railroad and he had to be removed, along with the others. The board had reached an impasse. To help resolve it, Lunding sent for Paul Gorman. When he arrived, Gorman was briefed on the situation. The directors asked for his opinion. In effect, they asked him to decide Saunders' fate, and Gorman did not shrink from the task.

Saunders had to be fired, Gorman said. The job could not be done if Saunders were permitted to remain. It would not be "practical" to have Saunders occupy an office on the eighteenth floor even though he was supposedly stripped of his powers. With the title of chairman still in his possession, Saunders could not be so easily unfrocked. Saunders was identified with policies that had failed and resulted in the directors assembling under crisis conditions. Finally, Gorman said, the banks wanted Saunders out.

"The reason for the June 8 meeting was that Gorman got a

phone call and he never said from who but it was one of the larger banks in New York," Gengras later told us. "He said the application [for government-guaranteed loans] would never be approved as long as Saunders and Bevan had anything to do with it.

"We were told this was the situation. I know this was the situation. Gorman said he was told that unless he was made chief executive officer we would not get the money. The banks and the government wouldn't go for it. I was told that on good authority and so were three or four others. The word didn't come from Washington, it came through New York, from the banks.

"It's not true that I was in touch with Volpe. A couple of very cute directors wanted to dump that in my lap. I know what they're trying to do. I know that the Federal Reserve, the banks, the Department of Transportation, the Navy, Packard,[6] they were all involved. There was a combination of things. It was not a question of one guy getting a call from Volpe.

"I simply as a member of the board stated that from what we had been told we had no choice but to remove them. At that meeting in June there was nothing new that hadn't been said at the May meeting in New York.

"Bevan had lost his credibility. This came not from any member of our own board but from the outside. Hanley was willing to let Saunders go, but he tried to save Bevan."

After delivering his opinion, which came across like a command, Gorman left the board room again to permit the directors to settle the matter in privacy. There was no longer any question about what action the board would take.

"It was all over after Gorman spoke," another director told us. "Everybody in that room respected Gorman. There was hardly any discussion about the rest of it. Nobody even mentioned Perlman."

The vote was unanimous. Saunders, Bevan and Perlman were to be fired. Gorman, in addition to staying on as president, was to become chairman and executive officer. Bevan was to be replaced by his assistant, Jonathan O'Herron. Perlman's job would not be filled. The minutes recorded the action this way: "Resolved that, effective immediately, Messrs. Stuart T. Saunders, David C. Bevan

---

[6] Deputy Secretary of Defense David Packard.

and Alfred E. Perlman are relieved of their duties and offices as chairman of the board, chairman of the Finance Committee and vice chairman of the board, respectively."

It was done. All that remained now was the distasteful job of informing the three men. Lunding appointed three directors to handle this chore — Gengras, Seabrook and Edward J. Hanley.

"Saunders took it like a man," one of the directors told us. "He had good control of himself. I had never been fond of him but I was impressed with his performance under that kind of stress."

Bevan accepted his fate graciously, the director said, but there was still Perlman.

"We had a serious problem," he said. "We had done this and we wanted to get the news out. We had to get this on the Dow-Jones ticker as quickly as possible. We went to see Perlman, but he refused to cooperate.

"Perlman absolutely refused to resign. His attitude was, 'Fuck you, see my lawyers.' He refused to make a move."

Seabrook, Gengras and Hanley were concerned about the possible impact the board's action would have on the railroad's stock. With their vast holdings in the company, Seabrook and Gengras were particularly anxious to see how the news would be received, hoping the board's decisive action would arouse the interest of investors. On that day, the stock was selling for $13.25 a share. International Utilities, Seabrook's firm, was in the midst of taking a loss of $8 million on its Penn Central holdings.

The three men rode the elevator down to the tenth floor and entered the office of William A. Lashley, the railroad's vice president for public relations and advertising. They asked Lashley to draw up a statement. Lashley drafted one that stated Saunders, Bevan and Perlman were retiring as officers and resigning as directors. Seabrook, Gengras and Hanley, with Lashley in tow, then raced back to the eighteenth floor. They had Saunders' and Bevan's permission to handle the matter as they saw fit. But they still needed Perlman's approval.

Perlman was not on the eighteenth floor. Seething with anger, the ousted vice chairman had stormed out of the Transportation Building and had ordered his private car hitched to a midafternoon train to New York. He was now en route. It would be five o'clock before the railroad could release its statement, long after the stock market had closed. Impatiently, the three directors placed a call to the station master's office in the railroad's Penn Station in New York. The station master was ordered to meet Perlman's train and to bring him directly to a telephone.

After a wait of more than an hour, Perlman was on the line. Lashley attempted to read the statement to him, but Perlman's voice, loud and angry, could be heard bubbling out of the receiver by the directors. Lashley put Hanley on the telephone to calm Perlman. As Hanley understood it, Perlman objected to any statement that indicated he agreed with the board's action and was vacating his post voluntarily. Perlman had a valid contract running through November 30, 1970, and he was not going to take a chance on losing five months' salary, more than $70,000, just so the board could make it appear as though the ouster of the railroad's management was actually accomplished under harmonious circumstances. Lashley made some quick repairs to meet Perlman's objections and the statement was finally released:

PHILADELPHIA, June 8 — The board of directors of Penn Central Transportation Company announced today the election of Paul A. Gorman as chairman of the board, president and chief executive officer, effective immediately. Directors of Penn Central Company, the parent holding company, will take similar action.

Mr. Gorman, who became president of both companies last December 1, succeeds Stuart T. Saunders as chairman and chief executive officer. Mr. Saunders and David C. Bevan, chairman of the Finance Committee, are retiring as officers and resigning as directors of the holding company, the transportation company and all other affiliates.

Alfred E. Perlman was relieved of duties as vice chairman and will resign from the board upon expiration of his contract on November 30, 1970.

The announcement was made after a special board meeting in Philadelphia today.

Saunders later said he believed, at the start of the June 8 meeting, that he would retain his title as chairman. He said nobody ever told him why this arrangement never was made. "Well, I don't know because I wasn't there," Saunders said. "But I think they felt their chances of getting the government loan would be improved if they made a clean sweep, so to speak. I think that's what it was. Besides, I told the board and they knew this, that I wanted to retire. And I stated at the beginning of the meeting that I was certainly willing to do anything they wanted me to in that regard. And I wasn't in there more than ten minutes."

The "clean sweep" was made. The next step was up to the government.

On June 9, the day after the railroad's management was ousted, some of the most powerful men in Washington gathered in the offices of Senate Republican Leader Hugh Scott of Pennsylvania, on the second floor of the Capitol, to discuss what should be done to save the Penn Central. The leaders of both houses of Congress were there, and so were the ranking majority and minority members of the Senate and House committees concerned with transportation and finance. Representatives from the departments of defense, transportation, commerce and the treasury were also present. John Volpe ran the meeting.

Volpe said he had a plan to keep the railroad out of bankruptcy. It was in two stages and it needed the approval of Congress.

The first stage involved the granting of up to $200 million in loans guaranteed by the government for a short-term period. The guarantees would be made under the provisions of the Defense Production Act of 1950, which authorized the Defense Department to enter into such arrangements with firms it deemed vital to the nation's defense efforts. As justification for this, the Defense Department could point to the fact that the Penn Central was the exclusive supplier to twenty-six defense installations. In addition, the railroad moved $2 billion worth of Defense Department freight each year, for which it was paid about $100 million. Government lawyers had studied the Defense Production Act and had concluded that the department could grant guarantees (known as V loans) without the approval of Congress.

The second stage did require congressional action. Volpe proposed that Congress approve legislation giving the Department of Transportation authority to guarantee loans to ailing railroads of up to $750 million. The loans would be long-term, and guarantees would be provided pretty much at the discretion of the Transportation Department. As soon as this legislation was passed, Volpe said, the Defense Department would turn over liability for the $200 million in loan guarantees granted the Penn Central to the Transportation Department.

"There was a good deal of yelling and screaming," Undersecretary of Transportation James Beggs recalled. "But in general no one said they wouldn't support us. They all asked to see a draft of the bill first. No politician really commits himself until he sees the bill. We sent them a draft of the bill and then went ahead and drew up the V loan instrument. The Federal Reserve made its determination and the Treasury went through its monkey business of contacting the financial community."

There was some grumbling from Congressman Wright Patman, chairman of the House Committee on Banking and Currency, and Democratic Sen. Vance Hartke, who was in a tight race for reelection from Indiana, but on the whole Volpe's plan was fairly well received. Senator Scott and Sen. Warren Magnuson, a Democrat from Washington, agreed to cosponsor the legislation establishing the $750 million in loan guarantee authority for the Department of Transportation. Magnuson was chairman of the Senate Commerce Committee.

The meeting in Scott's office ended with a semisolid consensus that Volpe's package would be pursued. Some of the details of the meeting were announced to the press and the news that the government intended to bail out the railroad made headlines around the nation. The next day, the reaction began to set in.

While Gorman was meeting with 120 bank officers in New York, Congressman George Mahon, the Texas Democrat who was chairman of the House Appropriations Committee, announced that he would hold hearings beginning on June 11 on the scheme to save the railroad. Mahon had a strong interest in the budget of the Department of Defense and he was concerned by its agreement to act as guarantor of loans for a private corporation. Mahon's committee had approved defense expenditures for the fiscal year starting July 1, 1970, of some $74 billion, but it had not approved the spending of $200 million to help the Penn Central solve its problems.[7] The government's lawyers might have determined that the Pentagon could act as guarantor without congressional approval, but the government would still have to justify this action by testifying before Mahon's committee.

Even if the Pentagon were so foolhardy as to fly in the face of congressional opposition and act as guarantor for the short-term loans, the problem would not have been solved. Volpe, and Penn Central officials, had made it clear that the short-term loan guarantees were just the first step. To regain its health, the railroad would need up to $500 million in long-term loan guarantees. There was no question that new legislation had to be passed by Congress to provide authority for long-term loan guarantees. There was also no question, therefore, that Congress had to be satisfied every step of the way. Hence, Mahon had no difficulty getting officials of the departments of transportation and defense to testify on the short-term guarantees even though Congress theoretically had no jurisdiction over that area.

Beggs presented the case for the Transportation Department. He was a careful, articulate witness who knew his subject. He outlined the financial condition of the railroad for the committee members, then discussed Volpe's two-stage plan. He said that a consortium of seventy-seven banks, headed by First National City and Chemical Bank New York Trust, was willing to loan the railroad up to $200 million if the government agreed to act as guarantor. It was at this point that Mahon expressed the doubts he was beginning to feel about the whole proposal. "Mr. Secretary, from where I sit, it looks as if we are being asked, or will be asked, to bail out the big banks and the big railroads, and the reason or the excuse for this is that the country cannot afford to let bad business procedures lead to bankruptcy because the bankruptcies might lead to the economic ruination of the country," Mahon said.

Mahon's point was well taken. The Nixon Administration was greatly concerned about the effect on the nation generally of a

---

[7] The railroad was indeed having problems. Besides the $106 million in long-term debt, the $110 million still outstanding in commercial paper, the $300 million revolving fund, Penn Central was daily running up bills it couldn't pay. By this time, it owed 61 other railroads $80 million in interline charges.

Penn Central bankruptcy. In particular, it was worried about the commercial paper market, which had quadrupled since 1965. In June 1970, largely because of the unavailability of funds through ordinary bank channels, there was about $40 billion in commercial paper outstanding.

The Penn Central had $110 million in commercial paper coming due over the next three to five months. Without new loans, there was no way for it to meet these obligations. What would be the impact of a default of this magnitude?

"The commercial paper market is a market that, as you know, is totally based on confidence," Beggs told the committee. "It has no other basis. There is no security behind them. It is a matter of judgment as to what the effect of $110 million going into default would be. . . . However, it is the belief of most financial people we have contacted that defaulting on that much paper at this time would have a very adverse effect on that market and might, indeed, send a shockwave through that market that could react all the way through the economy.

"In addition to that, of course, you have to judge the danger and the impact of the sixth largest company in the United States and the largest railroad going into reorganization, going in effect into a bankruptcy situation. While this, again, is a matter of judgment, the feeling is that this would have a very serious effect."

Despite Beggs' persuasiveness, the committee was still skeptical. This skepticism was heightened with the appearance of Assistant Secretary of Defense for Installations and Logistics Barry J. Shillito. Shillito made it clear that Defense had agreed to act as guarantor only because it was an emergency situation. As soon as Congress approved the legislation setting up the $750 million in long-term guarantees, under the Transportation Department, the Defense Department would wash its hands of the matter, Shillito said. "We are planning on the legislation coming to the floor hopefully in the next few months," Shillito told the committee. "We are planning on Defense coming off this note as guarantor as quickly as possible."

Although the navy would act as the guarantor, Shillito said, neither the navy nor the Defense Department had any spare funds with which to pay the banks if the railroad defaulted under the

END OF THE LINE 291

government guarantees. If a default occurred, he said, money would have to be withdrawn from some other Defense program. But, he added, "We are not planning on having to pay this note."

"An endorser never does," replied Congressman Robert Sikes, a Florida Democrat.

"In your experience as an endorser and as a guarantor you mean you have the hopeful and optimistic view that the railroad will pay it out, or that Congress will pass a bill?" asked Jamie Whitten, a Democratic congressman from Mississippi.

"That is not my point," Shillito said. "My point is, sir, that based on the comments of the Congress, the leaders of the Congress involved in the legislation and putting the legislation through, allowing the Department of Transportation to become the guarantor, that as far as Defense is concerned this is a very interim thing on our part."

"I have been here twenty-nine years and a lot of laws folks thought would pass the first year I got here still haven't passed," Whitten told Shillito.

Whatever "the leaders of the Congress" may have said earlier, they were clearly beginning to have second thoughts about Volpe's plan to save the railroad from bankruptcy. Other committees, such as the Senate Commerce Committee and the House Committee on Interstate and Foreign Commerce, also scheduled hearings on the Penn Central. Sen. John Stennis, the Mississippi Democrat who headed the Senate Armed Services Committee, and Congressman L. Mendel Rivers, the (late) South Carolina Democrat in charge of the House Armed Services Committee, both let it be known that they opposed using Defense Department resources in this manner. No legislators were treated with more deference and respect by the Defense Department than Stennis and Rivers. The most ominous rumblings of all came from Wright Patman of Texas. He said he would call representatives of Defense and Transportation before his Committee on Banking and Currency to air the whole question. The hearings would begin on June 22.

But it was already obvious that Patman was opposed to guaranteeing loans for the railroad. In conversations with officials of the Nixon Administration, he charged that Defense Department short-term guarantees of up to $200 million would be an "unlawful" use of the Defense Production Act. The Defense Production Act, he said, was designed to help small and medium-sized contractors perform specific contracts for the Defense Department. More than anything else, Patman said, he was opposed to the government's using taxpayers' money to bail out bankers and private investors who sought to make money in the free enterprise system and now wanted to be made whole because they lost their gamble.

"At the start, our feeling was that the leadership was not negative," Beggs recalled. "Maggy [Senator Magnuson] was for it. Then we went back one more time. We were getting some storm signals from committee staff members. We were definitely getting the impression that this was becoming a big political issue. The President had vetoed the hospital bill and now he was getting set to bail out a big railroad. Some people in Congress like to compare this sort of thing. Vance Hartke was obviously out to make a political issue of it. He was involved in a close race for reelection. Then Magnuson said he could not support the bill. They all started to back away from it."

The political implications of the plan to rescue the railroad were there for all to see, and nobody had better political eyesight than the man in the White House. President Nixon was trapped in the middle of a very messy situation. How could he, the candidate of big business, sit back and permit the most important railroad in the nation to go broke?

On the other hand, 1970 was an election year. Nixon was determined to have the Republicans win control of the Senate, thus enabling him to have an easier time winning confirmation for his appointees and removing from the leadership of committees Democratic senators — J. William Fulbright of Arkansas was a prime example — who continually criticized him. The Penn Central could destroy the president's hopes of his party's winning the Senate. There were simply too many ties between the railroad and the Nixon Administration. Could he risk throwing in government resources to save the Penn Central when there were apparently glaring cases of conflict of interest within his own administration?

David Kennedy, for example, was Secretary of the Treasury.[8]

---

[8] Kennedy resigned as Secretary of the Treasury on February 1, 1971, to become a roving ambassador specializing in economic affairs.

His department not only had to advise the Administration on the wisdom of providing loan guarantees, it also had to contact the financial community to see if it would be receptive to granting further loans to the railroad under government guarantees. In the end, Treasury, working through Undersecretary Paul A. Volcker, helped put together the consortium of seventy-seven banks that agreed to advance up to $200 million to the railroad. During this time, Penn Central owed $15 million to the bank that Kennedy headed before he joined the Cabinet — Continental Illinois Bank & Trust Company. If the railroad failed, there was no way of forecasting how much of a loss Kennedy's former bank would suffer.

Maurice H. Stans was Secretary of Commerce. Before joining the Cabinet, Stans had been head of Glore Forgan, Wm. R. Staats, Inc., Charlie Hodge's firm that had done so much work for the Penn Central. On March 21, 1969, a partnership to which Stans belonged exercised an option to purchase shares of Macco Corporation stock. The Macco stock was later exchanged for Great Southwest stock. Great Southwest was 90 percent owned by Penn Central. When he became Secretary of Commerce, Stans placed all his holdings in a "blind" trust with the United States Trust Company. But, after the Macco option was exercised, Stans and his sixty-five partners were notified that the stock had been bought and exchanged for Great Southwest shares. Stans thus learned in June 1969 that 37,955 shares of Great Southwest were being distributed to him through the "blind" trust. On June 12, 1970, despite the slump in Great Southwest, these shares were worth more than $300,000. Great Southwest was heavily dependent on the Penn Central for both cash and credit. If the railroad failed, the real estate company could be one of the ancillary victims. Stans said that, after the June 3 meeting in the White House, he disqualified himself from any further participation in the Penn Central matter. He did this, he said, during a meeting in David Kennedy's office on June 4 when "the full extent of the Penn Central's plight became apparent." At the request of the White House, Stans said, he made available his general counsel, James Lynn (who subsequently became Undersecretary of Commerce) to work on the loan guarantee arrangements. "Lynn was the only lawyer in town who knew

294 THE WRECK OF THE PENN CENTRAL

enough about this sort of thing to draw up the papers," said the Transportation Department's Beggs.

Walter H. Annenberg was Ambassador to England. An assignment to the Court of St. James's was the most prestigious prize the United States government could offer to a diplomat, amateur or professional. Nixon appointed Annenberg to the post in March 1969. The president had long been close to Annenberg and had been a guest in Annenberg's $5 million home in Palm Springs. While Annenberg was publisher of the Philadelphia *Inquirer,* he would not permit any criticism of Nixon in the newspaper.[9] When he became ambassador, Annenberg owned 177,000 shares of railroad stock and was a member of the Penn Central board. As the largest individual shareholder in the railroad, he could be expected to be hurt the most by the collapse of the railroad.

Randolph H. Guthrie was Nixon's former law partner. He had been retained to represent the railroad in legal matters connected with the government guarantees. There was no doubt the railroad hoped Guthrie could work wonders for it in Washington.

Any reasonably intelligent politician could probably construct an entire campaign around any of these issues, and this was not lost on the White House, where hard-eyed and skillful politicians abounded. Even if there were no *real* conflicts of interest, the mere fact that there *appeared* to be could be just as damaging. The political dangers inherent in the plan to help the railroad remained an unspoken factor throughout the drafting of plans for the loan guarantees.

A second major problem was the attitude of Congress itself. If the legislation authorizing the Department of Transportation to provide long-term loan guarantees of up to $750 million was not passed, it would be pointless for the Defense Department to act as guarantor for $200 million in short-term loans. Both the railroad and the Transportation Department had said that a combination of short- and long-term loans was necessary to restore the Penn Central to health. If Defense agreed to the short-term loans only to

---

[9] John R. Bunting, president of the First Pennsylvania Banking & Trust Company, subsequently said that if Annenberg were still in Philadelphia publishing his newspapers, the railroad would have had no difficulty getting loan guarantees from the Nixon Administration.

have Congress reject the second part of the package, the railroad would still be in trouble and Defense might very well be left holding a $200 million bag.

This possibility became more real every day. Senator Hartke, chairman of the Subcommittee on Surface Transportation, was among those who objected to the long-term guarantees. He told the Transportation Department that the legislation was poorly drafted, was too concessionary to the railroads, and did not provide adequate safeguards for the taxpayer.[10] Senator Stennis and Congressmen Rivers and Mahon told the Defense Department they mistrusted the plan.

The man who promised to cause the most trouble was Wright Patman. Patman had been in Congress continuously since 1929 and for most of that time he had railed against the power of bankers and the evils of high interest rates. Now he had a once-in-a-lifetime opportunity to prove that the banks had contributed to the problems of a major corporation. At the same time he could prevent the government from using the taxpayers' money to help save the railroad that he believed had been corrupted by the banks. Patman began preparing subpoenas that were awesome in scope. He demanded that the railroad supply him with details of all financial transactions between the railroad and its subsidiaries from 1963 on, with copies of all bank loan agreements the railroad and its 186 subsidiaries had entered into, with details of all bank deposits over $100,000 (the railroad had deposits with 142 banks, the subsidiaries with hundreds more). The list of data Patman wanted seemed endless, covering more than twenty pages. Each sentence in the specifications attached to the subpoenas encompassed huge areas, such as the request for all records of real estate sales by Arvida Corporation, the railroad's Florida land company. Patman wanted the minutes from board meetings of the railroad and its affiliates, lists of stockholders, names of officers and di-

---

[10] During the 1970 political campaign, John Volpe went to Indiana to try to help defeat Hartke, a somewhat reckless move for a Cabinet officer whose department had to work daily with the man Volpe was campaigning against. After he was reelected, Hartke summoned Volpe to a hearing on the Penn Central and criticized him mercilessly for two hours, telling him bluntly that he wasn't doing the job he was being paid to do. Volpe clenched his fists, but there was little he could do. Hartke had won.

rectors, when they joined the company, how much stock they owned, when they bought it, what they paid for it, when they sold it.

On June 18, Patman and five senior Democratic members of his committee publicly urged the Pentagon to delay signing the loan agreements until after additional hearings were held.[11] Patman's request came late. The guarantees were to be signed the following day.

The Penn Central board was having the latest in its series of emergency meetings when Patman called for a delay in the granting of government guarantees. Not surprisingly, the meeting dealt with the events in Washington and what could be done to improve the railroad's position there. Then Paul Gorman raised the question of Randolph Guthrie, Nixon's former law partner, who was not proving to be an unqualified blessing. Bayard Roberts, the railroad's secretary, recorded the discussion in a tersely worded, homemade shorthand. These handwritten notes never found their way into the official minutes of the meeting.

PAG [Paul A. Gorman]: Yesterday Jack Anderson [a syndicated Washington columnist] asked whether we were employing Mudge firm. We said yes and have used before — foreign financing — also predecessor firm going back fifteen years.

JMS [John M. Seabrook]: Let's put Guthrie on board [of directors]. Have not given up yet. He has done remarkable job with Studebaker (chairman). Guthrie think less political embarrassment if on Board.

RSR [R. Stewart Rauch]: Dubious. Will have to put fees in proxy statement. Democratic congress.

ECG [E. Clayton Gengras]: Apprehensive politically.

That ended, for the time being, the discussion of Guthrie. He was not asked to sit on the board of directors.

Despite the growing congressional opposition, Defense appeared to be going through with the plan. On the morning of June 19, Deputy Secretary of Defense David Packard telephoned Wright Patman and told him that Secretary of the Navy John Chafee

---

[11] The other five were Reps. William A. Barrett and William S. Moorhead, of Pennsylvania; Leonor K. Sullivan, of Missouri; Henry S. Reuss, of Wisconsin, and Thomas L. Ashley, of Ohio.

would sign the agreements that afternoon. The railroad sent three representatives to New York City to meet with representatives from nine banks. The railroad men and the bankers waited in a tenth-floor conference room of New York's Federal Reserve Bank. As soon as word got to them that Chafee had signed the papers, the banks were to advance the railroad $50 million of the $200 million principal amount. Another representative of the banks was seated outside Chafee's office in the Pentagon, waiting for the word.

The railroad needed the $50 million desperately. By the end of June, commercial paper amounting to $9,795,000 was due. In that same period, payments of principal and interest on debt and rental of equipment amounted to $21,900,000. The payroll on Tuesday, June 23, would cost $12 million, and on Thursday, June 25, the payroll would cost another $8 million. And the railroad had only a little more than $7 million in cash on hand.

The banks' representative was still sitting outside Chafee's office when David Packard arrived at the White House. Packard was the number-two man in the Pentagon, and he was not easily impressed. At fifty-seven, he was worth some $300 million, most of which he had earned as board chairman and chief executive officer of the Hewlett-Packard Company. From the start, Packard had struggled with his misgivings about the loan guarantees. His principal fear was that a collapse of the railroad could trigger a panic in an already shaky stock market. Now, however, the news of the railroad's problems had leaked out and, after some reaction, the market seemed to be absorbing the news with relative calm.

Inside the White House, Packard walked to the first-floor office of Peter M. Flanigan, a forty-six-year-old special assistant to the president. Flanigan was a wealthy investment banker who took a leave of absence in 1968 from his job as vice president of Dillon, Read & Company to work as Nixon's deputy campaign manager. His father, Horace Flanigan, had been chairman of Manufacturers Hanover Trust Company and was still an honorary director of that company. The railroad owed Manufacturers Hanover more than $12 million.

Besides Packard, those who attended the meeting in Flanigan's office were James Beggs from the Transportation Department,

James Lynn from the Commerce Department, Paul Volcker from the Treasury Department and Barry Shillito from the Defense Department. Flanigan acted as chairman.

"The Defense Department asked to contact the House Appropriations Committee, Mahon's committee," Beggs recalled. "They got what they considered a negative reaction. They thought a V loan [a loan guarantee] was the wrong way to do it, although they wanted to help. It was obvious that a V loan was only a temporary expedient, that it didn't make much sense to go ahead with a V loan without the long term guarantees that the legislation would provide.

"The Defense Department was very, very nervous. Dave Packard was very, very adamant. He thought the DOD [Department of Defense] shouldn't be asked to do this. It was pretty much decided that we weren't going to do it. Many had a gut feeling that this was not the right thing to do. There was a general feeling that railroads have run in bankruptcy and this one will, too."

Late that afternoon, a warm Friday that saw Washington residents streaming out of the city for the weekend, the meeting in Flanigan's office broke up. The Transportation Department had lost. Wright Patman had won. Thomas M. Timlen, a vice president in New York's Federal Reserve, walked into the tenth floor conference room and said a few words to the three railroad men and the representatives from the nine banks. When Timlen concluded, the men packed up their briefcases and walked out. Packard ordered this message released by the Defense Department:

The Department of Defense has decided not to guarantee bank loans to the Penn Central Transportation Company under the Defense Production Act.

The Department of Defense considered guaranteeing the loan based on indications from Congressional leaders that legislation could be passed promptly under which the guarantee could be taken over by the Department of Transportation.

In the light of growing uncertainty regarding enactment of that legislation, the Department of Defense has declined to make the guarantee.

Reporters in the White House sought out Press Secretary Ron Ziegler for comment, but Ziegler would say only that President

Nixon was "aware that the DOD has made this decision and concurred in it."

The decision did not sit well with the Transportation Department. John Volpe had climbed out on a limb for the Penn Central, only to have the Defense Department cut him down. Volpe did not expect to be treated this cavalierly. Just two years earlier, when he was governor of Massachusetts, Volpe had been pursued and wooed by Richard Nixon, who was then seeking the Republican nomination for president. In his quest for support, Nixon dropped hints that various powerful Republican politicians were being considered for the honor of being his running mate. He placed Volpe's name close to the top of the list. If things worked out, he would be the first Italian-American vice president. Volpe enthusiastically endorsed Nixon, then set out on a trip to the Orient to establish his credentials as a suitably experienced man to be second in command of the nation. At the 1968 Republican convention in Miami Beach, however, Nixon decided to make Spiro Agnew the first Greek-American vice president, and Volpe was offered the Transportation Department as his reward.

Now it was obvious that Volpe, who resigned his governorship to join the Cabinet, was not one of the most powerful men in Washington. He saw the president only infrequently and only after considerable difficulty. At one point, he had been unable to get in to see Nixon for nine straight weeks. But nothing could compare to the humiliation he suffered when his highly publicized plan to save the railroad from bankruptcy was aborted, almost at the moment of delivery, with the consent of the president.

Despite the embarrassment occasioned by the Defense Department's withdrawal of support at the last minute, Volpe and Beggs, his number-one aide, did not disclose their bitterness over the reversal. Inside the Transportation Department, however, other officials raged against the Pentagon and the White House. The setback, they knew, indicated the Transportation Department lacked the strength to put over its programs. Volpe had no muscle either on Capitol Hill or in the White House offices of the man who supposedly once thought of him as a likely candidate for vice president.

"Why did the Nixon Administration reverse itself on guaranteeing Penn Central loans?" one high-level Transportation Department official reflected. "The Department of Defense has no guts. We knew we were going to have tough political sledding. All the elements for the demagogues were there — the Nixon Administration vetoing Hill-Burton [hospital] funds but bailing out a seven billion dollar corporation. You've seen the cartoons — Nixon gives the railroads money but tells poor kids, 'Go away, you smell bad.' The Nixon law firm's involvement. Annenberg. David Kennedy's bank.

"They [Defense] weren't going to do it unless we could guarantee them the $750 million rail transport aid bill would pass. The DOD loan guarantee would keep the railroad out of bankruptcy for ninety days. Then, if the $750 million loan guarantee bill passed, the Secretary of Defense's name would come off the $200 million note and the Secretary of Transportation's name would go on. The Department of Transportation said, 'We'll take our lumps, but the bill will pass.'

"But then Patman gives a fire-eating speech and the DOD gets scared. The DOD is so used to having everything their own way on the Hill that they absolutely panicked. They don't live the way the rest of us do. They went rushing to the President and said, 'We're not going to get the legislation through.' The Treasury Department got all nervous and wanted guarantees that Maggy (Senator Magnuson) would vote for it. Between them, they got the White House nervous."

It was pleasantly warm along Philadelphia's Main Line on Saturday, June 20. William L. Day, chairman of the First Pennsylvania Banking & Trust Company and a Penn Central director, left his home in Devon in the morning to keep a golf date. He was on the fairway when the message reached him: Paul Gorman had set up an emergency meeting for one o'clock that afternoon with Wright Patman. Day's presence was requested.

It was a desperate final attempt, doomed to fail, but it had to be made. So, on that warm June day, five busy and important men traveled to Washington to plead the railroad's case before the granite-faced congressman from Texas. Besides Gorman and Day the others were John Seabrook and R. Stewart Rauch, both directors, and Jonathan O'Herron, the financial vice president. After two hours, the five men were forced to admit defeat.

"My position remains unchanged," Patman said, when the meeting ended. "As I have in the past, I expressed my deep concern that the government's interest be fully protected and that the taxpayers not be made liable for any financial losses resulting from a guarantee to this huge corporation."

The trip back to Philadelphia was gloomy, and the men were faced with even gloomier prospects when they arrived back in the city. The Transportation Building on Penn Center Plaza was relatively empty on what was by now a late Saturday afternoon. Gorman and the other directors went to the eighteenth-floor executive offices. Newsmen were not permitted to go higher than the tenth floor, where William Lashley, the railroad's vice president for public relations, had his offices. Lashley's job that day was to keep the news out of the newspapers.

Upstairs, Gorman was making arrangements to have a special board meeting the next day, Sunday, June 21. All the directors and top officers, and outside legal counsel, were asked to attend. In preparation for that meeting, Gorman and the members of the Executive Committee agreed on these recommendations to be made to the board the next day:

> That unless additional cash is made available in the meantime, the board authorizes the filing of a petition for reorganization under Section 77 of the Bankruptcy Act and that it take such action in ample time to publicize the filing of the petition prior to the opening of business on Monday morning;
>
> That every effort be made to continue the operation of train service and that widespread publicity be given to these efforts; and
>
> That no action be taken until it becomes absolutely mandatory with respect to filing a petition under the Bankruptcy Act by any other company subsidiary to, or affiliated with, this company.

While these recommendations called for "widespread publicity," the publicity was withheld on Saturday when reporters were searching for stories for their Sunday newspapers. The reason the news was withheld was that Gorman, and the others, still nursed a hope, however small, that lightning might strike and save the company on Sunday. Another reason was that Gorman could not very well announce the company was going to file a petition under the Bankruptcy Act without first obtaining formal board approval.

Ten members of the board were present at 11 A.M. when the special meeting began. Two others were absent. There had been nineteen directors on June 8; now there were only twelve. Saunders, Perlman and Bevan had been fired, reducing the number to sixteen on June 8. Since then, four others had resigned. On June 21, those present were Gorman, Seabrook, Day, Rauch, E. Clayton Gengras, Franklin Lunding, R. Walter Graham, R. George Rincliffe, Edward J. Hanley and Gaylord P. Harnwell. Otto Frenzel and Daniel E. Taylor were absent.

Others in the board room were Samuel H. Hellenbrand, the Penn Central's vice president for industrial development, real estate and taxes; E. A. Kaier, vice president and general counsel; Lashley; Jonathan O'Herron; R. W. Minor, senior vice president, legal and public affairs; Bayard Roberts, secretary; Carroll R. Wetzel, of the Philadelphia law firm of Dechert, Price & Rhoads, and Randolph H. Guthrie, of Mudge, Rose, Guthrie & Alexander, "the Nixon firm."

At this moment, with the railroad seemingly hours away from bankruptcy, when the directors could be expected to swing into action, the minutes of that meeting record the following as the first bits of business the board attended to:

The following resolutions were, on motion, adopted:
RESOLVED that, effective June 1, 1970, annual salaries of the officers named below are approved and authorized as follows:
J. R. Sullivan, vice president, marketing, $60,000;
E. L. Claypole, vice president, transportation, $52,500;
M. P. Richards, vice president, purchases and materials, $51,000.
RESOLVED that, effective June 1, 1970, annual salaries of the officers named below are approved and authorized as follows:
F. J. Gasparini, assistant vice president, real estate, $33,000;
R. C. Karvwatt, director, communications services, $32,500;
C. E. Ingersoll, assistant vice president, passenger service contracts, $32,000;
J. W. Diffenderfer, assistant vice president, special services, $32,000.
RESOLVED that the board approves and confirms the action taken

by the Executive Committee at its meeting on June 18, 1970, appointing Jonathan O'Herron as executive vice president at an annual salary of $66,000, plus contingent compensation of $14,000.

The board then turned to the rehiring of Frederick W. Rovet, who had left the company on October 31, 1968, and was now returning as assistant vice president for real estate. The minutes show that the directors discussed in great detail the pension benefits that would be granted to Rovet and his beneficiaries.

Some months later, E. Clayton Gengras said he had never seen a board of directors quite like the board that served the Penn Central.

"The first board meeting I attended in Philadelphia, I got in the car to drive home and I was sick," Gengras said. "At a board meeting, you talk about operating the business. It lasts three or four hours and you find out what's wrong and do something about it. You don't spend all your time talking about stock options for the executives.

"But they sat up there on the eighteenth floor in those big chairs with the plates on them and they were a bunch of, well, I'd better not say it. The board was definitely responsible for the trouble. They took their fees and they didn't do anything. Over a period of years, people just sat there. That poor man from the University of Pennsylvania [Gaylord P. Harnwell], he never opened his mouth. They didn't know the factual picture and they didn't try to find out."

After disposing of the problem of officers' salaries and pension benefits, the board finally turned to the question of the survival of the railroad. Gorman presented the recommendation of the Executive Committee that a petition for reorganization under the Bankruptcy Law be filed unless some alternative course appeared possible.

Gorman reviewed the refusal of the Defense Department to guarantee loans for the railroad and then turned to Guthrie, the former law partner of the president. Guthrie, according to Roberts' notes, told the board that Nixon was the man who made the decision that killed Volpe's plan. Nixon made this decision, Guthrie said, because David Packard did not want to commit Defense to so large an obligation and because of opposition by Democrats in Congress. If the Democrats had not resisted so strongly, Guthrie said, the president might have been willing to overrule Packard.

Roberts' notes show that Gorman told the men in the board room that the decision to renege on the government guarantees was "not in response to Patman." The notes said that Gorman described Patman as "all vindictive and not interested in helping. Patman couldn't care less whether Penn Central goes under or about effect on financial market." Gorman also said that Volpe "claimed to be thunderstruck at development."

Urgent telephone calls pulled Gorman from the board room a half dozen times during the meeting. Three of the calls were from Volpe and one was from Walter Wriston of First National City Bank. Wriston had been in telephone contact with Volpe, Treasury Secretary David Kennedy and Arthur F. Burns, chairman of the Federal Reserve. Wriston told Gorman that the banks could not advance another dollar to the railroad without government guarantees.

In one of his calls, Volpe demanded that the Penn Central discharge Guthrie. "Who hired Guthrie?" Volpe asked, according to Roberts. "End it now with publicity." Roberts also included this summary on Volpe's attitude about legislation providing long-term loan guarantees for railroads: "Volpe said he would go along with legislation only if Guthrie [is] dismissed." Volpe told Gorman he would try to reach the president to persuade him to reverse the Defense Department decision. He asked that the board await his call before doing anything, and then announced that he was going to a christening. When Gorman protested Volpe's planned absence during those crucial hours, Volpe assured the railroad's chief executive that he could be reached in his car. He also promised to have an answer by 5 P.M. for the board.

After this, Gorman and all other officers of the railroad left the room. The only ones remaining were the nine outside directors and Randolph Guthrie. Incredibly, the directors chose this moment to discuss what "arrangements" should be made for Stuart Saunders and David Bevan. It quickly became clear that there would be no "arrangements" for Bevan, despite the efforts of his old friend Edward J. Hanley to help him. Perlman had a contract until

November 30, 1970, so the directors did not discuss him. The minutes show this discussion concerning Saunders: "There was discussion of a possible arrangement in respect of the retention of Mr. Saunders as a consultant to the company for a substantial period of months. It was the consensus of the board that such an arrangement should be entered into on appropriate terms if it proved to be practicable after consulting with counsel and taking into account the Interstate Commerce Commission's order in the Penn Central merger case as to protection for employees."[12]

The board recessed and reconvened in midafternoon. When the meeting reopened, William L. Day announced that he intended to resign as a director if the railroad filed for reorganization under the Bankruptcy Act. As head of a bank that was a creditor of the Penn Central, Day said, he would find himself in a conflict of interest situation. The petition had already been drafted by Carroll Wetzel. The document noted that: "The debtor [the railroad] has been suffering large deficits since 1968 and is virtually without cash. The debtor is unable to meet its debts as they mature, has no means of borrowing or otherwise procuring funds to pay and discharge its debts and obligations. . . ."

Section 77 of the Bankruptcy Act would permit the railroad to suspend most of these debts. The Section, adopted by Congress in 1933, was drawn specifically to cover railroads that found themselves in bankruptcy situations. Unlike ordinary bankruptcies, Section 77 does not provide for liquidation. It is a means for railroads to reorganize while the trains keep running. Under court supervision, trustees are appointed to oversee the reorganization. During the period of trusteeship, virtually all obligations of the railroad, except for debts incurred to purchase equipment, are held in abeyance. The protection of the court prevents creditors from collecting on these debts, which include state and local taxes.

"A railroad in Number 77 proceedings is not a defunct organism but remains a live and going concern," Justice Felix Frankfurter of the United States Supreme Court wrote in 1954. "Indeed,

---

12 No such "arrangement" was ever worked out, and Saunders never became a consultant for the Penn Central. In April 1971, Saunders was admitted to practice law in Pennsylvania by the Pennsylvania Supreme Court.

the desire to provide a ready remedy for the overhauling of a railroad's financial structure without impairing its primary responsibility as a regularly functioning carrier was one of the principal reasons for the enactment of Number 77."

If ever there was a need for "the overhauling of a railroad's financial structure," it existed within the Penn Central on June 21, 1970. On that day, the company had current liabilities, including debt due within one year, of $748,974,342. Its current assets amounted to $462,472,382. There was a working capital deficit of $286,501,960. The balance sheet showed that cash on hand was $7,308,130.

The board was hoping for the best, but preparing for the worst. While the directors waited for Volpe's promised call, Carroll Wetzel was in telephone contact with Judge C. William Kraft, Jr., of the United States District Court for Eastern Pennsylvania. Judge Kraft, who was at his home in Delaware County, told Wetzel he would be available to receive a petition for reorganization under Section 77, if it became necessary.

Gorman was called out of the board room for the last time about 5 P.M. Volpe was on the telephone. The Secretary of Transportation, the former governor of Massachusetts who almost became vice president, could not reach Nixon. He had called the president, he told Gorman, but he could not get through to him. Volpe said he would continue to press for legislation to provide long-term loan guarantees for railroads of up to $750 million, but he could do no more to help the Penn Central out of its current crisis.

The directors knew it was all over as soon as Gorman returned to the room. There could be no mistaking the look on his face. Briefly, Gorman related what Volpe had told him. The end was at hand. The railroad had outrun the money. John Seabrook moved that the board approve the filing of the petition. William Day seconded the motion. It was carried unanimously.

RESOLVED that the board authorizes the Chairman of the Board to sign and cause to be filed a petition in the form presented at this meeting for voluntary reorganization of the company under Section 777 of the Bankruptcy Act.

It was done. The Great Merger had survived for 872 days. What had been conceived of as the most awesome transportation machine in the world had ended as the most monumental business failure in United States history.

The petition was dispatched to Judge Kraft's home via Penn Central courier Larry Turner. Wetzel reported that the document was filed at 5:35 P.M. At 5:40 P.M., Judge Kraft signed the order putting the Penn Central into reorganization under Section 77 of the Bankruptcy Act.

At the Transportation Building in Philadelphia, William Lashley, the railroad's vice president for public relations, was finishing up the statement the directors would release informing the public that the Penn Central Transportation Company had collapsed. The statement said:

> Because of a severe cash squeeze and having been unable to acquire from any source additional working capital, Penn Central Transportation Company today filed a petition for reorganization in the U.S. District Court for the Eastern District of Pennsylvania. Judge C. William Kraft, Jr., signed an order approving the petition.
>
> The action was taken under Section 77 of the Bankruptcy Act, which contemplates a reorganization of the company and continuance of its operation. This procedure is unlike ordinary bankruptcy, which contemplates liquidation.
>
> The court order permits Penn Central Transportation Company to retain possession of and continue operation of the railroad system and to conduct other normal business, pending the appointment of trustees by the court. The trustees must be approved by the Interstate Commerce Commission.
>
> The transportation company's board of directors met Sunday and authorized this action, which relates solely to the transportation company and does not apply to the Pennsylvania Company, the parent Penn Central Company or to the many other affiliated and subsidiary companies.
>
> The railroad is notifying its more than 94,000 employees to stay on the job and continue to perform their usual duties.

11

Thoughts from the Caboose

By this time the reader may have reached some tentative conclusions to explain the Penn Central's collapse: The railroad went broke because of bad management, divided management, dishonest accounting, diversion of funds into unprofitable outside enterprises, nonfunctioning directors or a basic disinterest in running, or even an inability to run, a railroad. Put even more bluntly, he may blame the bankruptcy on inefficiency, incompetency, gross miscalculations, practices bordering on fraud and a public-be-damned attitude.

But now hear Perlman. Now hear Saunders. It's their turn to explain what happened. Five months after he was dropped as pilot of the Penn Central, Saunders talked for three and one-half hours as a tape recorder spun in the library of his Ardmore home. Perlman refused an interview on the grounds that his testimony before a subcommittee of the Senate Commerce Committee on July 29, 1970, included everything he wanted to say on the subject of the bankruptcy. Indeed, he said a great deal that day. In his Washington testimony, Alfred Perlman, who never really wanted the merger and never had much faith in it, sounded very much like Stuart Saunders, who believed in it passionately. And they agreed completely on the crucial question of why the Penn Central collapsed.

Perlman and Saunders will be quoted here at considerable length. The skeptical reader — and one of the railroad industry's problems is its lack of credibility with much of the public — is invited to weigh their words against the record as it has been presented so far.

Perlman told the Senate Commerce Committee subcommittee:

We recognized almost from the beginning that we would have to pay certain penalties as a price for the merger, and that, for a time, these penalties would more than absorb any merger savings. We calculated that, during the first year after merger, these penalties would exceed the attained merger benefits by $82 million. This resulted from the fact that we were required to reinstate over 5,000 former employees who were no longer needed but had been on the payroll when the merger agreement was signed [in 1962]. These people could be removed only by normal retirement or death, unless they agreed to a separation upon the payment of a certain amount of salary. It averages about 16 months.

There were other penalties prescribed by the ICC. One of these required us to indemnify other railroads for fluctuations in their business caused by the merger.[1] We were also required to take over, at a fantastic cost,[2] the bankrupt New Haven, which had shown a $22 million deficit the previous year . . .

On top of that, in order to achieve merger savings, we had to spend a large amount of cash on the physical plant. For example, we had two passenger stations in Chicago. We had to construct a physical connection between the tracks so that one station could handle all the business previously handled by two. This was true of freight yards in thirty-five cities. Not only were connections required but, because one facility had to handle the business of both former railroads, very substantial increased capacity had to be added to ten of the yards. The cost of this work at the end of 1969 amounted to $121 million and resulted in savings of $74 million annually. Where we expected to get $81 million by 1975, we already had $74 million in two years of the merger.

We have heard a lot of carping from some sidewalk superintendents about what happened in the last two years. But I think this is an amazing performance to have been able to speed up the merger of these two companies physically as quickly as has been done. Because

[1] Perlman conceded in subsequent questioning that such fluctuations were minimal. Penn Central's business was so bad its competitors were generally not adversely affected.

[2] The ICC set $145.6 million as the sale price of the New Haven. The ruling has undergone protracted litigation and the issue remained unresolved at the time of the bankruptcy.

the more quickly these changes could be made, the more quickly we could achieve the savings necessary to offset the tremendous penalties we accepted as a price for approval of the merger.

Despite these penalties, Penn Central would not, in my opinion, be in reorganization today had it not been for other circumstances. These circumstances include a recession in the industries which provides a large part of our profitable traffic, the inflationary spiral in wages and material costs, coupled with our chronic inability to keep pace by increasing [freight] rates . . . and the unavailability of money, even at [interest] rates which would have been thought usurious a couple of years ago. This alone has added enormously to the burden of [Penn Central] . . . which had a high debt structure because it was not reduced through former reorganizations, as were many of the more marginal lines . . .

Railroads have one of the highest ratios of labor to overall operating expenses of any industry. Inflationary trends, which have increased wages far beyond any possibility of meeting these increases with increased productivity, have put a profit crunch on the industry that cannot be met by the present system of [freight] rate increases.

It is historical that rate increases follow wage increases in our industry by about a year, and in many cases are not achieved even at that time. With the tremendous inflation in wages, taxes and material prices, railroad rates are still lagging at 1958 levels.

Further, the securities markets have felt the effect of the inflationary spiral so that the value of collateral used to secure loans has tumbled to prices which can no longer support the loans. This also greatly aggravated the Penn Central cash situation. When we merged the N&W stock was around 130 and it is sixty today and this was collateral for a great many of the loans.[3]

On top of all this, both the Pennsylvania and the New York Central were, prior to merger, the largest handlers of mail in the United States. Just about the time of the merger, the Post Office Department diverted mail from rail passenger trains to air and other means, causing [railroads] a tremendous loss in revenue. Not only were we faced with the loss of revenues, but the thousands of employees on our payroll engaged in handling mail had to be kept on the payroll or paid off. The Government didn't pay off the mail handlers. Yet the passenger trains

---

[3] Perlman said later that if N&W stock had stayed around 100, he thought Penn Central would have succeeded in floating the $100 million debentures that went unsold in the spring of 1970, precipitating the bankruptcy.

which had been handling the mail were not permitted to be discontinued under what amounted to a freeze on discontinuances by the ICC.

The combination of all these factors makes necessary some method by which cash can be made available to meet the falling working capital position of railroads and to make funds available to provide rolling stock, physical improvements and automation. These investments in plant will help to attain an increased productivity to meet in some part the spiraling wage costs.

Perlman said that despite his earlier leanings toward a different configuration of eastern railroad mergers, "the Penn Central can be made to work and the resulting system can be viable." He warned, though, that neither the Penn Central nor railroads generally could survive without advocates in Washington and subsidies comparable those given their competitors in highway, waterway and airway transportation.

Asked if the American railroad industry was in fact a dying industry that could not support itself, Perlman replied:

I say that under the present system of regulation, under the present system of subsidies to the other three forms of transportation, under the system where we are not allowed to make competitive rates with other modes, it is a dying system; yes, sir . . . I still say the steel wheel on the steel rail is the most efficient form of transportation in the world. And it is being killed, we are not letting it die, it is being killed.

And, sir, I think that is the tragedy today, to see it being killed that way. All I say, as a taxpayer, is treat them all alike. Don't give any of them subsidies — or subsidize them all.

In his testimony that day, Perlman also leveled what are now familiar charges: that the merger wasn't a merger but a PRR "takeover"; that he was forced into a merger he didn't like and then found his hands tied by Bevan and Saunders. These allegations were made in response to often leading questions put by Sen. Vance Hartke, Democrat from Indiana, chairman of the subcommittee on surface transportation, and other senators. Sometimes, Perlman wouldn't go as far as Hartke apparently wanted him to.

Asked by Hartke if Bevan and Saunders were "diverting money from the railroad operations" for outside investments, and pledging securities for the "conglomerate," Perlman answered: "Well, it is very difficult to say. We did have a tremendous cash drain as far as the railroad is concerned in those first two years and we knew we were going to have it. They did make some advances to the Great Southwest at the time, but I do not think that they spent a great deal of money acquiring real estate companies and other companies."

Again, when Hartke asked if the failure of Bevan and Saunders to follow the budgetary procedures and railroad spending practices of the old Central was "one of the contributing causes for the collapse of the Penn Central," Perlman said: "I don't think so. I think that this tight money grabbed them and the fall of the collateral and things of that kind that they were not prepared for at all. I think a year and a half ago if one said this was going to happen, one would have been laughed at."[4]

Now it's time to pick up Stuart Saunders talking into the authors' tape recorder. The first question put to him concerned the ICC's requirement that Penn Central, as a condition of the merger, agree to take on the bankrupt New Haven.

Q: Do you view this in retrospect as one of the things that made it so difficult to make the merger work?

SAUNDERS: Oh, no. It was a problem, yes. Of course, the New Haven is a problem. But under conditions we had to operate, the New Haven is not enough to make a difference. The problems here are far deeper and much more deep-seated . . . This has been going on since World War II. Neither the Pennsylvania Railroad nor the New York Central have ever made any money. With the exception of one year, two years.

Q: You mean since World War II?

SAUNDERS: Well, I'll say since 1950. This is what people don't realize. They've *never* made any money . . . Neither the New York Central nor the Pennsylvania has paid any income tax since 1952 because they haven't made any money. With one single exception that

___

[4] Such self-delusions have long been common among railroad executives. "Even after the advent of automobiles, trucks, and airplanes," Theodore Levitt wrote in a 1960 article in *Harvard Business Review,* "the railroad tycoons remained imperturbably self-confident. If you had told them sixty years ago that in thirty years they would be flat on their backs, broke, and pleading for government subsidies, they would have thought you totally demented. Such a future was simply not considered possible . . . The very thought was insane."

I know of, and that was I think in 1966. They paid a small amount and that was actually refunded . . . That little bit of income in 1965–1966 represents one-tenth of one percent on investment. It's nothing. The only way that these railroads have survived is through their outside income. And cannibalizing themselves. These railroads have cannibalized themselves at the rate of about $50 million a year for over ten to fifteen years.

Q: When you say "cannibalize," what do you mean?

SAUNDERS: Sell off all their property. You take all of the development of Penn Center [office buildings in downtown Philadelphia on land formerly owned by the PRR]. Every damn piece of that property has been sold and poured back into operating the railroad. The railroad doesn't own any of it. That's just typical. We've — they've sold off properties everywhere along the line. They've sold lots of their N&W stock — all to operate the railroad and subsidize the railroad. So this isn't something that happened as a result of the merger. This is something that had been building up over a period of fifteen years or more. And by virtue of making no money they haven't spent the money on their property they ought to spend. They didn't have it. They ought to have spent twice as much as they did but they couldn't do it. They didn't have it and they couldn't get it.

Since 1963 we spent — these two railroads — a billion and six hundred million dollars. That's about 20 percent of all the money that was spent in this country by the railroads on railroad property. We ought to have spent twice that much. But we didn't have it; we couldn't get it . . .

But that's only part of the story. The fact is that the Pennsylvania and the New York Central are the two most expensive railroads in this country to operate . . . They have 67 percent of all the railroad passenger business in the East. And the passenger business is the biggest money-losing business in this country. I don't know of anything that loses as much money as the passenger business.

On the Penn Central, you start out every month, before you turn a wheel, on an out-of-pocket basis, you are roughly $6 million in the red [in passenger service]. Whereas these other railroads have no such problem to contend with. That is one of the great differences between the Penn Central and these other railroads . . . You have short [freight] hauls. Therefore, you don't make as much money off it as the western railroads do on their long hauls or the Southern Railroad on its long hauls or even the N&W on its long hauls. You have many more yards and terminals on the Penn Central, and in freight operations they are the most expensive things to operate. And that's where you lose your time. Classifying cars and things like that. But with short hauls and such highly industrialized territory you have to have these yards.

So you have short hauls and you have terrific terminal costs. Much greater relatively than any other railroad in the country. Then you have high port costs. New York is the highest cost port in the country . . . Philadelphia is relatively higher cost. So is Baltimore. I mean Norfolk is much cheaper; New Orleans is cheaper; San Francisco is cheaper.

Out of every operating dollar that you get, your labor cost on the Penn Central is roughly sixty cents. In the southern and western railroads, about forty cents. For the railroads as a whole it's under fifty cents. And that's a tremendous difference because your labor bill on the Pennsylvania is over a billion dollars a year. And this is also reflected in another thing: When you get, say, a 10 percent wage increase, or 8 percent increase, it hits the Pennsylvania 15 or 20 or 30 percent harder than the other railroads because it's got that many more employees. All of these are factors that are built into the basic problem or difficulty of making the Penn Central a viable railroad.

Q: To be blunt, then, what made you all think you could put two losers together and make a winner? You've said both railroads were losing money for many years. How could this have possibly worked?

SAUNDERS: Mind you, I'm not apologizing, but I didn't have anything to do with the concept of the Penn Central. The record had practically been made when I came here. My job was to get the thing put through, which we finally did. But . . . coming back to your question . . . I think that the Penn Central merger is basically sound. It could be made viable and I think it may be yet. It's going to take a lot of doing. The problem is that most people look at this as the failure of certain individuals. What they don't appreciate is that this is basically a sick industry. And it's been sick for years.

As a matter of fact, I testified before Senator Hartke's committee last November [1969]. I testified before the House committee last September. My testimony was printed and sent all over the country to every newspaper and to every member of Congress. And I said there in that testimony that this industry is sick, that this house is on fire, it is burning down. I said this over a year ago. And nobody paid any attention to it.

No industry can survive on a 1 or 2 percent rate of return, or less. And that's what we've been trying to do for fifteen years. AT&T says they've got to have 8 to 9, now 9½ percent, in order to live. And they're right. There's no industry in this country that's tried to operate on the rate of return that the railroads have got in the last fifteen years.

But coming back to your question, why did they think the merger would work? In the first place they thought that they'd get $80 million of savings out of the merger, and they will get that. But a number of factors enter into it. First of all, not in order of importance, it was a great handicap to have such a long hiatus between the time the merger was conceived and the time it was put into effect. Very demoralizing from the point of view of personnel. You couldn't make any capital plans of consequence because you didn't know whether they were going to put the merger through or not.

But then on top of that, we effect the merger and then, within a period of months after that you're hit with a recession. And most people don't realize that we've got a real recession. It's a depression in effect; the worst one since the 1930's by far. And then it's compounded by the fact that you have tight money and you have inflation. You take tight money, inflation and the recession coming almost on the heels of the consummation of the merger. Inflation alone cost Penn Central last year $100 million. And I'm not talking about wages; I'm talking about other aspects of inflation. The cost of money — our interest charges last year went up $35 million over the preceding year and they'll go up again that much this year. Well, they won't now because they're not paying any interest. Wage costs of the Penn Central went up $75 million roughly last year over the preceding year. They went up the preceding year about the same figure. And they're going up that much again this year, even more, over $100 million.

Q: Was there any way you could have gotten around those labor costs?

SAUNDERS: Oh, no. That's another thing there's been complete misunderstanding about, and it's been misrepresented, particularly by the *Wall Street Journal*.[5] The courts have interpreted Section 52F of the Interstate Commerce Act to mean that in any merger no person shall lose his job or be adversely affected by virtue of the merger for four years. They're protected in their jobs four years from the date of the merger or four years from the date on which the particular employee is affected, whichever is later. In other words, it might be ten years after the merger but if he loses his job because of a merger-related

---

[5] The *Journal* implied that Saunders, in negotiating the labor agreements, was unwisely and unnecessarily generous.

reason he's protected from that time. The C&O Railroad today, I understand, is still protecting employees or paying severance pay for employees in a merger that was effected in 1948.

The labor agreement we made is cheaper or certainly not more expensive than what we would have had to take under the settled law. In the first place, we got labor's opposition out of the case. We got the right to transfer the men or the work, or both. Under the normal condition, you don't have the right to move anybody. You have to transfer the work. You have to go to labor and negotiate special agreements. And it's endless to do it. We had most of this all accomplished before the merger took effect. So overall this labor agreement saved us considerable money and time. It was certainly expensive monetarily but that was what we would have had to accept under existing law.

Q: In retrospect, do you think now it would have been better to go slow and absorb smaller losses over a longer period?

SAUNDERS: That's a matter of business judgment. But who could foresee at the time the economic conditions that were going to develop — the recession, inflation, tight money?

Q: Why has there been so much criticism of the railroads? Why have people charged that their failure to make money has been due to bad management rather than to the restrictions and factors you've discussed?

SAUNDERS: Well, it's basically — some of it is the railroads' fault, I think — but basically it's an erroneous concept that has existed in this country for years. The railroads have been treated as if they had a monopoly when in fact they don't. In 1947 the railroads had 67 percent of the intercity freight business in this country; today they've got about 40. Now that's a tremendous loss.

Let me put it to you this way: Every year in this country you spend roughly $19 billion on highways. They passed a bill this session of Congress: $2.4 billion for airports. Billions of dollars for supersonic planes. All for the benefit of our competitors. The railroads have got nothing. The Pennsylvania Railroad spent about $70 million on the Metroliner project. The federal government was supposed to spend $11 million. They finally paid $4 million of it. I mean, that's the kind of handout that you've gotten for the railroad industry. If the railroads can receive $300–$400 million a year of subsidy — and that's what we've got to have — and had been receiving it for say ten years like our competitors have — and it would be miniscule compared to what they've poured into these other forms of transportation — the railroad industry would be strong and healthy today. But just the reverse has taken place.

But you asked me whether the railroads have been at fault. Yes, I think they have. In not espousing their case as they should. One of the great problems is that you have such difficulty in getting any uniformity of opinion among the railroads as to what they ought to do. For many years we could never get any agreement among the railroads as to any subsidy for passenger business. The western railroads had very little of it. And they were opposed to any subsidy. Only last year we did get them to go along with seeking a subsidy for passenger business. But the western railroads and the southern railroads went along reluctantly.

On freight rate increases, the railroads are the only industry in this country that can get together and fix prices because they have immunity under the antitrust laws. But they can't ever agree. Their competitive interests are so different. Last year we went for 6 percent — I wanted to go for 12 and I thought we should have it. And a number of western railroads agreed. But the Southern Railroad said no. It took months to get them to go for anything and they finally went along with 6. And the commission gave us 5.

Q: What about the diversification program?

SAUNDERS: The diversification program has been a lifesaver for Penn Central. They'd have been bankrupt long before this had it not been for the outside interests. And people have such false notions. You take for instance Buckeye. The Pennsylvania put about $100 million into Buckeye all told. But they've been getting between $12–$14 million a year back from Buckeye in earnings. We basically acquired Buckeye with some cash and Norfolk & Western stock. We took about 500,000 shares of Norfolk & Western stock. We had about 2.3 million of Norfolk & Western. But on these 500,000 shares which we bought Buckeye with we're getting $14 million whereas on the 2.3 million shares of Norfolk & Western we're getting less than $14 million. We're getting less than ten [million dollars]. On this one transaction, less than one-fifth of the stock, we get more than we got on all our Norfolk & Western stock . . .

I'm not trying to justify the Executive Jet investment. But look at the Lehigh Valley [railroad]. The Pennsylvania Railroad put twice as much money or more into the Lehigh Valley and it is now in re-organization. Nobody's ever sued the officers [of the PRR about that]. Never got a penny out of it. I mean all this hue and cry — you can't make perfect investments every time. I mean, nobody does. You've got to make mistakes. Who ever said that [the Lehigh Valley] was mis-management? Nobody's ever said a word about the Lehigh Valley.

Q: When you have a merger of two equals, more or less, can the thing be worked out? Is there a precedent for this kind of merger in any business?

SAUNDERS: No. This is the largest merger ever undertaken in this country. And to think that you can do it overnight — we said it'd take eight years. And we would have accomplished it within five if we hadn't had the recession and inflation and tight money. We'd have done it. But nobody seems to appreciate the complexity of this thing. What a tremendous undertaking it was. And the personalities you had to deal with, the problems, the complexities. I don't care if you'd had Moses or whoever it might have been running the company, it couldn't have been done. And while the results are not good, I think that under the circumstances we did the best job that could have been done. And I'm not ashamed of anything. I think there are aspects of it I didn't approve of. But that is not the big problem here. And I say you could have had any management in this country and it still wouldn't have done any better.

Q: The problems are really beyond the control of the company?

SAUNDERS: Many of them are. That's what I've said from the beginning. This talk about mismanagement — maybe some errors were made, of course. I don't claim we did everything right. But I don't care who was in there, they wouldn't have escaped these problems because they're built in. They're beyond the control of management. But nobody's going to make it a viable company unless they really get to the heart of this thing. And it doesn't involve personalities. It involves the basic problems that are inherent here.

Q: Do you think nationalization is the answer?

SAUNDERS: No. It may be the only alternative. It can't be avoided unless you get sympathetic consideration by government. And real money put into the railroads. I think it's [nationalization] wholly undesirable. And I think it'll cost the government a whole lot more money through nationalization than it will through subsidy. But your railroads are so run down from years of starvation rations that they can't revive themselves. I don't care who's running them.

There was a lot more from Saunders, of course, on all aspects of the merger and the personalities who failed to make it work. But the foregoing is a fair sample of his point of view on the overriding question of why the railroad didn't make a go of it. It was clearly his opinion that all of the executive suite entanglements, the red-green brouhaha, the corporate interlocks, insider trading, Penphil machinations, computer confusion — all of the fascinating stuff that attracted such congressional fire — amounted to mere flyspecks. Penn Central failed because, under the ground rules for railroads in this country, it couldn't succeed. So said Stuart Saunders.

Now come the trustees of the Penn Central Transportation Company in reorganization under Section 77 of the federal bankruptcy statute. After Penn Central on June 21, 1970, filed for reorganization in U.S. District Court in Philadelphia, Federal Judge John P. Fullam named four men as a kind of superboard of directors to oversee the reorganization of the company. The four he named were George P. Baker, former dean of the Harvard Business School; Richard C. Bond, former head of the Wanamaker department stores; Jervis Langdon, Jr., former head of the Chicago, Rock Island & Pacific Railroad, and former Secretary of Labor W. Willard Wirtz.

Working with Judge Fullam, the trustees picked a president to succeed Gorman. Their choice was William Moore, the rangy, energetic, former number-two man at the moneymaking Southern Railway. While Moore threw himself into the job of running the trains, the trustees probed and thumped the sick patient, trying to find out what ailed it. On February 10, 1971, they filed their preliminary report "concerning premises for a reorganization." The report was believed to have been written by James A. McDonald, former operating vice president of the Canadian National Railroad whom Perlman had hired as vice president of the Penn Central on March 1, 1969. McDonald was the son of a Manitoba railroad station agent, and an unusual railroader: an honor graduate in economics at the University of Saskatchewan, a Rhodes Scholar, a Royal Canadian Navy telegraphist in World War II. At the Penn Central, he scrupulously avoided internal politics and quickly won respect, from reds and greens alike, as a first-rate railroad industry economist.

The report that McDonald authored reached essentially the same conclusions as Perlman in his congressional testimony and Saunders in his long interview.

"Penn Central," said the trustees' preliminary report, "is presently locked by circumstances beyond managerial control into a situation which had best be recognized now as completely precluding viability unless certain constraints are removed, or other arrangements are made to compensate for their effects."

The key hurdle that must be overcome if Penn Central is to remain in the private enterprise system, the report continued, is its "obligation to perform as a public service company in certain areas and under certain conditions which simply do not lend themselves to profitable operations, *no matter who the operator is, or how efficient* [emphasis added]. The only possible remedy here is for public authority to lend its hand to a speedy elimination of the conditions which produce the losses, or respond with adequate compensation if it insists upon a continuance of the conditions."

The trustees quarreled with Perlman's assessment of the premerger situation. Perlman had termed the New York Central "depression-proof." He answered yes to Senator Hartke's question: "But basically then, as far as the New York Central was concerned, it was a healthy operation as far as an industrial unit of the United States was concerned?" This assertion fitted Hartke's own apparent conviction, and that of many other observers, that the merger was wrecked by the PRR people. Saunders, on the other hand, had told Hartke's committee: "Neither the New York Central nor the Pennsylvania had made any money of consequence in the last ten years."

The trustees sided with Saunders. "Penn Central, of course, is a merger of three major railroads, no one of which had any railroad earning power prior to the merger . . . The New Haven was then in bankruptcy and slowly being liquidated, and the Pennsylvania and New York Central entered the merger with marginal earnings that depended on so-called 'other' income . . . Add to this record of poor premerger earnings the postmerger spiraling of Penn Central's terminal expenses and deficits from passenger service and there comes into focus a clearer picture of what it takes to create Penn Central viability."

In the preliminary report and subsequent congressional testimony on March 9, 1971, the trustees offered a blueprint for improving Penn Central's earnings record by $200–$400 million a year.

[*1*] Plant reduction. "Penn Central's [20,000-mile] plant should be reduced by about 40 percent in terms of route miles. Nearly 20 percent of present route miles can be identified as redundant . . . The economics of transportation dictate that most of the traffic now moving on light density rail lines should be handled by truck and/or piggy-back trailers and containers." The ICC should determine the facts as to freight and passenger losses. If losses are established, the railroad should be subsidized or the service abandoned.

[*2*] Freight rate restructuring. "The Congress should condemn as unlawful any rate . . . which is below the cost of providing the service and should adopt long-term variable costs as the absolute floor for rate making by all regulated carriers. This would automatically require the raising of hundreds of below-cost rates that in the case of Penn Central are producing losses estimated at more than $80 million a year."

[*3*] Labor adjustments. "The rationalizing of employment and labor relation policies and costs is the most critical single condition to making the Penn Central viable and permitting its successful reorganization." Penn Central's 1970 labor costs of $1.1 billion "exceeded by at least $120 million anything which could be considered a 'rational cost' figure." As previously noted, the trustees found that Penn Central was carrying on its payroll about 10,000 more employees than it needed. They attributed this condition to full-crew laws, which labor critics term featherbedding, in Indiana, Ohio and New York, plus archaic work rules which continue in effect despite having repeatedly been found unjustified by fact-finding boards. "The enterprise cannot carry the labor costs it does now," the trustees said of the bankrupt railroad.

In practical terms, they reported, the choice is between establishing procedures for reducing labor costs or, if that can't be done, "passing the bill for the extra costs to government." The trustees recommended the creation of a joint labor-management standing committee at Penn Central with a "neutral member" as chairman to settle work-rules disputes. Penn Central would be allowed to reduce its work force so long as employees losing jobs received "full equitable compensation." Workers, in turn, would be required to accept changes in assignment dictated by reasons of economics or efficiency so long as the changes placed "no undue burden" on them.

[4] Passenger service. The trustees counted on help from the quasi-public National Rail Passenger Corporation, formerly called Railpax and now known as Amtrak. Amtrak took over most of the nation's long-haul passenger rail service on May 1, 1971. The Penn Central is one of nineteen railroads participating in the venture. Amtrak was created by Congress with a $40 million grant. It also has $100 million worth of federal loan guarantees and it expects to receive about $200 million in cash, loans or equipment from member railroads. These "initiation fees" are the price the railroads must pay for dropping their money-losing intercity passenger service. Penn Central's initiation fee was $52.4 million payable over a three-year period. However, Amtrak will reimburse Penn Central for running trains and these payments should more than offset the railroad's payments to Amtrak. In return, 140 long-distance trains, which cost the railroad more than $50 million a year in losses, were taken over by Amtrak, and thirty other trains were simply dropped.

As we write, Amtrak's future, like the Penn Central's, is uncertain. When Amtrak took over on May 1, public attention was focused less on the 186 trains it started operating than on the 180 it dropped. Penn Central's Broadway Limited began running daily between New York and Chicago under Amtrak's aegis. But its Manhattan Limited, which took the route of the old New York Central's Twentieth Century to Chicago by way of Buffalo and Cleveland, was dropped. The Wabash Cannon Ball made its last run between Detroit and St. Louis and the Atlanta-to-Savannah Nancy Hanks carried its final passengers. Cleveland was at first without train service of any kind. More than 15,000 railroad employees reportedly faced loss of their jobs due to Amtrak's cutbacks. The new corporation appeared to be critically undercapitalized. And the *New York Times,* terming Amtrak "a pitiful apology for a rail system," complained editorially that direct "responsibility for train operation" would remain in the "inept hands" of "bumbling rail managements that did more than either airlines or buses to drive away past passenger traffic." As far as the *Times* and other critics were concerned, Amtrak was merely a paper organization set up to justify reductions in long-haul passenger service. But Secretary of Transportation John A. Volpe promised that Amtrak would "compete directly and aggressively" with airlines, buses and automobiles. He said that clean passenger cars, on-time schedules, appetizing meals and prompt service "can and in time will be restored to rail operations." However, he pleaded for patience. He said Amtrak should begin to break even in about three years.

Time will tell. Penn Central's trustees were confident that Amtrak would "compensate Penn Central for all costs that can be identified as related to its intercity passenger service." And they said that if their four primary conditions — concerning plant reduction, freight rate reforms, labor adjustments and Amtrak operations — were met, Penn Central might pick up an additional $200–$400 million a year. "When gains of this magnitude are taken into account," they said, "the effect on earning power, even when discounted for the known impact of continuing inflation, is substantial, and a basis for the reorganization of Penn Central begins to emerge."

It seems very unlikely that all of the trustees' conditions will be met in the foreseeable future. Yet, in retrospect, one might argue that Penn Central's bankruptcy was the best thing that could have happened to the railroad industry and even to Penn Central. Previously, when the railroads cried wolf the politicians and public paid them little heed. It was hard to feel much sympathy for transportation companies that provided terrible service yet rarely — in the old PRR's case, never — missed a dividend. After June 21, 1970, everything changed. Penn Central's dividends were gone, its stock fell to less than 5, its directors quit, and some of the banks tied to the railroad through "corporate interlocks" were owed millions and had no immediate prospects of collecting. Penn Central was clearly in desperate shape. And when its trustees described this situation and offered remedies they were listened to and possibly even believed.

Now that the railroad industry has the public's ear at last, what is its solution? In 1969, the Association of American Railroads created America's Sound Transportation Review Organization (ASTRO) and assigned it the task of preparing a report on what needed to be done to restore the railroad industry to health. By coincidence, the ASTRO Report was published on June 30, 1970, nine days after Penn Central went broke. The document set a precedent: America's railroads had never before been able to agree on major policy guidelines. The ASTRO Report, by ASTRO's general counsel, former U.S. senator George A. Smathers, a Florida Democrat, said that the failure of American railroads to agree on "basic matters" helped explain why they were in such trouble. The railroads, the report said, "have forfeited initiative in such elemental areas as car ownership, rates and divisions. They have often been lacking in policy leadership, choosing to react rather than to think positively and imaginatively. They have constantly bemoaned a surfeit of regulation while scurrying again and again to the [Interstate Commerce] Commission for protection against their own errors or resolution of their many internal differences . . . It is simply too late in the day for the luxuries of corporate individualism and the balkanized disunity of self-contained empires. If the industry will not surrender a large measure of its individuality, major decisions will either be made by others or not made at all . . . The industry must also command the management skills to meet the challenges of the next decade. It has been singularly remiss in not aggressively recruiting young leaders from colleges and business schools."

But this candid self-criticism aside, ASTRO reached conclusions strikingly similar to those later ones of Penn Central's trustees. It blamed the railroads' plight primarily on federal and state transportation policies which "have weakened the [railroad] industry and taxed the public with higher costs." Its theme is familiar by now: Lopsided support of competing air, road and waterway carriers. Starved railroads are subject to "outdated laws and unwarranted restrictions" — just as though they still enjoyed their nineteenth-century monopolies. Assistance to railroads is the best and cheapest transportation investment the government can make. In essence, the clear choice is not whether there will be a national rail network but what kind. It can be strong, vibrant, growing. Or it can keep deteriorating to the point where nationalization is the only course. And nationalization is the worst of all solutions — the most costly and disruptive and the least efficacious.

ASTRO urged major changes to put railroads on an even foot-
ing with their competitors:

[*1*] Railroads must be relieved of the burden of local property
taxation. They pay about $300 million a year in state and local
property taxes. [Penn Central's local tax payments amounted to
about $64 million a year.] Congress should reimburse the states for
their loss of railroad real estate tax receipts. The railroads' present
tax burden is intolerable. More than 20 percent of all rail revenues
go for taxes and other costs relating to basic right-of-way facilities.
The comparable proportion for trucks is 5.1 percent; for buses,
5.7 percent; and for airlines, 3.3 percent. By contrast, the government has invested $305 billion in highways used by trucks and
buses, $21.6 billion in airways and airport facilities and $14.6
billion in waterways. The railroads absorb all their own expenses.
The nineteenth-century land grants they received for 10 percent of
the nation's present rail trackage have all been repaid.

[*2*] The present highway trust fund should be converted into a
general transportation fund which would include railroad aid. The
states should be required to spend 10 percent of the federal highway trust funds they receive each year on railroad grade-crossing
improvements. More people die in grade-crossing accidents each
year than are killed in airplane crashes. Thirty thousand crossings
need improvements.

[*3*] Congress should create a new agency to regulate all modes
of transportation. Trains, planes and barges all would come under
the jurisdiction of this agency. The ICC, Civil Aeronautics Board
and Federal Maritime Commission would thus be drawn into it.

[*4*] Railroads should be allowed to become parts of total
transportation companies. Policies that make it difficult if not impossible for railroads to own trucking companies, shipping companies and airlines are rooted in the "antiquated premise" that the
other means of transport need protection against predatory railroads. There should be appropriate safeguards against abuses. The
regulatory agency would retain the right to revoke franchises and
even to order divestiture where necessary.

[*5*] Until railroads can earn a reasonable rate of return, they
should be granted automatic annual increases in general rates to
meet higher wage and material costs. Such increases should not be

subject to state regulation. Railroads should be allowed to reduce prices on particular commodities where lower rates would improve earnings.[6] They should be allowed to abandon lines that fail to meet costs.

[6] The federal government should guarantee $400 million annually in private loans for railroad right-of-way improvements. It should guarantee loans for the purchase of 50,000 freight cars a year for five years.

[7] The federal government should spend more for railroad research. "The United States lags far behind other nations in promoting technical research in such areas as railroad dynamics, high-speed freight trains, higher loads and cybernetics."

[8] "Realism must be introduced in every aspect of the passenger problem . . . The governing principle . . . is that railroads should be relieved of continuing and severe losses on unprofitable service required in the public interest." Commuter service must be continued regardless of deficits. The federal government can play a large role, but substantial local and regional participation is essential. "No railroad should have to operate unprofitable commutation service . . . Discontinuances should be permitted . . . unless public bodies present feasible programs to relieve railroads of recurring operating deficits and to provide for capital improvements."

The Metroliner experience, the ASTRO Report continued, suggests the existence of a definite market in the New York–Philadelphia–Baltimore–Washington corridor, but its profitability potential is unclear. Further experimentation is needed. "If [rail] corridors are to be preserved, cooperation will be required among federal and local agencies and the railroad industry."

Long-haul passenger service is the largest single burden imposed by government on the railroads. "Despite the nostalgic emotionalism which it sometimes generates, the service has been in an irreversible decline for years. With few exceptions, the commercial market has been pre-empted by the airlines and the buses which

---

[6] At present, railroads must file with the ICC for permission to reduce rates as well as raise them. In the so-called "Big John" case, the Southern Railway had to wait two years for permission to reduce rates on grain shipments and two years more for final approval.

have clear inherent advantages. The obligation to operate long-haul passenger trains at a loss has been the largest single burden imposed by government on the rail industry."

"Properly funded and soundly managed," the report continued, Amtrak could become "the overdue vehicle for rationalizing the intercity rail passenger structure." It said that a rail passenger network could be preserved where patronage and potential so warrant. At the same time, operating contracts with railroads serving points within the network could relieve these roads of heavy losses they were incurring.

How would Congress react to ASTRO's recommendations? Congress represents the people, and when most people think of railroads they think of (often deteriorating) passenger service. Yet in its eighty-two pages, the ASTRO Report devoted only three and a half pages to the subject of passenger service. And these came at the very end. Congress is likely to shift priorities and put major stress on matters that the industry itself has assigned secondary or tertiary importance. As Senator Hartke puts it: "Measures to force railroaders to turn their attention back to railroading may well be popular."

Senator Hartke, at a conference in Washington in March 1971, on "Railroads in Crisis," offered his views on what the future might hold for American railroading. As chairman of the Senate subcommittee on surface transportation, he was in a pivotal position. He made these points. "First, Congress is not eager to put up money for the railroads . . . The lesson is clear that, despite the industry's continuing financial problems, the public treasury is not going to be its salvation — at least as it is now constituted. Public funds will be made available only as part of a substantial over-haul — as with the Rail Passenger Service Corporation.

"It is also clear that industry dogma must be reexamined. The Penn Central's collapse throws into serious question the idea that mergers between railroads are the answer for sick roads. Further, evidence uncovered to date indicates that conglomerate mergers were not the remedy for the Penn Central's low earnings. Penn Central's diversification program appears to have had the follow-ing effects: Management's time was diverted from solving the hard problems of the railroad business to buying easy profits — and shortlived, paper profits, at that — in other companies. Cash that the railroad desperately needed was drained off in two ways: high dividends were paid to keep the Penn Central's stock price high and to make it an attractive merger partner. In addition, cash was funneled downstream to the conglomerate's subsidiaries. When the real pinch came, the subsidiaries were as short of cash as the parent railroad and could not give it the help it needed."

On the subject of the ICC, Hartke said that calls for its abolition — as suggested by Sen. Mike Mansfield, Senate majority leader — or for reduction of its regulatory powers — as urged by ASTRO — "cannot be dismissed as reckless extremism." However, Hartke himself was not prepared to abolish the ICC. He thought that continued regulation, updated to take changing economic circumstances into account, might well be needed to protect the interests of shippers and consumers. "And that," he said, "means retaining the ICC — in one form or another."

Hartke did not rule out eventual nationalization of American railroads. Because of continuing frustration over rail problems and prolonged crisis, nationalization is "no longer a nasty word" on Capitol Hill. Response to the rail crisis could result in such drastic action but Hartke thought that the costs of nationalization would prove "prohibitive." Railroaders oppose nationalization almost to a man. In its report, ASTRO thought that merely to acquire the privately owned rail facilities in this country might cost the government $60 billion. Such a transfer in ownership would leave untouched the rail industry's enormous capital needs. And so deep is the national commitment to private enterprise, said ASTRO, that a government takeover of the trains could only be accomplished painfully and piecemeal, after steady slippage of rail service. Nor would nationalization necessarily solve anything. "The establishment of a monolithic Federal rail system offers only the certainty of size. At best, the results of government operations are highly controversial and uncertain."

The United States is the only country on earth where virtually all railroads are privately owned.[7] With about half the world's

---

[7] The small Alaskan Railroad is owned by the government and run through the Department of Transportation. It claimed $300,000 in profits

trucks and automobiles on American highways, railroads here face stiffer competition than anywhere else. Wage rates are higher, problems are different. For these reasons, foreign experience with nationalized railroads may not be relevant. But there's much interest here in the foreign experience, and also much misunderstanding and misinterpretation of profit-and-loss figures.

In July 1970, the month after Penn Central's bankruptcy, the *Wall Street Journal,* in a lead article on page one, took a look at the nationalized rail network in Britain. Under the tagline "Thriving RR," the *Journal* reported: "British Railway System Makes Money Stressing Its Passenger Service." The story was an implied rebuke to Penn Central and other American railroads that claim they can't turn a profit on passenger trains. British Rail, said the *Journal,* posted a profit of $30 million in 1969 following a $353.8 million loss in 1968. Passenger revenues were up 10 percent and freight revenues up 4 percent. The story did say that branch line trackage in Britain had been reduced from 20,000 miles at the time of nationalization, January 1, 1948, to 12,000. And 40 percent of the 17,000 daily passenger trains ran behind schedule. But the report was generally euphoric. It described the impressive all-first-class trains traveling the 194 miles between London and Liverpool in two hours and thirty-five minutes — at a modest round-trip cost of $11.76. British Rail, "long in the red," said the *Journal,* "is finally earning a small profit. And it's doing it by paying close attention to passenger service."

Later, the Associated Press checked out the *Journal's* story. It found that British Rail's claimed paper profit in 1969 did not take into account $36 million the government granted for elimination of surplus trackage or $146 million in government subsidies for uneconomic commuter and rural passenger services. Without these grants, British Rail's loss, said AP, would have run to over $150 million, or close to half a million dollars a day. The Associated Press also surveyed nationalized railroad systems in France, West Germany, Switzerland, Italy, Japan and Canada. Except for the

---

in 1969. Sen. Marlow Cook (D-Ky) points out, however, that it paid no local, state or national taxes. It depreciated $2.4 million worth of equipment, he says, even though it had no reserve for depreciation. The Long Island Rail Road is owned by New York State.

Swiss railways, which posted a genuine profit of $200,000, all the nationalized networks studied lost money. Italy's 1969 rail losses were put at $504 million, France's at $355 million and West Germany's at $273 million. Japanese National Railways lost $365 million while private railroads in Japan dropped $88 million. Canadian National Railways lost about $25 million while the privately owned Canadian Pacific reported a profit of $35 million, which was roughly the amount of its government subsidy.

A month after its report on British trains, the *Wall Street Journal* examined the Japanese National Railways and found the situation "dismal indeed." Conditions on most Japanese trains, reported the *Journal,* belied that nation's "bullet-train" image of providing the world's fastest, most efficient rail service. True, a second-class passenger could make the 331-mile trip from Tokyo to Osaka at top speed for $11.50. But such a run was hardly typical of Japanese trains.

"The railroad system in this nation," said the *Journal's* correspondent in Japan, "is in as much trouble as many of its American counterparts. JNR is stuck with money-losing lines and with jammed, aging commuter trains. Politics controls its rates. Couple this with increasing wage costs and a tough union and the system's deficit soars to more than $1 million a day.

"In fact, JNR is beginning to look rather like an Oriental Penn Central, deeply in debt and becoming rapidly liquid. The road's debt of more than $5 billion carries annual interest charges greater than its entire income from commuter operations."[8]

Following this grim report, the *Journal* editorialized that while U.S. rail critics often point to government-run trains in such countries as Britain and Japan as examples for the U.S. to emulate, it should be apparent that "nationalization offers no miracle solution, either here or abroad."

Certainly, nationalization is no panacea. But many Americans

---

[8] The *Journal's* findings were confirmed by *Business Week* magazine. Its April 24, 1971, issue carried an article on "Japan's Troubled Railroads" which said the JNR had lost $2 billion in seven years and was running in the red on all but 1,488 miles of its 13,000-mile system. It concluded that the Japanese railway system "resembles a hugely magnified nationalized Penn Central."

come home from Europe convinced that government-run train service there is faster, cheaper and more pleasant in every way than is train riding in this country. In any event, the writing is on the wall: The federal government may not physically take over passenger trains, but public bodies and quasi-public bodies will increasingly subsidize this service. And in all subsidized endeavors, whether they are in the field of education or transportation, government aid almost invariably leads to a measure of government control. Of course, the Long Island Rail Road, the nation's biggest commuter line, has already been taken over. For $65 million in 1965 the Pennsylvania Railroad turned over to the state of New York the Long Island's 754 miles of track, 3,415 acres of land, 285 buildings, 275 bridges, eighty locomotives, 1,192 passenger cars, twenty-four freight cars, thirty-nine substations, a tunnel — plus gallons of red ink. The PRR had purchased 57 percent of the Long Island's stock for about $8 million in 1900 and the balance of the stock in 1929. It carried this investment on its books at $47.6 million when Bevan and Saunders negotiated the sale to the state. At that time, the Long Island had been in bankruptcy for sixteen years and had not paid a dividend for twice as long. In the summer of 1969, four years after the state takeover, Governor Nelson Rockefeller, of New York, in a burst of optimism, pledged to make the Long Island the best commuter line in the United States. Its 170,000 daily riders are still waiting for this promise to be fulfilled. Even the Long Island's numerous and vociferous critics concede that some improvements have followed state ownership, but there have been no gains on the balance sheet. The Long Island lost $24 million in 1970.

Meanwhile, Penn Central's commuter service between New York and New Haven is now operated under contract with the New York Metropolitan Transportation Authority and the Connecticut Transportation Authority. In October 1970, Connecticut agreed to lease 106 miles of Penn Central's track in that state for sixty years at $815,000 a year. The MTA agreed to buy fourteen miles of right-of-way from the New York City line to the Connecticut state line for $7.2 million. And the two state agencies agreed to pay Penn Central $2.9 million a year for sixty years for use of the trackage between the New York City line and Grand

Central Station. They also agreed to continue to pay Penn Central $100,000 a year to operate the New Haven commuter service and, additionally, to make up whatever losses the line incurred in carrying 27,000 daily riders. Deficits have been averaging $2 million a year. The New Haven service has received substantial federal subsidies as well. In 1971, Washington pledged to provide $40 million for the purchase of 144 high-speed commuter cars. The old New Haven never received such treatment at taxpayers' expense.

Governor Rockefeller said confidently late in 1970 that the New Haven commuter service had been "saved" by the two-state takeover. Penn Central's Hudson and Harlem commuter lines are to operate under similar arrangements negotiated by the railroad and the Metropolitan Transportation Authority. Northern New Jersey commuter service to Manhattan is subsidized in part by the New Jersey Department of Transportation. Thus, close to a quarter of a million commuters to the nation's largest city ride trains that are state owned or are heavily subsidized by public agencies. If this isn't "nationalization" it is something quite close to it. Perhaps it should be called "regionalization."

In Philadelphia, six Penn Central commuter lines with 35,000 daily riders receive more than $5 million a year from the Southeastern Pennsylvania Transportation Authority. SEPTA obtains its funds from the state, the city and surrounding counties. It is seeking federal aid to buy new passenger cars and to build a midcity tunnel linking Penn Central's Penn Center Station, in the heart of Philadelphia, with the Reading Company's terminal six blocks away. The Reading's six commuter lines are also subsidized by SEPTA. If the two railroads fail to maintain their commuter schedules or if their trains are chronically late, their subsidies are cut. The Reading's record has generally been better than the Penn Central's. But since the bankruptcy, the coming of gung-ho William H. Moore as president and the creation of a separate commuter division within Penn Central, its interest in improving service seems to have been rekindled. In 1970, it boosted its on-time performance[9] from 73 percent to 94 percent. On January 14,

---

[9] To be on time, according to SEPTA's contract with the Penn Central and Reading, trains must complete their runs within four minutes of their scheduled time of arrival.

1971, following sleet and freezing rain the night before, all 413 Penn Central trains on its six Philadelphia commuter lines ran on time. Not in many years could the railroad point to such an achievement. It sent around a press release reporting that Pat King, general manager, Philadelphia commuter area, gave his more than 1,000 employees "a pat on the hand."

Moore views recent regional-aid developments as evidence that "the concept of support of commuter service by local governing authorities is gaining in acceptance." But he doesn't see such support growing fast enough to "relieve Penn Central of commuter service deficits during the crucial period of reorganization." Yet the prospects of steady improvements in commuter rail service in this country must be considered bright. In any region, commuters are very important and influential people. "Never underestimate commuters," says the Penn Central's James McDonald, who rides the Paoli Local. "The guy who does is out of his cotton-pickin' mind." One "guy" who did was Stuart Saunders. By pointedly avoiding the commuter trains himself and by talking as he did to Harold E. Kohn, in what he thought was a private conversation, Saunders convinced Philadelphia's commuters that he considered them public nuisances. Actually, Saunders fought hard and quite effectively for subsidies to improve commuter service. The fact that riding levels on Philadelphia commuter trains are now higher than at any time since World War II gasoline-rationing days is in part due to his efforts. But his living style and some off-hand remarks hurt his image just as the "public-be-damned" retort attributed to William H. Vanderbilt tarnished the reputation of that nineteenth-century mogul.

It's not likely that railroad executives or politicians will in the future underestimate commuters or commuter rail service. Not only are commuters important people but their trains can help relieve highway congestion that is strangling cities and pollution that is poisoning their environment. Commuter trains are the obvious answer to the problem of moving workers into and out of cities quickly, cleanly and efficiently. Nothing else makes much sense, and it's inconceivable that the trains' advantages won't finally be fully exploited.

As commuter service gets increasing public assistance so may the comparatively few remaining intermediate-length and long-haul passenger trains. Since World War II, these trains have been steadily vanishing from America's landscape. In 1944, 75 percent of the people who traveled between cities by "common carrier" — rail, bus or air — chose trains. In 1969, more than 90 percent of these travelers used planes or buses; fewer than 8 percent rode trains. Amtrak is not expected to reverse this trend overnight, if ever. But it is expected to maintain a skeleton service while relieving Penn Central and other railroads of heavy losses. It may be that high-speed trains in the Northeast Corridor, such as Penn Central's Metroliner and the Department of Transportation's New York–Boston TurboTrain, will eventually make money. Saunders thinks the Metroliner will. Even if they don't, they probably will continue to run because it is so clearly in the public interest to retain them as regionally assisted or federally assisted trains.

To restore Penn Central to solvency, however, and to keep other American railroads from failing may take hundreds of millions of dollars in government aid. The money is needed not just to prop up passenger service but, even more important from the railroads' point of view, to assist in strengthening freight service as well. When the emphasis shifts from passenger-service subsidies to subsidies for railroad operations generally, the prospects of government aid grow steadily more murky. There's no precedent to point to. For more than half a century, since enactment of the 1920 Transportation Act requiring the ICC to develop a workable national transport network, this country has vacillated. We still lack such a network. We don't even have the outlines of one. With the railroad industry now facing its moment of truth, efforts to develop a feasible transportation system will be redoubled. Already, of course, steps have been taken; creation of Amtrak is a major example. But most of the efforts to date have been aimed at solving immediately pressing problems on a piecemeal basis. Nothing much has been done about the deep-seated problems that have been steadily growing for decades.

The railroad industry's position is precarious. As a group, American railroads have earned as much as 6 percent on their investment in only one year since the twenties. And that was the war year of 1943 when the rails hummed with government-generated business. To replace equipment and make improvements, American railroads have gone heavily into debt. In the last ten years their equipment obligations have mounted to a record $4.3 billion. Meanwhile, their income has been slumping. Of the nation's seventy-one major railroads, thirty-four began the year 1971 with deficits in working capital. Railroad revenues reached $12 billion, highest figure ever, in 1970, but ordinary net income skidded to $126.8 million, only one-fourth the total of the previous year. Penn Central was just one of twenty-one railroads that operated at a loss in 1970. And even eliminating Penn Central's mammoth reverses, the rail industry's 1970 net income was lower than at any time since World War II.

Railroads continue to be strangled by government regulations and shackled with burdensome work rules. Early in 1971, the Indiana legislature refused to repeal that state's so-called full-crew laws requiring, among other things, that freight trains of seventy cars or more all have firemen (even though there are no fireboxes on diesel engines). William H. Moore, Penn Central's president, said that the Penn Central and other railroads operating in Indiana face $22 million in "extra and unnecessary labor costs" in 1971 because the work rules remain on the books. "Unless changes are made, and made very soon," Moore warned, the entire railroad industry "will drown in this sea of inequities."

With the situation so fluid, it would be foolhardy at this time to predict the future of American railroads or the future of the Penn Central. Certainly, Penn Central's trustees and its new management team headed by Moore were unable to reverse its downward spiral in the first year after the bankruptcy. Losses in the early months of 1971 were almost as great as were those in the early months of 1970. A federal district judge, Robert P. Anderson, of the U.S. Southern District Court of Connecticut, in opposing a refinancing of some of Penn Central's debts, said: "It appears preferable to face up to the possible necessity of a present resort to reorganization than to contemplate a decade and a half of probable death by attrition with insolvency and bankruptcy at the end."

Does that sad fate await the Penn Central? Certainly much depends on what happens to the national economy and what other steps, if any, are taken by the federal government to assist the stricken giant. Whatever the outcome, it does seem clear that certain lessons have already been learned from the wreck of the Penn Central.

(*1*) Bigger does not necessarily mean better. Bigness has always been admired in this big country, and for quite a while investors put great store by the Penn Central's sheer size. They thought that because the nation's largest railroad was created by the nation's largest corporate merger, its future success and happiness were assured. They were wrong. After June 21, 1970, many American businesses may be expected to heed the warning of Robert Townsend, author of *Up The Organization:* "Don't catch growth fever. Most firms use acquisitions as the Penn Central did — to cover up big problems."[10]

(*2*) Mergers of "equal" partners pose special problems. The Penn Central merger was not a PRR "takeover," despite Alfred Perlman's claim that it was. Maybe it should have been. Then everyone would have known who was boss and the former PRR executives would have assumed full responsibility for the merged railroad's success or failure. Instead, there was an attempt to intermingle "red" and "green" at all levels. At the top, the ruling troika so divided authority that it was never clear who could finally be blamed for the crash.

(*3*) The functioning of boards of directors needs close scrutiny and reform. Penn Central's board paid out nearly $100 million in dividends while the railroad's debt was soaring and its working-capital position was deteriorating by $140 million. Why? E. Clayton Gengras, former maverick on Penn Central's board, thinks the answer is obvious: The board was asleep. Nor is this unusual. Townsend again: "A director is someone who barely knows the name of your company, knows nothing about your people, your product or your problems. He ought to pay you to sit on the board." According to Stanley C. Vance, author of *The Corporate Director,* directors of American corporations are well-meaning and often competent in their own fields but "they just don't have the time to run an enterprise the size of the Penn Central." As a consequence, he says, "they are, in a sense, derelict in their duties." Penn Central's board certainly seems to have been derelict.

---

[10] The Chesapeake & Ohio Railway and the Norfolk & Western Railway got the message. In the spring of 1971, they voted to cancel their six-year-old merger plan which would have created the nation's largest railroad in terms of trackage — 27,500 miles compared to the Penn Central's 20,000 miles and the Burlington Northern's 25,400 miles. The decision was apparently based in part on the Penn Central's woes and uncertainty over restructuring eastern rail systems.

Ralph Nader may succeed in democratizing boards of directors. Perhaps more important is an examination of the role of these boards in carrying out their assigned functions to manage and control corporations about which they often know very little. In the case of railroads seeking financial help from government, self-examination seems essential. Congress is hardly likely to give or loan much money to railroads with ties to banks through interlocking directorates. Before its collapse, Penn Central was a prime example of such a railroad.

(4) Corporate financial statements often conceal more than they tell. Penn Central's quarterly reports in 1968 and 1969 gave no hint of the impending disaster. In fact, they conveyed a contrary impression that the merger was working out even better than anticipated. In December 1968, Saunders predicted that "consolidated net income for 1968 will be considerably better than for 1967," and: "We expect in 1969 to reap greater benefits of merger than we did in 1968." When we interviewed him in August 1969, he insisted that all was well, that the toughest times were over and that the merger would be fully effectuated in five years, three years ahead of schedule.

These overoptimistic statements and financial reports that did not tell the true story misled the investing public, the press and, apparently, even the railroad's own board of directors. Yet there was probably nothing unusual about any of this. Companies do it all the time to protect their stock prices. The difference was that the Penn Central got caught.

(5) Railroads that diversify may cut themselves off from public assistance. Between 1962 and 1970, ten U.S. railroads formed holding companies, in effect transforming themselves into railroad-based conglomerates. While Penn Central's holding company was getting all the publicity, other rail holding companies such as Northwest Industries, Inc., Kansas City Southern Industries, Inc., and Katy Industries, Inc., were extremely active. Penn Central's outside interests may or may not have drained money from the railroad; as far as Congress is concerned, it doesn't really matter. The point is that Washington won't appropriate funds to railroads if there's the slightest possibility that the money could be used for nonrailroad purposes. Penn Central's decision to sell most of its nonrail assets probably means that, for better or worse, it aims to stick solely to the railroad business. This should greatly improve its chances of getting public assistance.

(6) The railroads, finally, need a break. James McDonald, Penn Central's Canadian-born vice president for staff, thinks Americans have a "death wish" about their railroads, and he may be right. The romance

is gone. The flamboyant excesses of the nineteenth-century titans, the making of the West, the "golden spike," are gone too. What's left are some massive marble stations and dreadful service. James McDonald, who once got soaked by rain pouring through a leaky roof while he was riding in a Penn Central parlor car between New York and Philadelphia, understands the reasons for the bitterness and even the death wish. Personal experience conditions thinking. And after a few such experiences riders cease believing in railroads or the good intentions of railroaders.

This time, though, the railroaders are telling it true. Theirs is a very sick industry and it suffers from more than bad management. Nothing shows this more clearly than the wreck of the Penn Central. Between February 1, 1968, and June 21, 1970, there converged on the hapless railroad an astonishing combination of adverse forces that made disaster virtually inevitable. In retrospect, it's a wonder that so many people — not only Stuart Saunders but cautious bankers, supposedly well-informed security analysts and the shareholding public — thought the merger could work. It couldn't work. It faced too many disadvantages.

First, it was subject to all the frustrations, red tape and delays of federal regulation but got none of the benefits of federal aid that went, directly or indirectly, to its airline and trucking competitors. Second, it was "capital intensive" — burdened with an enormous capital structure that had to be kept rolling come what may. It couldn't stop running the Morning Congressional or the Paoli Local while trying to sort out the merger. Nor could it stop paying its $20 million a week payroll. Third, its financial structure was enormously complicated. Neither the Pennsylvania nor the New York Central had previously been forced through the catharsis of bankruptcy and reorganization. As a result, both were badly disorganized. Putting together their tangle of wholly owned and partly owned properties, their real estate holdings, trucking affiliates, pipelines, hotels and other interests created more confusion. Fourth, the merged railroad was obliged to accept costly and cumbersome work rules which added, according to postbankruptcy estimates of the trustees, 10,000 unneeded employees to its work force. Fifth, beyond the anticipated merger expenses were the many unanticipated ones. The thousands of expensive man-hours wasted on trivia. The high-salaried board chairman and high-salaried president spending time trying to decide whether their railroad cars would be painted red or green, and more time trying to agree on a symbol for the merged colossus. Time and energy expended on minutiae is apparently part of the price one pays for a big merger. The question arises whether it is worth it. In Penn Central's case the futility of it all was heightened and made absurd by the fact that the business it was selling — what Perlman calls the steel wheel on the steel rail — had long ago been given up for dead by much of the traveling public and many of the shippers of freight. The federal government had given up on railroads and was putting its money in other modes of transport. And the railroads themselves had given up on railroads. Hence their diversification into profit-making (they hoped) sidelines.

So here was the record-sized merger bringing together two badly disorganized, unprofitable companies in a discredited industry regulated by an unsympathetic federal agency, denounced by public and politicians for its poor performance record, and hemmed in by powerful unions clinging to archaic work rules. To this mishmash add management blundering, corporate disloyalty, executive-suite bickering, board-room slumbering, tight money, a national economic recession, inflation — and an unusually severe winter that struck just as recovery seemed possible. With this combination of bad luck and bad management, the merger couldn't work. The "money-eating monster" — the railroad — simply ran wild.

In the end, possibly even in the beginning, there wasn't anything anybody could do about it. The adversity under which Penn Central labored may have made Stuart Saunders' vision an "impossible dream." Maybe the best corporate brains in America couldn't have got the Penn Central running down the track. Certainly, Saunders, Perlman and Bevan couldn't. And didn't. Their way didn't work. It was, in fact, a hell of a way to run a railroad.

———

It's just before five o'clock on a hot August afternoon in Manhattan. All over the city tense, unsmiling people seem ready to explode in rage, frustration and despair. Sidewalks and subways are jammed. In the clogged streets taxis, trucks, buses and autos bawl and snarl and poison the air.

In Penn Station's subterranean vastness, the mood is different.

The Broadway Limited, started in 1902 by the Pennsylvania Railroad, was once the proudest of trains. In its later years, the crew sometimes outnumbered the passengers during stretches of the New York City to Chicago run. (Courtesy of the Penn Central)

On an outbound platform, an archaic, civilized ritual is being performed. The Broadway Limited is getting ready to roll to Chicago. All seats are reserved and 216 persons have booked places for the 907-mile run. Now the conductor peers down the platform for late arrivals. There are none. He draws out his pocket watch and makes a small ceremony of looking at it. 4:55 P.M.

"Boh-ARD!" He steps inside the train and tugs twice on an overhead cord. Up front, in the cab of Locomotive No. 4935, Richard B. Kline, a stocky, sandy-haired engineer in khakis and a baseball cap, has been awaiting this signal. He sounds the engine bell. Then, reaching for the master control, he pulls the throttle forward one notch. More than 600 volts of electric current course from the engine's transformer to its traction motors. The motors start up. Quietly, seemingly effortlessly, the fading star of the Penn Central's once-proud long-distance passenger fleet glides out of Penn Station and under the Hudson River toward Newark, first stop on its 16-hour-and-45-minute daily run.

At fifty-one, Dick Kline still gets a special kick out of driving the Broadway. He's a railway mail clerk's son, the father himself of six sons and two daughters, a thirty-year railroad man. He lives in Paxtang, Pennsylvania, near Harrisburg, and works out of Penn Central's Harrisburg yards. Most of his days are spent in the cabs of freight engines. The Broadway is something else. "This is our best train," he says. "They see that you get over the road. You get good signals. You get preference."

Kline's job this humid afternoon is to get the Broadway, with its three coaches, seven sleepers, coach-lounge, twin-unit diner-kitchen and baggage car, over the electrified tracks to Harrisburg. There it will switch to a diesel engine. Another crew, one of six scheduled to operate the train, will take over. Kline is heading home. It's been a long day. A telephone call from the Harrisburg terminal awakened him at 2:30 this morning. He dressed, ate breakfast, and signed on at 3:27 A.M. for the New York–bound Penn-Texas night train[11] from St. Louis. At 4:34 A.M. he throttled the Penn-Texas locomotive out of Harrisburg and, at 8:15, reached New York. Once the train was unloaded in Penn Station,

---

[11] Since Kline made this run, the Penn-Texas has been discontinued.

Kline drove it through the East River tunnel to Penn Central's Sunnyside Yard, at Long Island City. After signing off there he was free for six hours before signing on with the Broadway.

Now, crossing New Jersey's grim, industrial landscape on his homeward journey, Kline is intent on the roadbed ahead and on his speedometer. Trains travel mainly on momentum and there's no stopping them suddenly. Sixty-five or seventy is a good clip for the Broadway except on the longest straightaways where it may go faster. If its speed becomes excessive, a signal flashes in the cab: "SAND." This tells Kline to pull a knob dropping sand under the wheels and causing the train to slow down. Kline explains all this. He tells how Locomotive No. 4935's various valves and gauges work and how, every ten miles, an electric substation along the right-of-way feeds juice to the overhead catenary wires which, in turn, provide power for the train.

The Broadway picks up passengers at Newark and Trenton ("Trenton Makes / The World Takes"), crosses the Delaware, passes alongside Bucks County's 17,311-house Levittown and eases into drab North Philadelphia Station. As the train heads west into the setting sun, Kline puts on dark glasses. A sweeping American panorama opens before his eyes. On the Schuylkill River, scullers who might have been painted in deep pastel shades by Thomas Eakins a century ago bend over their oars. Beyond the Main Line, in Pennsylvania Dutch farm country, the train speeds past sheep, cows, Amish buggies and heavily fertilized cornfields. The smells are rich, yeasty farm smells and the Broadway seems worlds away from Manhattan.

Outside Lancaster, as it's getting dark, two black-hatted, barefoot Amish boys scamper playfully across the tracks in front of the onrushing engine. "That's what gives you white hair," says Dick Kline, wiping his brow. "You can't stop this thing in less than half a mile, but they don't realize it."

It's dark when the Broadway pulls into Harrisburg. Locomotive No. 4935 is unhooked and a diesel takes its place. Dick Kline signs off and heads home. He has covered 388 miles in seventeen hours. Since Penn Central engineers get a day's pay for every 100 miles they travel, Kline will receive almost four days' pay for his

Five miles outside of Altoona is the famed Horseshoe Curve, one of the wonders of raildom. (Calendar painting by Grif Teller. Courtesy of the Penn Central)

Harrisburg–New York round trip. But he may not get another assignment for two days.

With new engine and train crews, the Broadway snakes westward into the night. In the diner, Steward H. E. Steck's staff serves drinks and dinner to 100 travelers. Three cooks roast the beef over a fire of pressed logs from Tennessee. The meat is cooked to order and very good. The dinner costs $5.95 and Steck donates a small bottle of red wine to each customer. Service is excellent and the linen is fresh. Diners linger over their coffee. A feeling of euphoria pervades the car.

About five miles west of Altoona, where there's been another crew change, the Broadway rises out of a valley. Traversing a mountainside, it takes a route cut by men and horses in the 1850's at the direction of the Pennsylvania Railroad's great John Edgar Thomson. The Broadway begins a long turn. As the twinkling cars describe a graceful arc in the night, those riders in the middle of the train look out windows. They can see the engine up front and the caboose at the rear. This is the Horseshoe Curve, one of the wonders of raildom. At the midpoint in the curve, off on a siding with floodlights trained on it, is a black, beautiful PRR locomotive about fifty-five years old, a gift of the railroad to the city of Altoona. It is a perfect gem. "Every time I see it," says a railroadman named Howard Gilbert, who is riding the Broadway tonight, "it makes me want to weep."

Back in Palm Falls, Conewego Creek, Catawissa Rapids and other sleeping cars, the towels are clean and the water is hot. Everything works. After slipping between starched sheets, one traveler flicks on his night-light and dips into a mystery novel as the Broadway hurtles across Ohio through a blinding thunderstorm. It seems to him that this is the only civilized way to travel.

At 7:35 next morning, the sun shines on the puddles in the Fort Wayne, Indiana, station. On the platform, the Broadway's new conductor is talking to its new engineer by walkie-talkie. The Broadway begins its final 148-mile leg to Chicago. The conductor, a veteran employee from Fort Wayne, complains about the deterioration of Penn Central's rolling stock.

"This is the only recent train we've got," he says. "The rest of 'em are a bunch of junk. The equipment's terrible and everything's pretty well wore out. Too many men are laid off and they're not fixing the cars. The tragedy is that nobody seems to give a damn."

The Broadway is twenty minutes late into Chicago's Union Station. It's been a great ride, though. Worth every penny of the $98.69 fare for a first-class seat and a roomette. (The coach fare is $52.60.) But one traveler who rode the Broadway Limited to Chicago flies home on a jet. The cost is similar and the trip takes only two hours. The airline stewardess turns out to be the granddaughter of a Pennsylvania Railroad engineer. She loves jets and wouldn't travel any other way. She has a lot of company. Even with Amtrak the long-distance trains seem to be dying out. Soon the great Broadway Limited, born in 1902, may be the only one left. And then it, too, will be gone. As the conductor said: "The tragedy is that nobody seems to give a damn."

Index

The following abbreviations are used: B&O, Baltimore & Ohio; C&O, Chesapeake & Ohio; NYC, New York Central; PC, Penn Central; PRR, Pennsylvania Railroad.

Business Council, 96, 267
Business Week, 102, 119, 330n
Butcher, Elizabeth, 270
Butcher, Howard, III, 83, 239; resignation from PC board, 160, 172, 225–226; and PC, 269–270
Butcher, Washington, 269
Butcher & Sherrerd, 239, 269, 270, 271

Cabot, Louis, 265, 272
Cabot Corp., 265, 272
Caledonian Airways, 193
California, 13, 30
Campbell Soup Co., 83, 96, 236, 265, 272
Canada, railroads, 329, 330
Canadian National RR, 319, 330
Canadian Pacific RR, 330
Canals, 26
"Cannibalizing," 63, 313
Cannon, Francis A., 150n
Carbon County, Pa., 25
Carl Byoir & Associates, 49–50
Carnegie, Andrew, 37
Casey, Robert P., 77, 78
Casnoff, Alan, 145
Cassatt, A. J., 43, 92
Cassatt, Mary, 43
Cassidy, Leslie M., 151n
Central America, 30
Chafee, John, 296, 297
Chamberlain, Melville A., 158–159
Chase Manhattan Bank, 96, 265, 271
Chemical Bank New York Trust Co.: and Penphil, 157–160, 169; loan to Bevan, 171n; and PC, 230, 271, 289; Building, 243
Chesapeake & Ohio RR, 50; and NYC and PRR, 43, 44; and NYC, 55, 57, 58; merger with B&O, 57, 58, 59, 66, 117, 214, 316; shareholder parties, 133; cancels merger with N&W, 336n
Chestnut Hill, Philadelphia, 38
Cheston, George and Peggy, 96
Chicago, Ill., 28, 29, 31, 36, 38, 39, 48, 49, 66, 103, 118, 138, 347
Chicago, Burlington & Quincy RR, 124n

Chicago, Rock Island & Pacific RR, 319
Chubb, John E., 233n
Cincinnati, O., 28, 29, 118
Civil Aeronautics Board: and Executive Jet–PC (PRR), 139, 177, 178, 183, 184–185, 187, 188, 191–192; proposed transportation agency, 325
Civil War, 29, 30
Clary, Thomas J., 50
Classification. *See* Freight
Claypole, E. L., 302
Clement, Martin W., 93
Cleveland, O., 103, 118, 138, 322
Cole, Basil: quoted, 126, 149; investigation of Executive Jet, 179–182
Colony Life Insurance Co., 150n
Columbia, Pa., 26
Commercial and Financial Chronicle, quoted, 24
Commercial paper: and PC, 224–225, 231, 253, 256, 263–264, 269, 271, 290, 297; federal concern over market, 290
Commodore Hotel, 243
Community antenna television systems, 72
"Community of interest," 42–43, 45
Commuter service: development, 38; PC's, 129, 131, 132, 139–140, 142–147, 331–333, 334; in ASTRO report, 326. *See also* Passenger service
Conace, Frank, 199
Conemaugh River, 27
Connecticut, transit authorities and commuter service, 140, 331–332
Connor, John T., quoted, 78
Consolidated Edison, 123, 268n
Continental Illinois Bank & Trust Co., 230, 267, 279, 293
Continental Mortgage Investors, 148, 166
Cook, Marlow, 329n
Cook, William S., 223–224
Corning, Erastus, 29
Corsair, 22, 23, 36
Corsair Compact, 19, 22–24
Covington & Burling, 183, 184

Interstate Commerce Commission
(cont.)
mercial paper, 225, 231, 252–253;
and PC bond issue, 255; Perlman
on, 309, 311; Hartke on, 328
Irving Trust Co., 230
Italy, rail system, 329, 330

Japan, railroads, 134, 136, 329, 330
Japanese National Railways, 330
Jerrold Electronics Corp., 72
Jersey Central RR, 44
Jewel Companies, Inc., 160, 260,
266, 272
Jews, at PRR, 97
Johns-Manville, 151n
Johnson, Lyndon B.: and Saunders,
67, 74, 75, 76, 85–86, 96, 279;
and merger, 77, 78, 86, 88; and
Metroliner, 134, 136
Johnson Flying Service, 184–185,
190, 191, 192, 195
Johnston, Harvey F., 81–82
Johnstown, Pa., 27
Josephson, Matthew, quoted, 36, 38,
42

Kahn, Otto, quoted, 45
Kaier, E. A., 302
Kaminsky, Simon, 160, 225, 226
Kaneb Pipeline Co., 149, 150n, 158,
159, 165–166, 172
Kansas City Southern Industries,
Inc., 337
Karafin, Harry J., 81
Karvwatt, R. C., 302
Katy Industries, Inc., 337
Katzenbach, Nicholas, 77
Kelly, James McGirr, quoted, 146–
147
Kenefec, John C., 113
Kennedy, David, 259, 300, 304; and
government assistance to PC, 230,
267, 274, 292–293; and PC man-
agement, 279
Kennedy, John F., 72, 75, 257; and
PC merger, 66
Kennedy, John F., Library Corp., 96
Kennedy, Miles C., and George H.
Burgess, quoted, 45, 47
Kennedy, Robert, 72

Kennedy International Airport, 244
Kirby, A. P., 99
Kirby, Fred M., 266
Kline, Richard B., 342–343
Kling, Vincent G., 150n
Knight, Guy W., 233n; quoted, 222n
Knight Newspapers, Inc., 84
Knox, Seymour H., 160, 259, 266,
280
Kohler, Saul, 81
Kohn, Harold, 129, 131, 333
Kraft, C. William, Jr., 306, 307
Kreyling, Edward G., 122
Krim, Arthur B., 85–86
Kuhn, Loeb & Co., 45

Labor: 19th-century strikes and riots,
39–40; unionization, 40; opposi-
tion to merger, 45, 66; Merger
Protective Agreement, 67, 220–
223, 229, 315–316; PC costs, 217–
223, 229, 310, 314, 315, 335; full-
crew laws, 219, 321, 335; adjust-
ments recommended, 321–322
Lackawanna RR, 44, 46
Lake Shore RR, 39
Lamont, Thomas, 54
Lancaster, Pa., 26, 343
Langdon, Jervis, Jr., 319
Langtry, Lily, 35
Larchmont, N.Y., 5, 49n
Large, Henry W., 115–117, 119–122,
233n
LaSalle and Bureau County Railroad
Co., Inc., 215
Lashley, William, 233n, 301, 302;
quoted, 91, 117; on executive fir-
ings, 285, 286; on bankruptcy, 307
Lassiter, Olbert F., 126, 150n, 190;
and Executive Jet, 176–185
passim, 191–199 passim, 203, 204
Lassiter Aircraft Corp., 197
Lausche, Frank J., 50
Lawrence, David L., 66, 74, 75–76,
77
Lawson, Robert, 103
Lebanon, Pa., 79
Lehigh Valley RR, 44, 46, 138,
317–318
LeMay, Curtis, 178, 183, 187, 190
Levine, Harvey A., quoted, 102

Wynne, Toddie, 162, 163
Wynne family, and Great Southwest
    Corp., 161, 162, 163
Wynnewood, Pa., 78, 92

Yale Club, 243
Yarnall Biddle & Co., 150n, 151n

Yonkers, N.Y., 119
Young, Robert R., 44; control of
    NYC, 46, 52; and Symes, 53; sui-
    cide, 54; and Perlman, 54n, 99
Youngstown, O., 48

Ziegler, Ron, 298